Modern Critical Views

Modern Critical Views

HENRIK IBSEN

Edited and with an introduction by
Harold Bloom
Sterling Professor of the Humanities
Yale University

CHELSEA HOUSE PUBLISHERS
Philadelphia

© 1999 by Chelsea House Publishers, a division of
Main Line Book Co.

Introduction © 1999 by Harold Bloom

Printed and bound in the United States of America

10 9 8 7 6 5 4 3 2

∞ The paper used in this publication meets the minimum
requirements of the American National Standard for
Permanence of Paper for Printed Library Materials,
Z39.48-1984

Library of Congress Cataloging-in-Publication Data

Henrik Ibsen / edited and with an introduction by Harold
Bloom.
        p.   cm.—(Modern critical views)
    Includes bibliographical references and index.
    ISBN 0-7910-4784-9
    1. Ibsen, Henrik, 1828-1906—Criticism and
interpretation.
I. Bloom, Harold.   II. Series.
PT8895.H43   1998
839.8'226—dc21   98-30508
                                           CIP

Contributing Editor: Tenley Williams

Contents

Editor's Note

This volume brings together a representative selection of the best criticism available in English upon the plays and dramatic career of Henrik Ibsen. I am grateful to Tenley Williams for her skilled and erudite assistance in editing.

My Introduction briefly analyzes Brand and Hedda Gabler as characters in the mode of Shakespeare's hero-villains. The chronological sequence of commentaries begins with Ibsen himself describing his purposes as a poetic dramatist, and then continues with the novelist E. M. Forster's tribute to Ibsen's High Romanticism.

Francis Fergusson uncovers Ibsen's idea of the theater in *Ghosts*, while Eric Bentley states a total view, balancing the dramatist's genius and his limitations.

Hedda Gabler is the center of Una Ellis-Fermor's discussion, after which Michael Meyer comments upon *The Pillars of Society* and John Northam on *The Wild Duck*.

Ibsen's intricate role in the history of modern drama is sketched by Richard Gilman, while Steve Arestad traces the fortune of the Ibsen hero.

In an illuminating overview, Robert Brustein rightly argues against those who see Ibsen primarily as a playwright of social protest. Inga-Stina Ewbank's reflections upon Geoffrey Hill's version of *Brand* indirectly support Brustein's emphases.

Trolls in Ibsen are examined by Barbara Fass Leavy in regard to Hedda Gabler, and by the editor concerning *Peer Gynt*.

Michael Goldman meditates upon the pathos of *Little Eyolf*, after which Thomas Van Laan concludes this book with an informed critique of Shakespeare's influence upon Ibsen.

Introduction

Ibsen's vast range is allied to his uncanny ability to transcend genre; in both respects he is like Shakespeare, the dominant though frequently hidden influence upon his work. Shakespeare wrote his 38 (or so) plays in a quarter century; Ibsen composed for 50 years, and gave us 25 plays. His masterpieces, in my judgment, include *Brand, Peer Gynt, Emperor and Galilean*, in the period 1865–1873, with *Hedda Gabler* as a great postlude in 1890. *Peer Gynt* and *Hedda Gabler* retain their popularity, but do not seem so frequently performed as what are taken to be Ibsen's "social dramas": *A Doll's House, Ghosts, An Enemy of the People, The Wild Duck*, and the earlier *Pillars of Society*. His final period, after he turned sixty, gave us four great visionary plays: *The Lady from the Sea, The Master Builder, John Gabriel Borkman*, and *When We Dead Awaken*. Yet all of Ibsen is visionary drama; he inherited Shakespeare's invention of the human, characters capable of overhearing themselves, and his mastery of inwardness is second only to Shakespeare's. I will confine myself, in this Introduction, to brief accounts of only two plays: *Brand* and *Hedda Gabler*, or rather to the two sublime characters who give their names to these dramas. Since this volume contains my essay on *Peer Gynt*, my Introduction seeks to supplement that essay by extending some of its concerns from Peer Gynt to Brand and to Hedda Gabler.

Ibsen, who could be caustic, had a powerful aversion to Strindberg. "I have always liked storms," he wrote in a letter to his sister, a fondness that helps explain his purchase of a large portrait of Strindberg, which he hung on the wall of his study. Under the baleful gaze of his enemy, whom he considered "delightfully mad," Ibsen was spurred on to even more exuberance in his final plays, *John Gabriel Borkman* and the apocalyptic *When We Dead Awaken*. Earlier, in response to *Hedda Gabler*, where he found himself portrayed as Løvberg, the poet inspired to suicide by the demonic Hedda, Strindberg expressed his own fury:

1

It seems to me that Ibsen realizes that I shall inherit the crown when he is finished. He hates me mentally. . . . And now the decrepit old troll seems to hand me the revolver! . . . I shall survive him and many others, and the day *The Father* kills *Hedda Gabler*, I shall stick the gun in the old troll's neck.

The wild Strindberg was more overtly trollish than the socially conforming Ibsen, but Strindberg accurately diagnosed his unwelcome precursor as an "old troll." Trolls are not easy to define, particularly when they are thoroughly mixed into the human. If you think of the later Freudian myth of the rival drives of love and death, Eros and Thanatos, you get close to human trollishness. Ibsen's trollish figures are both doom-eager and desperate for more life; they are Ibsen's Shakespearean energies personified. Thomas Van Laan traces Hedda Gabler's debt to Shakespeare's Cleopatra, and on the level of deliberate allusion, that is definitely correct. But the deeper, more implicit model for Hedda is "honest Iago," the most trollish of all Shakespearean characters. Ibsen once told an interviewer that: "There must be troll in what I write," and one can wonder if he ever fully enjoyed the appparent Shakespearean detachment that he cultivated. No one should miss either the troll in Ibsen himself, or the presence of Ibsen in Brand, Hedda Gabler, Peer Gynt, and all their fellow protagonists. Perhaps Falstaff and Hamlet each had a link to Shakespeare's own personality and character, but such a surmise can only be imaginative. Ibsen is not Shakespeare; the dramatist of the great trolls was as late Romantic as they were: vitalistic, close to nihilistic, determined to turn life into the true work of art.

Brand speaks of "the poem of my life"; if he is a man of God, that god seems more Dionysus than Yahweh. Guilt, to a Dionysiac hero, has nothing to do with Original Sin, but rather reflects a failure to sustain ecstasy. Compromising in any way, with anything or anyone, is totally alien to Brand. He seeks only the Sublime, which he calls God, yet other names (including Brand's own) seem more accurate. Destroying the lives of those one loves best is hardly a path to God. Brand's capacity for suffering seems infinite, but why need he immerse those who care most for him in suffering that they cannot sustain? Ibsen is aware that *Brand* is not a "religious drama"; Brand, according to the dramatist, could also have been a sculptor or politician. W. H. Auden strongly disagreed. Himself a Kierkegaardian, Auden regarded Brand as an Apostle, someone who knows only "that he is called upon to forsake everything he has been, to venture into an unknown and probably unpleasant future." One can wonder if Auden was correct in so assimilating Brand to Kierkegaard's difficult question of "becoming a

Christian" in a country ostensibly already Christian. Auden himself points to the clear Nietzschean elements in Brand's exaltation of the will. If Brand is an Apostle, then the message he carries was given to him by the god Dionysus, who in one of his aspects is something of a troll.

II

Brand fascinates, though he also alienates himself from us. Even as he beholds the avalanche coming down upon him, he cries out to God: "Answer!" We shudder at the sublimity of the Brandian will, and yet we are not allowed to sympathize with Brand. Hedda Gabler, even more fascinating, powerfully provokes something of the same *dramatic* sympathy that Iago inspires in us. Hedda is the greatest figure in all Ibsen, possibly because she is Ibsen. "Men and women don't belong in the same century," the playwright enigmatically remarked. I think Ibsen would have said the same of the twentieth century, or the twenty-first, or any whatsoever.

As a demon or half-troll, Hedda emulates Iago by writing a tragic farce in which she and the other protagonists are caught in the net of her devisings. Oscar Wilde, accurate always, said he "felt pity and terror, as though the play had been Greek." Just as deftly, Wilde could have added: "or *Othello*." Hedda, who fears boring herself to death, finds Iago's cure for *ennui*: murder (or ruin) your fellow characters. Ibsen's marvelous woman shoots herself in the forehead, in the mode of Iago affirming: "from this time forth I never shall speak word," as he prepares to die silently under torture. Both Hedda and Iago are sublime solipsists, dramatists of the self at the expense of all others. And both are too grand for our mere disapproval. They stimulate our fear and our pity, as do Brand and Solness and so many of Ibsen's titans. The exception is Peer Gynt, who escapes into comedy, but that is another story, pursued by me elsewhere in this volume.

HENRIK IBSEN

The Task of the Poet

. . . And what does it mean, then, to be a poet? It was a long time before I realized that to be a poet means essentially to see, but mark well, to see in such a way that whatever is seen is perceived by the audience just as the poet saw it. But only what has been lived through can be seen in that way and accepted in that way. And the secret of modern literature lies precisely in this matter of experiences that are lived through. All that I have written these last ten years, I have lived through spiritually. But no poet lives through anything in isolation. What he lives through all of his countrymen live through with him. If that were not so, what would bridge the gap between the producing and the receiving minds?

And what is it, then, that I have lived through and that has inspired me? The range has been large. In part I have been inspired by something which only rarely and only in my best moments has stirred vividly within me as something great and beautiful. I have been inspired by that which, so to speak, has stood higher than my everyday self, and I have been inspired by this because I wanted to confront it and make it part of myself.

But I have also been inspired by the opposite, by what appears on intro-spection as the dregs and sediment of one's own nature. Writing has in this case been to me like a bath from which I have risen feeling cleaner, healthier, and freer. Yes, gentlemen, nobody can picture poetically anything for which he himself has not to a certain degree and at least at times served as a model. And who is the man among us who has not now and then felt and recognized within himself a contradiction between word and deed, between will and duty, between life and theory in general? Or who is there among us who has not, at least at times, been egoistically sufficient unto himself, and half unconsciously, half in good faith, sought to extenuate his conduct both to others and to himself?

I believe that in saying all this to you, to the students, my remarks have found exactly the right audience. You will understand them as they are meant to be understood. For a student has essentially the same task as the poet: to make clear to himself, and thereby to others, the temporal and eternal questions which are astir in the age and in the community to which he belongs.

In this respect I dare to say of myself that I have endeavored to be a good student during my stay abroad. A poet is by nature farsighted. Never have I seen my homeland and the true life of my homeland so fully, so clearly, and at such close range, as I did in my absence when I was far away from it.

And now, my dear countrymen, in conclusion a few words which are also related to something I have lived through. When Emperor Julian stands at the end of his career and everything collapses around him, there is nothing which makes him so despondent as the thought that all he has gained was this: to be remembered by cool and clear heads with respectful appreciation, while his opponents live on, rich in the love of warm, living hearts. This thought was the result of much that I had lived through; it had its origin in a question that I had sometimes asked myself, down there in my solitude. Now the young people of Norway have come to me here tonight and given me my answer in word and song, have given me my answer more warmly and clearly than I had ever expected to hear it. I shall take this answer with me as the richest reward of my visit with my countrymen at home, and it is my hope and my belief that what I experience tonight will be an experience to "live through" which will sometime be reflected in a work of mine. And if this happens, if sometime I shall send such a book home, then I ask that the students receive it as a handshake and a thanks for this meeting. I ask you to receive it as the ones who had a share in the making of it.

Translated by Evert Sprinchorn

E. M. FORSTER

Ibsen the Romantic

"My book is poetry, and if it is not poetry, then it will be."
—Ibsen to Björnson.

Ibsen was a poet during the earlier part of his life. He began as a lyricist, and his first plays are either in verse or are inspired by an imaginative contemplation of the past. When he was about forty, a change occurred, the importance of which has been differently estimated. Certain critics, both friendly and hostile, regard it as a fundamental change. They argue that with *The League of Youth* the real or realistic Ibsen begins to emerge, the singer dies, the social castigator is born, the scene clarifies and darkens, and ideas come to the front which do not necessarily contradict previous ideas, but which are given a prominence that entirely alters the dramatic emphasis. We pass from the epic to the domestic. Peer Gynt becomes Hjalmar Ekdal, and Brand as Gregers Werle tears the spectacles of illusion from his eyes, and they work out their tragedy, not among forests and fjords, but in a photographic studio opening into a sort of aviary. The aviary contains a few dead Christmas trees, also a water trough, some rabbits but no bears, one wild duck and that a damaged one. We could not be further from romance, the critics say, and turn, if we are friendly, to the character drawing, the technique, and the moral and social issues; if they are hostile, to the squalor. "Somewhere in the course of the battle of his life Ibsen had a lyric Pegasus

From "Ibsen the Romantic" by E. M. Forster from *Abinger Harvest* by E.M. Forster. 1936. Reprinted in *Ibsen: A Collection of Critical Essays*, ed. Rolf Fjelde. Copyright © 1965 by Harcourt Brace & Company. Reprinted by permission of Harcourt Brace & Company.

killed under him," writes Brandes. "Novel and perilous nonsense," wrote the *Daily Telegraph*. The critics agree in thinking that the poetry, if ever there was any, has gone.

Has it gone? Can the habits of forty years be set aside? Of twenty years—yes; most people are romantic at twenty, owing to lack of experience. As they grow older life offers various alternatives, such as worldliness or philosophy or the sense of humor, and they usually accept one of these. If, in spite of more solid temptations, they still cling to poetry, it is because a deep preference has to be satisfied. Ibsen was a poet at forty because he had that preference. He was a poet at sixty also. His continued interest in avalanches, water, trees, fire, mines, high places, traveling, was not accidental. Not only was he born a poet—he died one, and as soon as we try to understand him instead of asking him to teach us, the point becomes clearer.

He is, of course, not easy to understand. Two obstacles may be noted. In the first place although he is not a teacher he has the air of being one, there is something in his method that implies a message, though the message really rested on passing irritabilities, and not on any permanent view of conduct or the universe. In the second place, he further throws us off the scent by taking a harsh or a depressing view of human relationships. As a rule, if a writer has a romantic temperament, he will find human relation- ships beautiful. His characters may hate one another or be unhappy together, but they will generate nobility or charm, they will never be squalid, whatever their other defects. And the crux in Ibsen is that, though he had the romantic temperament, he found personal intercourse sordid. Sooner or later his char- acters draw their little knives, they rip up the present and the past, and the closer their intimacy the better their opportunities for exchanging pain. Oswald Alving knows how to hurt his mother, Rosmer his mistress, and married couples are even more favorably placed. The Helmers, the Tesmans, the Wangels, Solnesses, Allmers, Borkmans, Rubeks—what a procession, equally incapable of comradeship and ecstacy! If they were heroic or happy once, it was before the curtain rose, and only survives as decay. And if they attain reconciliation, like the Rentheim sisters, the curtain has to fall. Their intercourse is worse than unfriendly, it is petty; moral ugliness trespasses into the aesthetic. And when a play is full of such characters and evolves round their fortunes, how can it possibly be a romantic play? Poetry might perhaps be achieved if Ibsen's indignation was the straight-hitting sort, like Dante's. But for all its sincerity there is something automatic about it, he reminds us too often of father at the breakfast table after a bad night, sensitive to the defects of society as revealed by a chance glance at the newspaper and apt to blame all parties for them indiscriminately. Now it is the position of women that upsets father, now the lies people tell, now their inability to lie, now the drains, now the newspaper itself, which he crumples up, but his helpers and servers have to retrieve it, for bad as are all political parties he must really see who got in at Rosmersholm. Seldom can a great genius have had so large a dose of domestic irritability. He was cross with his enemies and friends, with theater-managers, professors, and students, and so cross with his countrymen for not volunteering to help the Danes in 1864 that he had to go to Italy to say so. He might have volunteered in person—he was in the prime of life at the time—but this did not occur to him; he preferred instead to write a scathing little satire about a Norwegian mother whose son was safe at the front. And it is (if one may adopt the phrase) precisely the volunteer spirit that is absent from his conception of human relationships. He put everything into them except the strength of his arm.

"Not a great writer . . . almost great, but marred by this lack of generosity." How readily the phrases rise to the lips! How false they are! For this nagging quality, this habitual bitterness—they are essential in his greatness, because they beckon to the poetry in him, and carry it with them under the ground. Underground. Into the depths of the sea, the depths of the sea. Had he been of heroic build and turned to the light and the sun, his gifts would have evaporated. But he was—thank heaven—subterranean, he loved narrow passages and darkness, and his later plays have a romantic intensity which not only rivals the romantic expansion of their predecessors, but is absolutely unique in literature. The trees in old Ekdal's aviary are as numerous as a forest because they are countless, the water in the chickens' trough includes all the waves on which the Vikings could sail. To his impassioned vision dead and damaged things, however contemptible socially, dwell for ever in the land of romance, and this is the secret of his so-called symbolism: a connection is found between objects that lead different types of existence; they reinforce one another and each lives more intensely than before. Consequently his stage throbs with a mysteriousness for which no obvious preparation has been made, with beckonings, tremblings, sudden compressions of the air, and his characters as they wrangle among the oval tables and stoves are watched by an unseen power which slips between their words.

A weaker dramatist who had this peculiar gift would try to get his effect by patches of fine writing, but with Ibsen as with Beethoven the beauty comes not from the tunes, but from the way they are used and are worked into the joints of the action. *The Master Builder* contains superb examples of this. The plot unfolds logically, the diction is flat and austere, the scene is a villa close to which another villa is being erected, the chief characters are an elderly couple and a young woman who is determined to get a thrill out of her visit, even if it entails breaking her host's neck. Hilda is a minx, and though her restlessness is not so vulgar as Hedda Gabler's it is quite as pernicious and lacks the saving gesture of suicide. That is one side of Hilda. But on the other side she touches Gerd and the Rat-Wife and the Button-molder, she is a lure and an assessor, she comes from the non-human and asks for her kingdom and for castles in the air that shall rest on solid masonry, and from the moment she knocks at the door poetry filters into the play. Solness, when he listened to her, was neither a dead man nor an old fool. No prose memorial can be raised to him, and consequently Ibsen himself can say nothing when he falls from the scaffolding, and Bernard Shaw does not know that there is anything to say. But Hilda hears harps and voices in the air, and though her own voice may be that of a sadistic school-girl the sound has nevertheless gone out into the dramatist's universe, the avalanches in *Brand* and *When We Dead Awaken* echo it, so does the metal in John Gabriel Borkman's mine. And it has all been done so competently. The symbolism never holds up the action, because it is part of the action, and because Ibsen was a poet, to whom creation and craftsmanship were one. It is the same with the white horses in *Rosmersholm*. the fire of life in *Ghosts*, the gnawing pains in *Little Eyolf*, the sea in *The Lady from the Sea*, where Hilda's own stepmother voices more openly than usual the malaise that connects the forces of nature and the fortunes of men. Everything rings true and echoes far because it is in the exact place which its surroundings require.

The source of Ibsen's poetry is indefinable; presumably it comes from the same place as his view of human nature, otherwise they would not harmonize as they do in his art. The vehicle in which poetry reached him— that can easily be defined; it was, of course, the scenery of western and south-western Norway. At some date previous to his Italian journey he must have had experiences of passionate intensity among the mountains, comparable to the early experiences of Wordsworth in the English lakes. All his life they kept returning to him, clothed in streams, trees, precipices, and hallowing his characters while they recriminated. In *Brand* and *Peer Gynt* they filled the stage; subsequently they shrank and concentrated; in the two last plays they again fill the stage and hasten the catastrophes by a shroud of snow. To compare Ibsen with Wordsworth is to scandalize the faithful in either camp, yet they had one important point in common: they were both of them haunted until the end of their lives by the romantic possibilities of scenery. Wordsworth fell into the residential fallacy; he continued to look at his gods direct, and to pin with decreasing success his precepts to the flanks of Helvellyn. Ibsen, wiser and greater, sank and smashed the Dovrëfjeld in the depths of the sea, the depths of the sea. He knew that he should find it again. Neither his satire nor his character drawing dwelt as deep; neither the prob-lems he found in human conduct nor the tentative solutions he propounded lay at the roots of his extraordinary heart. There, in that strange gnarled region, a primeval romanticism lurked, frozen or twisted or exuding slime, there was the nest of the Great Boyg. The Great Boyg did not strive, did not die, lay beneath good and evil, did not say one thing more than another:

> Forward or back, and it's just as far;
> Out or in, and it's just as strait.

What do the words mean, and apart from their meaning, are they meant to be right? And if right, are the prayers of Solveig, which silence them for a moment, wrong? It is proper that we should ask such questions as these when focusing on the moral and social aspect of his work, and they have been brilliantly asked and answered by Bernard Shaw. But as soon as we shift the focus the questions go dim, the reformer becomes a dramatist, we shift again and the dramatist becomes a lyric poet, listening from first to last for the movements of the trolls. Ibsen is at bottom Peer Gynt. Side whiskers and all, he is a boy bewitched:

> The boy has been sitting on his mother's lap.
> They two have been playing all the life-day long.

And though the brow that bends over him can scarcely be described as maternal, it will assuredly preserve him from the melting ladle as long as books are read or plays seen.

FRANCIS FERGUSSON

Ghosts: *The Tragic Rhythm in a Small Figure*

The Plot of *Ghosts:* Thesis, Thriller, and Tragedy

Ghosts is not Ibsen's best play, but it serves my purpose, which is to study the foundations of modern realism, just because of its imperfections. Its power, and the poetry of some of its effects, are evident; yet a contemporary audience may be bored with its old-fashioned iconoclasm and offended by the clatter of its too-obviously well-made plot. On the surface it is a *drame à thèse*, of the kind Brieux was to develop to its logical conclusion twenty years later: it proves the hollowness of the conventional bourgeois marriage. At the same time it is a thriller with all the tricks of the Boulevard entertainment: Ibsen was a student of Scribe in his middle period. But underneath this superficial form of thesis-thriller—the play which Ibsen started to write, the angry diatribe as he first conceived it—there is another form, the shape of the underlying action, which Ibsen gradually made out in the course of his two-years' labor upon the play, in obedience to his scruple of truthfulness, his profound attention to the reality of his fictive characters' lives. The form of the play is understood according to two conceptions of plot, which Ibsen himself did not at this point clearly distinguish: the rationalized concatenation of events with a univocal moral, and the plot as the "soul" or first actualization of the directly perceived action.

From "*Ghosts*: The Tragic Rhythm in a Small Figure" by Francis Fergusson from *The Idea of a Theater* by Francis Fergusson. Reprinted in *Ibsen: A Collection of Critical Essays*, ed. Rolf Fjelde. Copyright © 1965 by Prentice-Hall, Inc.

Halvdan Koht, in his excellent study *Henrik Ibsen*, has explained the circumstances under which *Ghosts* was written. It was first planned as an attack upon marriage, in answer to the critics of *A Doll's House*. The story of the play is perfectly coherent as the demonstration and illustration of this thesis. When the play opens, Captain Alving has just died, his son Oswald is back from Paris where he had been studying painting, and his wife is straightening out the estate. The Captain had been accepted locally as a pillar of society but was in secret a drunkard and debauchee. He had seduced his wife's maid, and had a child by her; and the child, Regina, is now in her turn Mrs. Alving's maid. Mrs. Alving has concealed all this for something like twenty years. She was following the advice of the conventional Pastor Manders and endeavoring to save Oswald from the horrors of the household: it was for this reason she sent him away to school. But now, with her husband's death, she chooses to get rid of the Alving heritage in all its forms, in order to free herself and Oswald for the innocent, unconventional "joy of life." She wants to endow an orphanage with the Captain's money, both to end any rumors there may be of his sinful life and to get rid of the remains of his power over her. She encounters this power, however, in many forms, through the Pastor's timidity and through the attempt by Bertrand (a local carpenter who was bribed to pretend to be Regina's father) to blackmail her. Oswald wants to marry Regina and has to be told the whole story. At last he reveals that he has inherited syphilis from his father—the dead hand of the past in its most sensationally ugly form—and when his brain softens at the end, Mrs. Alving's whole plan collapses in unrelieved horror. It is "proved" that she should have left home twenty years before, like Nora in *A Doll's House*; and that conventional marriage is therefore an evil tyranny.

In accordance with the principles of the thesis play, *Ghosts* is plotted as a series of debates on conventional morality, between Mrs. Alving and the Pastor, the Pastor and Oswald, and Oswald and his mother. It may be read as a perfect well-made thriller. The story is presented with immediate clarity, with mounting and controlled suspense; each act ends with an exciting curtain which reaffirms the issues and promises important new developments. In this play, as in so many others, one can observe that the conception of dramatic form underlying the thesis play and the machine-made Boulevard entertainment is the same: the logically concatenated series of events (intriguing thesis or logical intrigue) which the characters and their relationships merely illustrate. And it was this view of *Ghosts* which made it an immediate scandal and success.

But Ibsen himself protested that he was not a reformer but a poet. He was often led to write by anger and he compared the process of composition to his pet scorpion's emptying of poison; Ibsen kept a piece of soft fruit in his cage for the scorpion to sting when the spirit moved him. But Ibsen's own spirit was not satisfied by the mere discharge of venom; and one may see, in *Ghosts*, behind the surfaces of the savage story, a partially realized tragic form of really poetic scope, the result of Ibsen's more serious and disinterested brooding upon the human condition in general, where it underlies the myopic rebellions and empty clichés of the time.

In order to see the tragedy behind the thesis, it is necessary to return to the distinction between plot and action, and to the distinction between the plot as the rationalized series of events, and the plot as "the soul of the tragedy," The action of the play is "to control the Alving heritage for my own life." Most of the characters want some material or social advantage from it—Engstrand money, for instance, and the Pastor the security of conventional respectability. But Mrs. Alving is seeking a true and free human life itself—for her son, and through him, for herself. Mrs. Alving sometimes puts this quest in terms of the iconoclasms of the time, but her spiritual life, as Ibsen gradually discovered it, is at a deeper level; she tests everything— Oswald, the Pastor, Regina, her own moves—in the light of her extremely strict if unsophisticated moral sensibility: by direct perception and not by ideas at all. She is tragically seeking; she suffers a series of pathoses and new insights in the course of the play; and this rhythm of will, feeling, and insight underneath the machinery of the plot is the form of the life of the play, the soul of the tragedy.

The similarity between *Ghosts* and Greek tragedy, with its single fated action moving to an unmistakable catastrophe, has been felt by many critics of Ibsen. Mrs. Alving, like Oedipus, is engaged in a quest for her true human condition; and Ibsen, like Sophocles, shows on-stage only the end of this quest, when the past is being brought up again in the light of the present action and its fated outcome. From this point of view Ibsen is a plot-maker in the first sense: by means of his selection and arrangement of incidents he defines an action underlying many particular events and realized in various modes of intelligible purpose, of suffering, and of new insight. What Mrs. Alving sees changes in the course of the play, just as what Oedipus sees changes as one veil after another is removed from the past and the present. The underlying form of *Ghosts* is that of the tragic rhythm as one finds it in *Oedipus Rex*.

But this judgment needs to be qualified in several respects: because of the theater for which Ibsen wrote, the tragic form which Sophocles could develop to the full, and with every theatrical resource, is hidden beneath the clichés of plot and the surfaces "evident to the most commonplace mind." At the end of the play the tragic rhythm of Mrs. Alving's quest is not so much completed as brutally truncated, in obedience to the requirements of the thesis and the thriller. Oswald's collapse, before our eyes, with his mother's screaming, makes the intrigue end with a bang, and hammers home the thesis. But from the point of view of Mrs. Alving's tragic quest as we have seen it develop through the rest of the play, this conclusion concludes nothing: it is merely sensational.

The exciting intrigue and the brilliantly, the violently clear surfaces of *Ghosts* are likely to obscure completely its real life and underlying form. The tragic rhythm, which Ibsen rediscovered by his long and loving attention to the reality of his fictive lives, is evident only to the histrionic sensibility. As Henry James put it, Ibsen's characters "have the extraordinary, the brilliant property of becoming when represented at once more abstract and more living": i.e., both their lives and the life of the play, the spiritual content and the form of the whole, are revealed in this medium. A Nazimova, a Duse, could show it to us on the stage. Lacking such a performance, the reader must endeavor to respond imaginatively and directly himself if he is to see the hidden poetry of *Ghosts*.

Mrs. Alving and Oswald: The Tragic Rhythm in a Small Figure

As Ibsen was fighting to present his poetic vision within the narrow theater admitted by modern realism, so his protagonist Mrs. Alving is fighting to realize her sense of human life in the blank photograph of her own stuffy parlor. She discovers there no means, no terms, and no nourishment; that is the truncated tragedy which underlies the savage thesis of the play. But she does find her son Oswald and she makes of him the symbol of all she is seeking: freedom, innocence, joy, and truth. At the level of the life of the play, where Ibsen warms his characters into extraordinary human reality, they all have moral and emotional meaning for each other; and the pattern of their related actions, their partially blind struggle for the Alving heritage is consistent and very complex. In this structure, Mrs. Alving's changing relation to Oswald is only one strand, though an important one. I wish to consider it as a sample of Ibsen's rediscovery, through modern realism, of the tragic rhythm.

Oswald is of course not only a symbol for his mother, but a person in his own right, with his own quest for freedom and release and his own anomalous stake in the Alving heritage. He is also a symbol for Pastor Manders of what he wants from Captain Alving's estate: the stability and continuity of the bourgeois conventions. In the economy of the play as a whole, Oswald is the hidden reality of the whole situation, like Oedipus' actual status as son-husband: the hidden fatality which, revealed in a series of tragic and ironic steps, brings the final peripety of the action. To see how this works, the reader is asked to consider Oswald's role in Act I and the beginning of Act II.

The main part of Act I (after a prologue between Regina and Engstrand) is a debate, or rather agon, between Mrs. Alving and the Pastor. The Pastor has come to settle the details of Mrs. Alving's bequest of her husband's money to the orphanage. They at once disagree about the purpose and handling of the bequest; and this disagreement soon broadens into the whole issue of Mrs. Alving's emancipation versus the Pastor's convention-ality. The question of Oswald is at the center. The Pastor wants to think of him, and to make of him, a pillar of society such as the Captain was supposed to have been, while Mrs. Alving wants him to be her masterpiece of libera-tion. At this point Oswald himself wanders in, the actual but still mysterious truth underlying the dispute between his mother and the Pastor. His appear-ance produces what the Greeks would have called a complex recognition scene, with an implied peripety for both Mrs. Alving and the Pastor, which will not be realized by them until the end of the act. But this tragic develop-ment is written to be acted; it is to be found, not so much in the actual words of the characters, as in their moral-emotional responses and changing rela-tionships to one another.

The Pastor has not seen Oswald since he grew up; and seeing him now he is startled as though by a real ghost; he recognizes him as the very rein-carnation of his father: the same physique, the same mannerisms, even the same kind of pipe. Mrs. Alving with equal confidence recognizes him as her own son, and she notes that his mouth-mannerism is like the Pastor's. (She had been in love with the Pastor during the early years of her marriage, when she wanted to leave the Captain.) As for Oswald himself, the mention of the pipe gives him a Proustian intermittence of the heart: he suddenly recalls a childhood scene when his father had given him his own pipe to smoke. He feels again the nausea and the cold sweat, and hears the Captain's hearty laughter. Thus in effect he recognizes himself as his father's, in the sense of his father's *victim*; a premonition of the ugly scene at the end of the play. But at this point no one is prepared to accept the full import of these insights. The whole scene is, on the surface, light and conventional, an accurate report of a passage of provincial politeness. Oswald wanders off for a walk before dinner and the Pastor and his mother are left to bring their struggle more into the open.

Oswald's brief scene marks the end of the first round of the fight, and serves as a prologue for the second round, much as the intervention of the chorus in the agon between Oedipus and Tiresias punctuates their struggle, and hints at an unexpected outcome on a new level of awareness. As soon as Oswald has gone, the Pastor launches an attack in form upon Mrs. Alving's entire emancipated way of life, with the question of Oswald, his role in the community, his upbringing and his future, always at the center of the attack. Mrs. Alving replies with her whole rebellious philosophy, illustrated by a detailed account of her tormented life with the Captain, none of which the Pastor had known (or been willing to recognize) before. Mrs. Alving proves on the basis of this evidence that her new freedom is right; that her long secret rebellion was justified; and that she is now about to complete Oswald's emancipation, and thereby her own, from the swarming ghosts of the past. If the issue were merely on this rationalistic level, and between her and the Pastor, she would triumph at this point. But the real truth of her situation (as Oswald's appearance led us to suppose) does not fit either her rationalization or the Pastor's.

Oswald passes through the parlor again on his way to the dining room to get a drink before dinner, and his mother watches him in pride and pleasure. But from behind the door we hear the affected squealing of Regina. It is now Mrs. Alving's turn for an intermittence of the heart: it is as though she heard again her husband with Regina's mother. The insight which she had rejected before now reaches her in full strength, bringing the promised pathos and peripety; she sees Oswald, not as her masterpiece of liberation, but as the sinister, tyrannical, and continuing life of the past itself. The basis of her rationalization is gone; she suffers the breakdown of the moral being which she had built upon her now exploded view of Oswald.

At this point Ibsen brings down the curtain in obedience to the principles of the well-made play. The effect is to raise the suspense by stimulating our curiosity about the facts of the rest of the story. What will Mrs. Alving do now? What will the Pastor do—for Oswald and Regina are half-brother and sister; can we prevent the scandal from coming out? So the suspense is raised, but the attention of the audience is diverted from Mrs. Alving's tragic quest to the most literal, newspaper version of the facts.

The second act (which occurs immediately after dinner) is ostensibly concerned only with these gossipy facts. The Pastor and Mrs. Alving debate ways of handling the threatened scandal. But this is only the literal surface: Ibsen has his eye on Mrs. Alving's shaken psyche, and the actual dramatic form of this scene, under the discussion which Mrs. Alving keeps up, is her pathos which the Act I curtain broke off. Mrs. Alving is suffering the blow in courage and faith; and she is rewarded with her deepest insight:

> I am half inclined to think we are all ghosts, Mr. Manders. It is
> not only what we have inherited from our fathers and mothers
> that exists again in us, but all sorts of dead ideas and all kinds of
> old dead beliefs and things of that kind. They are not actually

alive in us; but they are dormant all the same, and we can never be rid of them. Whenever I take up a newspaper and read it, I fancy I see ghosts creeping between the lines. There must be ghosts all over the world. They must be as countless as the grains of sand, it seems to me. And we are so miserably afraid of the light, all of us.

This passage, in the fumbling phrases of Ibsen's provincial lady, and in William Archer's translation, is not by itself the poetry of the great dramatic poets. It does not have the verbal music of Racine, nor the freedom and sophistication of Hamlet, nor the scope of the Sophoclean chorus, with its use of the full complement of poetic and musical and theatrical resources. But in the total situation in the Alving parlor which Ibsen has so carefully established, and in terms of Mrs. Alving's uninstructed but profoundly developing awareness, it has its own hidden poetry: a poetry not of words but of the theater, a poetry of the histrionic sensibility. From the point of view of the underlying form of the play—the form as "the soul" of the tragedy—this scene completes the sequence which began with the debate in Act I: it is the pathos-and-epiphany following that agon.

It is evident, I think, that insofar as Ibsen was able to obey his realistic scruple, his need for the disinterested perception of human life beneath the clichés of custom and rationalization, he rediscovered the perennial basis of tragedy. The poetry of *Ghosts* is under the words, in the detail of action, where Ibsen accurately sensed the tragic rhythm of human life in a thousand small figures. And these little "movements of the psyche" are composed in a complex rhythm like music, a formal development sustained (beneath the sensational story and the angry thesis) until the very end. But the action is not completed: Mrs. Alving is left screaming with the raw impact of the calamity. The music is broken off, the dissonance unresolved—or, in more properly dramatic terms, the acceptance of the catastrophe, leading to the final vision or epiphany which should correspond to the insight Mrs. Alving gains in Act II, is lacking. The action of the play is neither completed nor placed in the wider context of meanings which the disinterested or contemplative purposes of poetry demand.

The unsatisfactory end of *Ghosts* may be understood in several ways. Thinking of the relation between Mrs. Alving and Oswald, one might say that she had romantically loaded more symbolic values upon her son than a human being can carry; hence his collapse proves too much—more than Mrs. Alving or the audience can digest. One may say that, at the end, Ibsen himself could not quite dissociate himself from his rebellious protagonist and see her action in the round, and so broke off in anger, losing his tragic vision in the satisfaction of reducing the bourgeois parlor to a nightmare, and proving the hollowness of a society which sees human life in such myopic and dishonest terms. As a thesis play, *Ghosts* is an ancestor of many related genres: Brieux's arguments for social reform, propaganda plays like those of the Marxists, or parables *à la* Andreev, or even Shaw's more generalized plays of the play-of-thought about social questions. But this use of the theater of modern realism for promoting or discussing political and social ideas never appealed to Ibsen. It did not solve his real problem, which was to use the publicly accepted theater of his time for poetic purposes. The most general way to understand the unsatisfactory end of *Ghosts* is to say that Ibsen could not find a way to represent the action of his protagonist, with all its moral and intellectual depth, within the terms of modern realism. In the attempt he truncated this action, and revealed as in a brilliant light the limitations of the bourgeois parlor as the scene of human life.

The End of *Ghosts:* The Tasteless Parlor and the Stage of Europe

Oswald is the chief symbol of what Mrs. Alving is seeking, and his collapse ends her quest in a horrifying catastrophe. But in the complex life of the play, all of the persons and things acquire emotional and moral significance for Mrs. Alving; and at the end, to throw as much light as possible upon the catastrophe, Ibsen brings all of the elements of his composition together in their highest symbolic valency. The orphanage has burned to the ground; the Pastor has promised Engstrand money for his "Sailor's Home" which he plans as a brothel; Regina departs, to follow her mother in the search for pleasure and money. In these eventualities the conventional morality of the Alving heritage is revealed as lewdness and dishonesty, quickly consumed in the fires of lust and greed, as Oswald himself (the central symbol) was consumed even before his birth. But what does this wreckage mean? Where are we to place it in human experience? Ibsen can only place it in the literal parlor, with lamplight giving place to daylight, and sunrise on the empty, stimulating, virginal snow-peaks out the window. The emotional force of this complicated effect is very great: it has the searching intimacy of nightmare. But it is also as disquieting as a nightmare from which we are suddenly awakened; it is incomplete, and the contradiction between the inner power of dream and the literal appearances of the daylight world is unresolved. The spirit that moved Ibsen to write the play, and which moved his protagonist through her tragic progress, is lost to sight, disembodied, imperceptible in any form unless the dreary exaltation of the inhuman mountain scene conveys it in feeling.

Henry James felt very acutely the contradiction between the deep and strict spirit of Ibsen and his superb craftsmanship on the one side, and the little scene he tried to use—the parlor in its surrounding void—on the other.

> If the spirit is a lamp within us, glowing through what the world and the flesh make of us as through a ground-glass shade, then such pictures as Little Eyolf and John Gabriel are each a chassez-croisez of lamps burning as in tasteless parlors, with the flame practically exposed. There is a positive odor of spiritual paraffin. The author nevertheless arrives at the dramatist's great goal—he arrives for all his meagerness at intensity. The meagerness, which is after all but an unconscious, an admirable economy, never interferes with that: it plays straight into the hands of his rare mastery of form. The contrast between this form—so difficult to have reached, so "evolved," so civilized—and the bareness and bleakness of his little northern democracy is the source of half the hard frugal charm he puts forth.

James had rejected very early in his career his own little northern democracy, that of General Grant's America, with its ugly parlor, its dead conventions, its enthusiastic materialism, and its "non-conducting atmosphere." At the same time he shared Ibsen's ethical preoccupation, and his strict sense of form. His comments on Ibsen are at once the most sympathetic and the most objective that have been written. But James's own solution was to try to find a better parlor for the theater of human life; to present the quest of his American pilgrim of culture on the wider "stage of Europe" as this might still be felt and suggested in the manners of the leisured classes in England and France. James would have nothing to do with the prophetic and revolutionary spirit which was driving the great continental authors, Ibsen among them. In his artistry and his moral exactitude Ibsen is akin to James; but this is not his whole story, and if one is to understand the spirit he tried to realize in Mrs. Alving, one must think of Kierkegaard, who had a great influence on Ibsen in the beginning of his career.

Kierkegaard (in *For Self-Examination*) has this to say of the disembodied and insatiable spirit of the times:

> . . . thou wilt scarcely find anyone who does not believe in—let us say, for example, the spirit of the age, the *Zeitgeist*. Even he who has taken leave of higher things and is rendered blissful by mediocrity, yea, even he who toils slavishly for paltry ends or in the contemptible servitude of ill-gotten gains, even he believes,

firmly and fully too, in the spirit of the age. Well, that is natural
enough, it is by no means anything very lofty he believes in, for
the spirit of the age is after all no higher than the age it keeps
close to the ground, so that it is the sort of spirit which is most
like will-o'-the-wisp; but yet he believes in spirit. Or he believes
in the world-spirit (*Weltgeist*) that strong spirit (for allurements,
yes), the ingenious spirit (for deceits, yes); that spirit which
Christianity calls an evil spirit—so that, in consideration of this,
it is by no means anything very lofty he believes in when he
believes in the world-spirit; but yet he believes in spirit. Or he
believes in "the spirit of humanity," not spirit in the individual,
but in the race, that spirit which, when it is god-forsaken for
having forsaken God, is again, according to Christianity's
teaching, an evil spirit—so that in view of this it is by no means
anything very lofty he believes in when he believes in this spirit;
but yet he believes in spirit.

On the other hand, as soon as the talk is about a holy spirit—
how many, dost thou think, believe in it? Or when the talk is
about an evil spirit which is to be renounced—how many, dost
thou think, believe in such a thing?

This description seems to me to throw some light upon Mrs. Alving's
quest, upon Ibsen's modern-realistic scene, and upon the theater which his
audience would accept. The other face of nineteenth century positivism is
romantic aspiration. And Ibsen's realistic scene presents both of these aspects
of the human condition: the photographically accurate parlor, in the foreground, satisfies the requirements of positivism, while the empty but stimulating scene out the window—Europe as a moral void, an uninhabited
wilderness—offers as it were a blank check to the insatiate spirit. Ibsen
always felt this exhilarating wilderness behind his cramped interiors. In *A
Doll's House* we glimpse it as winter weather and black water. In *The Lady from
the Sea* it is the cold ocean, with its whales and its gulls. In *The Wild Duck* it
is the northern marshes, with wildfowl but no people. In the last scene of
Ghosts it is, of course, the bright snow-peaks, which may mean Mrs. Alving's
quest in its most disembodied and ambivalent form; very much the same
sensuous moral void in which Wagner, having totally rejected the little
human foreground where Ibsen fights his battles, unrolls the solitary action
of passion. It is the "stage of Europe" before human exploration as it might
have appeared to the first hunters.

There is a kinship between the fearless and demanding spirit of
Kierkegaard, and the spirit which Ibsen tried to realize in Mrs. Alving. But

Mrs. Alving, like her contemporaries whom Kierkegaard describes, will not or cannot accept any interpretation of the spirit that drives her. It may look like the *Weltgeist* when she demands the joy of living, it may look like the Holy Ghost itself when one considers her appetite for truth. And it may look like the spirit of evil, a "goblin damned," when we see the desolation it produces. If one thinks of the symbols which Ibsen brings together in the last scene: the blank parlor, the wide unexplored world outside, the flames that consumed the Alving heritage and the sunrise flaming on the peaks, one may be reminded of the condition of Dante's great rebel Ulysses. He too is wrapped in the flame of his own consciousness, yet still dwells in the pride of the mind and the exhilaration of the world free of people, *il mondo senza gente.* But this analogy also may not be pressed too far. Ulysses is in hell; and when we explore the Mountain on which he was wrecked, we can place his condition with finality, and in relation to many other human modes of action and awareness. But Mrs. Alving's mountains do not place her anywhere: the realism of modern realism ends with the literal. Beyond that is not the ordered world of the tradition, but *Unendlichkeit,* and the anomalous "freedom" of undefined and uninformed aspiration.

Perhaps Mrs. Alving and Ibsen himself are closer to the role of Dante than to the role of Ulysses, seeing a hellish mode of being, but free to move on. Certainly Ibsen's development continued beyond *Ghosts,* and toward the end of his career he came much closer to achieving a consistent theatrical poetry within the confines of the theater of modern realism. He himself remarked that his poetry was to be found only in the series of his plays, no one of which was complete by itself.

ERIC BENTLEY

Ibsen: Pro and Con

It must have been a pleasure to welcome Ibsen with open arms when all one's primmer relatives were shaking their fist at him, but the great days of Ibsenism are past. Today the mention of the Norwegian's name elicits in many quarters a certain feeling of tedium. After all, the Ibsenites won all too complete a victory: their man was accepted into the dull ranks of fame; he was an academic figure.

A supremely great writer like Shakespeare can survive such acceptance—with whatever wear and tear. It is harder for a genius of the second rank. The livelier reader—the only reader that counts—is apt to think Ibsen well deserves his dim respectability. It would be better if he belonged to the third rank and did not raise such high expectations! Ibsen so often leads us to expect the highest things, we are disturbed when he falls short. He is an author one worries about. From time to time one wonders—as one does not wonder about Shakespeare—: is he really good or have I been imposed upon?

If we are to return to him, if we are to read and see him freshly, it cannot be by ignoring such worries. Before hearing a spokesman *for* Ibsen, let us hear a devil's advocate voice our misgivings.

From "Ibsen: Pro and Con" by Eric Bentley from *Theatre Arts* XXXIV:7 (July 1950): 39–43. Copyright © 1950 by John D. MacArthur.

CON

When we open our Ibsen we enter an unconvincing world: a world created by bad prose, clumsy dramatic structures, and stale ideas. Since you will tell me that the bad prose is the work of his translators, I will concentrate on the structures and the ideas.

How could H. L. Mencken feel that Ibsen abolished the artificial "well-made play" and just let the facts "tell themselves"? Hadn't he read "Ghosts"? At the end of Act 2 Mrs. Alving's story is just "telling itself" when—lest it all come blurting out before our evening at the theatre is done—Ibsen has a sanatorium catch fire. This is a disastrously clumsy dramatic construction. The craftsman's machinery overwhelms the poet's vision.

Is not the same true of "A Doll's House"? Krogstad, for example, is a mere pawn of the plot. When convenient to Ibsen, he is a blackmailer. When inconvenient, he is converted. Ibsen the craftsman is busy constructing relationships between two couples—Torvald and Nora, Krogstad and Mrs. Linde. The parallels and contrasts must work out right, even if the characterization is impaired.

Dr. Rank is not the pawn of the plot—he is not even necessary to it—but he is the pawn of an idea. When Ibsen wants to bring the theme of hereditary disease and death before us he has only to write "Enter Dr. Rank." You will tell me that Dr. Rank is a symbolic character, and that symbolism is one of the elements in the total structure of an Ibsen play. The trouble is that Ibsen's symbolism is so portentous—what with the sanatorium burning to show us that the Alvings are burning and Rank dropping his black cross in the letter box to show us that death is in the background.

In "An Enemy of the People," "A Doll's House," and "Ghosts" the symbolism is obvious to the point of being tiresome; in "The Master Builder" it is obscure to the point of being confused. I don't mean that the reader of "The Master Builder" has nothing to hold on to. Every little Freudian nowadays knows what to say about the towers and Solness's inability to climb them. Biographers are at hand to explain that Ibsen was tired of writing "social" plays as Solness was tired of building homes for human beings. What then? The play as a whole is bewildering. Whatever human reality Ibsen may have meant to show us is hidden behind a wilderness of trolls, birds of prey, helpers and servers, devils (good and bad, blond and brunette), fairy kingdoms, and castles in the air. The symbolism proliferates. The total result is a mess.

Then there are the ideas, Ibsen's famous ideas: there should be votes for women, women's rights are equal to men's, hereditary syphilis is a bad thing, mercy killing is sometimes justified, keep germs out of the bathwater, don't be jealous of the younger generation, and so forth. If my phrasing is flippant, blame Ibsen, whose presentation of problems is always either ridiculous or vague: the greatest actress who ever played Mrs. Alving—Eleanore Duse—admitted as much. What, for instance, lies behind the nebulous Victorian terms in which Mrs. Alving's life with her husband is dressed? As a critic has already asked: did she never enjoy it when she went to bed with him? Not the least little bit? Again, if the phrasing is flippant, Ibsen asks for it: his kind of drama raises such questions without revealing the answers. Consequently it is impossible to grasp his characters in the way he seems to want you to grasp them.

Oswald in Paris is as cloudy a figure as his mother in his father's bedroom. A matter we must be clear about is whether his disease *must* have come from his father or whether he could not have contracted syphilis from his own sexual activities. At one moment he seems to say No to the latter question. "I have never lived recklessly in any sense . . . I have never done that," but soon thereafter he says "I ought to have had nothing to do with the joyous happy life I had lived with my comrades. It had been too much for my strength. So it was my own fault . . . My whole life incurably ruined—just because of my own imprudence." This last speech is not conclusive, but that is precisely the trouble: conclusiveness is called for. Perhaps one does not care what the doctors say of Oswald's collapse in Act 3. Perhaps one can forgive Ibsen for his unscrupulously melodramatic timing of the collapse. But there are many details which could be clear and aren't. For example: Oswald argues that the Parisian artists prefer living unmarried with their children's mothers because it is cheaper. But is it?

A picture composed of such unclear details can only come together in our minds as a fog. Is any clear attitude defined to the famous "modern ideas" to be found in the play? And how far do they go? One assumes that the books Mrs. Alving reads—and which Ibsen does not name—are typical of nineteenth-century liberalism. Yet in one curious passage she goes far beyond ordinary enlightenment into the assumption that we should accept even incest. Ibsen being Ibsen, the suggestion is not clarified.

If "Ghosts" is not exactly a "drama of ideas" it will be better to instance a play that *is*—"An Enemy of the People." Dr. Stockman expects his fellow-townsmen to accept the truth, however they may be affected by it. He finds, however, that people refuse to accept a truth if it interferes with their interests, that the liberal opposition goes along with the interested minority, and that the masses soon follow suit. He therefore decides—in Act 4—that he is against majority rule.

This is straightforward, if not profound. It is in the fifth Act that Ibsen proves himself a muddlehead. Vehement as Stockman is in rejecting common folk as "curs" he firmly intends to educate them. He will begin by educating his own boys and a handful of street urchins. He will train the curs to the point where they can drive out the wolves. "You shan't learn a blessed thing . . . but I will make liberal-minded and high-minded men out of you." That is to say: "The voice of the people is not the voice of God till the people has been educated by me."

Even if we share Stockman's high opinion of himself we must ask how he can secure his position as an educator in a country where the majority are curs?

Even in a more fortunate land, how can we make the philosopher a king? "An Enemy of the People" is a manifesto for the petty bourgeois, the petty snob, and petty intellectual. The masses are ignorant, you are cultured, therefore you disbelieve in democracy, you believe in culture. What of it? You have not made it clear how you can attain power. In any case, as a leader you are self-appointed, and that is a game many can play at: *anyone* can declare himself a leader, cultured or otherwise.

Are you going to say that Stockman is not Ibsen? There is precious little evidence within the play that the latter is critical of his creation. The whole play breathes the perennial self-complacency of the arrogant idealist— from the Pharisee of the first century to the Communist intellectual of today. That Ibsen felt compelled to show the other side of the medal in "The Wild Duck" can hardly comfort the critic of "An Enemy of the People." It takes more than two one-sided plays to make a single two-sided masterpiece. And "An Enemy" is one-sided, a play of moral blacks and whites. To read it as a subtle study in self-righteousness, like "Le Misanthrope," would be to conceive another play. Stockman is an Alceste taken pretty much at his own valuation.

As a piece of thinking, "An Enemy of the People" is too superficial to be instructive. As a piece of art, it is too feeble to be influential. In 1950 it would be as easy as it is wise to let Ibsen rest in peace.

PRO

I do not find either Ibsen's ideas or his forms as disastrously "dated" as you assume.

Let me begin where you left off—with the ideas. Are even the ones you mentioned really outmoded? I believe they only *sound* so. "Women's rights," for example. The phrase itself is not in use today—but for that matter it isn't used in "A Doll's House." The problem as to what women's rights are is still real enough. The world is still a man's world, and if the status of women has been raised, it is still a secondary and an awkward status.

In 1950 there are still many "doll's houses." As for "Ghosts," hereditary disease is still with us, mercy killing is still a controversial question. And as for "The Master Builder," the conflict of the generations is as real as ever.

Even the play you take as the very type of outmoded "drama of ideas"—"An Enemy of the People"—is neither as transparent nor as wrong as you make it appear. Certainly Stockman's philosophy is superogatory in a country like Germany where too many people already share it. In America it might be a salutary challenge. The American philosophy of the common man needs constant criticism if it is to be preserved from demagogic sentimentality. The idealism of many people today begins in self-contempt and functions as a flight from the self: Stockman, whatever his failings, knew that morality must start from self-respect. You seem to consider the Ibsen who wrote "An Enemy" trivial, facile, journalistic. Just compare the portrait of a Norwegian community given in Steinbeck's "The Moon is Down." There can be no doubt who gives the keener, stricter, more deeply-pondered view.

But these are side issues. More essential is the fact that in discussing Ibsen's ideas you mentioned only those that jump to the eyes, the famous "social" ideas that scandalized conservative Victorians and delighted the Ibsenite rebels. Led astray, perhaps, by some of the latter, you too seem to expect Ibsen to be primarily a "brain." Perhaps you demand that his ideas be brilliant and original and that he juggle them with the skill of a logician. I, on the other hand, shall argue that you have failed to notice what are the most active ideas in Ibsen's plays and that you are thus unable to see what use he put them to.

What ideas are most active in "Ghosts"? Surely not those you have mentioned. Behind the question of mercy killing is the question of "modern ideas" generally—as against the "established ideas" of Pastor Manders. To perpetrate a mercy killing, a person would have to be emancipated entirely from established ideas. Ibsen brings the matter up, one might almost say, to show that Mrs. Alving is *not* so emancipated. Thus he is less interested in "modern ideas" themselves than in certain ideas that go behind them. In Ibsen one must always seek the idea behind the idea.

Ibsen did not by any means stop with the conflict of modern and established ideas. His special achievement is the depth and body he gives to each of these philosophies as it exists in people's lives. He does this not as an agile arguer but as a poet with a country, a people, a tradition behind him. Abstract ideas take concrete form through (for example his use of folk imagery. Established ideas he sees as ghosts, as the spirits of the dead of popular belief, and if Mrs. Alving strives after modernity she does so not as the "new woman" of the Paris boulevards, but as a daughter of the Vikings. Below the surface of modern, Christian civilization Ibsen finds primitive, pagan forces. It is to Norse paganism he looks alike for images of evil and for images of human dignity: here, rather than in those modern books which, so you insinuate, he doesn't even know the titles of. His superior people are to be understood as Vikings *manqués*. Mrs. Alving thinks she ought, like some rash pagan, to countenance incest, but she can't bring herself to do so. The great surprise of "A Doll's House" is our discovery of a Viking spirit in Torvald's little squirrel. Halvard Solness is a man who *had been* a Viking—ten years earlier. If you will agree to call *this* Ibsen's "idea" you will not find "The Master Builder" so bewildering.

Compared with Mrs. Alving, Solness is a strong man. But if the weaker Ibsen characters are held back by the spirits of the dead, the stronger are goaded on by the trolls of the mountain. Early in "A Doll's House" Nora is characterized as a "mad creature," and later when she dances the tarantella the troll in her takes over. In "The Master Builder" the trolls come for Solness in the person of Hilda Wangel—or that part of her which is a bird of prey. They goad him into attempting the impossible. Being a Viking no longer he cannot climb as high as he builds. He falls to his death.

I am not offering Norse mythology as a magic key to Ibsen. My point is simply that one can always look in Ibsen for something beyond the cliches of the problem drama. Take the most famous play of them all. "A Doll's House" seems to you to be about votes for women, a topic that does not come up in the play at all. What does come up is the matter of woman's place in a man's world, a much larger topic that still bristles with interest today. It even seems to me that Ibsen pushes his investigation towards a further and even deeper subject, a tyranny of one human being over another; in this respect, the play would be just as valid were Torvald the wife and Nora the husband.

Re-read the opening pages of "A Doll's House." Since the text is familiar, you are not just picking up the facts of the story, you are noticing the terms in which Ibsen presents his subject. No words are lost. Nora's tipping the porter a shilling instead of sixpence not only gives us her character but establishes money as one of the topics of the play. The borrowing of money—which lies at the heart of the action—is mentioned soon and is opposed to the possibility of freedom and beauty. The making of lots of money is seen by Torvald and Nora as a basis for security, a life free from care, yet when we meet someone who actually married for money we have a sense of foreboding. I am mentioning only a few of the references to money. They all lead into the play—taken as a play. You must after all regard "A Doll's House" as drama even when your topic is the ideas. The ideas thread their way in and out, as it were, as themes. The theme of money, for example. Money is at the root of so much that happens in "A Doll's House." Ibsen has, if you like, an "idea" about money. He doesn't philosophize about it. He lets it find expression through the action and the characters.

You managed to speak of four Ibsen plays without noticing an "idea" common to them all—an idea about disease. For Ibsen, disease is not only one of the facts of life in general but a symbol of modern life in particular. You doubtless recall Solness's sickly conscience, Oswald's rotting body and mind, and you mentioned Dr. Rank. Don't you find Ibsen adroit when he introduces the disease-theme in Rank's opening discussion of Krogstad, at once transfers it from the physical to the moral sphere, then applies it to society at large?

Admittedly, a formula such as "modern life—a disease" is little or nothing in itself. Ibsen makes dramatic use of it. He sets it in motion. He makes it grow. In "An Enemy of the People," Act 2, Hovstad explains that the morass which the town is built on is not physical but moral. In Act 3, Stockman realizes that "it is the whole of our social life that we have got to purify and disinfect." The idea gathers momentum, and has, as it were, a climax, along with the rest of the play's action, in Act 4. "It is not they who are most instrumental in poisoning the sources of our moral life and infecting the ground on which we stand . . . it is the masses, the majority."

When I turn your attention from the ideas themselves to Ibsen's use of them I don't mean Ibsen didn't take ideas seriously but that his seriousness about them—and the force of the ideas themselves—come out more in the way he has them operate than in anything he explicitly says. His criticism of life is made less in general formulations than in ironical juxtaposition of the facts. It has often been shown that Ibsen interweaves, intertwines, interlocks his materials. His dialogue is all implication, all cross-reference. This is his famous method. It is important to see in it not a system of meaningless theatrical trickery, but an exquisitely apt expression of Ibsen's awareness.

I grant you that when he became a virtuoso Ibsen succumbed to some of the virtuoso's temptations. His technique is sometimes obtrusive, and often the lines creak and groan beneath the load of double, treble, and quadruple significance. I only ask you not, in protesting against the defect, to forget the quality. As to the overall structure of an Ibsen play, for example it is misleading to observe that Ibsen used a highly artificial, not to say sensational, pattern borrowed from the Parisian hacks and handed back to them afterwards, if we do not add that this pattern exactly suited Ibsen's deeper purpose. For the hacks, it was a toy—and thus an end in itself, though by definition, a childish one. For Ibsen, it was the instrument of a vision.

Historians of the drama explain that Ibsen took over from the Parisian hacks the story of the long-buried secret which eventually leaks out with sensational results. They sometimes forget to add that Ibsen saw life itself as a placid surface through which, from time to time, what seemed dead and buried will break—a present into which the "vanished" past returns. Perhaps they are indifferent to the meaning of all this—that there is moral continuity between past and present, that concealment (repression, hypocrisy) is the enemy, openness (candor, light, truth) the one thing necessary. If so they miss the point of Ibsen's famous expositions: as pure technique they would be barren exercises; what justifies them is the way they tender the interaction of past and present. The curtain goes up ten years after Nora and Mrs. Linde last met, ten years after the death of Alving, ten years after the meeting of Solness and Hilda. Ibsen confronts one decade in his people's lives with another. The plot-pattern gives exact expression alike to his direct vision of life and to his subsequent interpretation of it.

To your contention that Ibsen's plots ride him, rather than he them, I reply that I could give more examples of the contrary. One is to be found at the end of "A Doll's House." If the plot dominated the play, the culminating point would be Torvald's discovery of Nora's secret. Ibsen's achievement is to have subordinated this external event to Nora's inner realization that Torvald is incapable of nobly taking the blame for what she has done. The dramatically active question of the last act is whether the "wonderful thing" will happen or not. The scene in which Nora realizes that it won't is one of the great scenes in modern drama, not only in precipitating the same mordant speeches ("It is a thing hundreds of thousands of women have done"), but in occasioning a magnificently dramatic silence—that of Nora gradually realizing that Torvald is a broken reed. (A few words escape her but the process of realization is silent.)

I should not leave the subject of Ibsen's dramatic art without a word on his mastery of the theatrical occasion. He isn't writing novels in dialogue form, he is writing for actors before the eyes of an audience. I suspect that, like so many moderns, you are primarily a novel-reader who resents not finding in Ibsen all that he finds in fiction. If you think Ibsen lacks the skills of Henry James you should recognize that he has others which James lacks, the skills of the theatre rather than the book. If, of course, you simply prefer the novel to the drama, there is no more to be said; you will naturally prefer James's gradual. word-by-word definition of his subjects to Ibsen's definition by upheaval. If, on the other hand, you can respect the theatrical medium you will appreciate the effect on the spectator of, say, Hilda Wangel's first irruption onto the stage with her alpenstock and knapsack, Mrs. Alving "registering" the offstage laughter of Regina and Oswald, Nora's suddenly appearing in her street-clothes. Such things are addressed to the eyes of an audience, not to the imagination of a solitary reader.

"Ibsen and the Actor" is a huge topic, for not only did he write for actors (like every other playwright); he gave the actor something essentially new and asked him for something essentially new in return: a new style. He brought to completion a development in the art of acting that had been under way for centuries—the humanizing of the actor, the conversion of a hierophant into a man. In Ibsen that part of man which the ancient mime kept covered—the face—is the very center of the performance. The individual spirit looks out of the eyes and shapes its thoughts with the lips.

But this is no doubt too special a subject for your taste. Let me try and sum up my rejoinder to your protest. I think you have too limited a conception of the way in which an artist teaches. Ibsen, for example, is not—or not in the first instance—providing a list of recommended virtues and deplored vices. In this regard, he is singularly modest. He has written only a preface to morals. He asks for that degree of honor, honesty, integrity, truth, what you will, that is needed before a moral life can exist. We have seen that he tells over and again the story of the disastrous effects of concealment and burial. He is asking us not necessarily to be saints and heroes, but at least to stand upright; at least—like Goethe's Faust—to assume responsibilities and make ethical distinctions; at least to be authentic human beings. Ibsen does not have his people follow the track of any particular virtue. He shows Nora and Mrs. Alving trying to discover themselves and reach the threshold of morality, the point where virtues—and of course vices—begin. So much of our life is too meaningless or too infantile even to be called vicious.

This criticism of life places Ibsen, not in the piddling tradition of the problem play, but at the very heart of our contemporary discussion of ourselves. He is one of the great modern writers. Like most of the others he has presented modern life to us in the form of fable, parable, myth, and once you realize that his medium was theatre and not the book, you will not find his fables inferior to those of other masters. Ibsen is a poet. Although he gave us verse, he managed to enrich and intensify his work by so many other means that the verse plays of the best poets since his time—T. S. Eliot's, for example—seem dilute and "unpoetic" by comparison.

Forty years ago a decadent poet—who evidently despised Ibsen's dialogue in general—could refer to Hilda Wangel's "harps in the air" as a feeble, if praiseworthy, attempt at lyricism. Strange that he hadn't more feeling for the *context* of Hilda's phrase, for that dry, prose understatement against which "harps in the air" come as a contrast, an intentionally brief glimpse of another order of experience! I do not mean to interpret the dry, prose understatement as a merely negative factor. A generation that has read Gertrude Stein and Ernest Hemingway knows better than that. Ibsen is a great realist, not least in his imaginative use of unimaginative language.

Of recent years those of us who admire Ibsen's poetry have probably understressed his realism. It is a pity the two words are used antithetically. Ibsen was a great poet—that is, he had a great imagination which found its outlet in words—but it would be foolish to try and detach him from the realist movement. He quite consciously channeled his energies into it. It was as a realist that he made his first impact, and, in closing my counter-statement, I shall maintain that it is partly as a realist that he must still make his impact today.

In refusing to squeeze Ibsen into the narrow category of the problem play we need not neglect to view him historically. There is a pedantry of historical scholarship that reduces artists to statistics and vaguely defined abstractions, but there is also history itself—man and all his works in the flux of time. I should prefer to see *any* artist in this context rather than in context of timeless forms and timeless ideas—and Ibsen above all. For, however we stress his artistry and the breadth of his mind, he was a man up to the neck in his time. We find him relevant today partly because we have still not put his time behind us, partly because the artists who become permanent are precisely those who grasp the ephemeral most firmly and not those whose eyes are fixed upon eternity.

A more historical view of Ibsen will keep us from exaggerating the other-worldness of a play like—to come back to your bugbear—"The Master Builder." For once we realize that Ibsen was not obsessed with syphilis or votes for women there is a danger of our locating his interest only in the deepest recesses of the individual consciousness. This would be to consider him just as narrow a specialist—only at the other extreme. The glory of Ibsen is that he refused to make certain fatal separations. He refused (for example to separate the individual from the collective, the personal from the social. Halvard Solness is seen in both aspects. There is Solness the individual artist: *the symbolism of the play drives inwards*, to the rich inner life of the man. There is also Solness the builder of actual houses: I should not be as much inclined as I once was to regard him as a mere front for the more spiritual figure. As Miss Bradbrook says: "Solness belonged to a class which transformed Norway. The replacing of the old wooden house . . . by modern buildings effected a domestic revolution." *The realism of the play drives outwards*, to the rich outer life of the man. If the symbolism and the realism of "The Master Builder" are imperfectly fused—and that may be the source of your difficulty with the play—one realizes that Ibsen could have perfected his work by simplifying his problem, by writing a narrowly "symbolic" or a narrowly "realist" play. Surely one prefers a heroic failure.

Not that the word failure applies to Ibsen's work as a whole. Artistic failures seldom outlive the artist, yet one-hundred years since Ibsen's first play was written his words sting and burn, if we let them, as fiercely as ever. No playwright has managed to project into his scenes more of the pressure of modern life, its special anxiety, strain, and stress. The life of our times courses through his plays in a torrent. And if we are a little more conscious than our grandparents were of the care with which Ibsen controlled the flood—his mastery of form—we must still begin where they began—with shock, with enthrallment, with illumination, as Ibsen's world, which is so large a sector of the modern world, social and personal, outer and inner, unfolds before us.

UNA ELLIS-FERMOR

Introduction to Hedda Gabler *and Other Plays*

This is an attempt to translate into the English of today three plays written in Norwegian at the end of the nineteenth century. The original itself is no longer the speech that would be used by a contemporary dramatist such as Helge Krog or Nordahl Grieg; some words have slightly different associations and overtones and there are turns of phrase here and there that represent the conversation of that period rather than of the present day. Moreover, the Norwegian language has changed rather more in the last half-century than has English in the corresponding period. Yet, because Ibsen is a great dramatist, the presence of these faint but subtle differences does not date the dialogue as it would that of a man who was wholly of his age. His language (like his thought and his technique) has less in it that is old-fashioned to modern Norwegian ears than has Henry Arthur Jones's to modern Englishmen. Nevertheless, it poses some pretty problems for the translator, who must try to render that dialogue in an English which sounds natural to the modern reader and, without so using the ephemeral as to put the translation itself out of date in ten years, nevertheless avoid that safe and colourless neutrality which would do an even graver injustice to the original. I am all too keenly aware that I have not achieved this; only Ibsen, writing in English, could. I can only plead that this is what I believe should be done.

This is primarily a reader's translation. But it has been my intention throughout to write dialogue which could be spoken by the actor, the cadences and the word-order such as can be put across from the stage without undue effort. This is more difficult in translation than in original writing; and the superb ease and power with which Ibsen does it in his own language is at once a stimulus and a responsibility. Nevertheless, this is not a 'stage version' or a free translation. No one who has lived for twenty years in close association with Ibsen's mind and thought would dare to tamper deliberately with the close-wrought and precise expression to which he gave the care and labour of constant revision. To the question of particular problems in the language of these three plays I shall return later.

Ibsen was the first Norwegian of modern times to lead the world in any of the arts; he is one of the five greatest dramatists of history. He inherited the stern moral tradition of a race accustomed to hardship and in love with liberty, a race of fine integrity and of a strenuous intellectual habit. His cultural heritage derived from the ancient and the modern world alike and, more immediately, from that of nineteenth-century Europe. But though the great age of Norwegian literature lay in the far past, its spirit was still potent; and in the Renaissance which he dominated he had Wergeland before him and Björnson beside him. The effect of Ibsen upon the European theatre and drama, and through them on European thought, is hard to calculate. He found the drama, in every literature but Germany's, moribund or fixed in its traditions; he left it vital and fertile. Apart from a few dramatists in Scandinavia and France, there was less attempt to imitate him than is sometimes supposed. Like Shakespeare, he affected his contemporaries by the stimulus and inspiration of his example, not by the conventions which found schools. There are no fixed traditions in Ibsen's work, though certain ideals persist from the beginning to the end. He left the world his integrity as a thinker and as an artist. And that can only be 'imitated' in the noblest, the Aristotelian sense.

The plays by which Ibsen is best known in this country are still the naturalistic studies of contemporary life, the work of his middle and late years, and three of those are presented here. But it is impossible to value Ibsen aright, even the Ibsen of the social problem plays, without an understanding of the poet who, like his contemporary Björnson, began with romantic historical verse plays and only gradually took upon himself the task of exposing the makeshift morality of his contemporaries in private and public life. To think of him solely as the great (though never undramatic) moralist of those middle plays is to forget the poet of *Peer Gynt* and its predecessors and of the late plays after *The Master Builder*, to lose sight of the slow and complex evolution of poet into moralist and of the moralist again into the individualist of the final years. Ibsen was no Shakespeare; he was never wholly an artist and never wholly a dramatist. But he was as much of both as was the great dramatic moralist, Aeschylus, before him. He was never, after the early years, content to contemplate the world as it is with the strange Shakespearian balance of eager affection, sympathy and non-critical detachment. His sympathies threw him headlong into criticism. He was a fighter, a prophet, an accuser of souls, and between this mood and the mood of the poet-dramatist there is perpetual conflict. But because of his power and integrity as an artist, he again and again subdued this conflict, so that only the clear runnings, the decantation of his thought, enter the plays; and it takes a knowledge of the whole of his work to see, beneath the flawless form, the volcanic forces that have moulded it. The poems give us the clues. And we are further helped by the letters, the posthumous papers and the passages in *Peer Gynt*, *The Master Builder* and *When We Dead Awaken* where the problems of the artist become themselves the matter of his art.

The three plays chosen for this volume, *The Pillars of the Community*, *The Wild Duck* and *Hedda Gabler*, cover the whole of the period during which Ibsen was preoccupied with the problems of personal and social morality in the world immediately about him. *The Pillars of the Community* initiates, almost with enthusiasm, the group of five which concentrate upon this theme; *The Wild Duck* ends the group in seeming disillusionment, and *Hedda Gabler* is a partial return to that world at a later period.

The Pillars of the Community, when it was finished in 1877, had cost Ibsen two years of unremitting labour and several re-writings. The result is a play whose thought is so profound and clear, whose craftmanship is so natural and easy, that it puts to shame alike the emptiness of the contemporary *pièce bien faite* in France and the turgidity of the serious British drama of the next two decades. His concern here is with the function of truth in life. This is, in fact, his concern throughout his life, and it links the early *Vikings at Helgoland* with the last play, *When We Dead Awaken*. But in the group of five upon which he now entered, *The Pillars of the Community*, *A Doll's House*, *Ghosts*, *An Enemy of the People* and *The Wild Duck*, Ibsen brings to the test of his ideal the society of his own times, observing it pitilessly, exactly and at close range, studying the immediate and the particular in terms of the universal and the continuing. He exposes in these five plays the effect of lies, shams and evasions, showing the tragedy and the degradation that accompany the forfeiting of integrity. In *The Pillars of the Community* he examines the lie in public life, the tragic struggle of Karsten Bernick to hide his sin and preserve his reputation at the expense of another man's good name. The lie in the soul so works upon him that, like Macbeth in a more primitive world, he is drawn step by step into actual crime and plans (and all but carries through) what is virtually a murder. Ibsen allows his Karsten Bernick to redeem himself by confession and to save his soul at the cost of his long-guarded reputation. But this is the first play of the series and it is, for Ibsen, optimistic. Lona Hessel's life-long love for Karsten saves him, as does Solveig's for Peer Gynt, by preserving the image of the man he should have been. In *A Doll's House* and in *Ghosts* the subject is the lie in domestic life; the first shows the destruction of a marriage by an unreal and insincere relationship between husband and wife, and the second the destruction of the lives and souls of the characters by the oppressive tyranny of convention. There is a ray of hope still in *A Doll's House*; in *Ghosts* there is no consolation but the integrity of mind to which Mrs. Alving has won her way through the wreckage of her life. In *An Enemy of the People* Ibsen returns to the lie in public life; but here the odds are against the honest man, solitary, outmanoeuvred and overpowered by the corrupt community. The plays had stirred and shocked his contemporaries, and Ibsen had become more famous but less popular; it is his voice that speaks when Stockmann exclaims at the end of the play, 'The strongest man in the world is he who stands most alone'.

The Wild Duck ends this group and yet, at the same time, begins the next. The apprehension of truth, which had for Karsten Bernick been a relatively simple psychological process, is now something more difficult, more doubtful and more dangerous. Gone is Lona Hessel who, with her robust affection and good sense, lets in the fresh air from the American prairies, and in her place is Gregers Werle, whose conception of truth is like an icy, fanatical wind from the frozen fjelds. Under his ministration the unfortunate Hjalmar Ekdal, a weakling with none of Bernick's fighting pluck, makes shipwreck of his life and of those of his wife and child. It takes two to tell the truth: one to speak and one to hear. It is obvious from the first that Hjalmar is incapable of hearing it, and before the play is out we realize that Gregers is in fact incapable of speaking it. His self-imposed mission has nothing to do with the truth which is an attitude of mind, and his harsh presentation of destructive fact bankrupts the lives he touches. Ibsen has not lost his faith in truth. He has only seen that it sometimes demands a subtler service than the first two plays of the series had supposed.

These three plays, and the two that fall between them, are sometimes called realistic, fourth-wall dramas. This is true if we give a liberal connotation to the word 'realism', but not if we identify it with photography. In fact, as a study of his craftsmanship will make clear, Ibsen does anything but photograph. Even his material is seldom wholly naturalistic. In all five plays, and most clearly in our two, a part at least is used (and we must suppose introduced) for its symbolic value as well as for its contribution to the action. The coffin-ships in *The Pillars of the Community* offer us one of the most artistically exquisite pieces of functional symbolism in modern drama. They are simultaneously an important factor of the action, a clear representative instance of the corruption and greed of the shipowners and, finally—but only in addition to these two strictly dramatic functions—a symbol of the rottenness of society. The wild duck is not quite so finely subordinated, but it plays the same three parts in its play; the symbolism, though more insistent than that of *The Pillars of the Community*, has not broken faith with dramatic form, as it was to do in *The Master Builder* and some later plays.

Hedda Gabler, finished in 1890, six years after *The Wild Duck*, is separated from it by two plays, *Rosmersholm* and *The Lady from the Sea*, which form a natural sequence with the last four, *The Master Builder*, *Little Eyolf*, *John Gabriel Borkman* and *When We Dead Awaken*. These six are all concerned with the problems of the individual, not as a member of society, but as a spiritual being. Society, the world outside the mind, enters indeed into all of them, and in *Rosmersholm* it is the man's public life that is the chief issue of the outward action and of the inner debate. But the emphases have changed. Ibsen is no longer concerned, as in the five earlier plays that we have just considered, with the moral responsibility of a man to the society around him, but with the potency of the inner life of thought. Public life, his contact with the surrounding society and even with his family, are significant now because of their effect upon that world of thought, imagination or spiritual development. In the last two plays of all, the impact of that world is itself a thing of the past, and the mind's reading of its experience and discovery of itself make up the action of the play.

Now, in this sequence *Hedda Gabler* was a little out of place, for it is not, as all of these are in one way or another, the study of the progress of a soul. The sharp, distinct detail in the picture of the two societies, bourgeois and aristocratic, whose conflict forms the background of the play, appears to link it with the sequence from *The Pillars of the Community* to *The Wild Duck*. But in fact it is not entirely at home in this group either, for the action is initiated by the central character, and not until the end does the control pass out of her hands into those of the other characters. The play is a member of both groups and of neither. The figure of Hedda dominates the play as do those of the great individualists of the later group, and her society is important only in so far as it affects her mind and determines her thought and action. But it is not, as they are, a study of a mind's progress into self-discovery, because Hedda's mind remains the same at the end as at the beginning; it has merely gone round and round the cage she has built for herself, looking for a way of escape. And yet it offers the same kind of negative comment on the dominant thought of the later plays as parts of *The Wild Duck* do on the main theme of its four predecessors. For Hedda refuses to discover herself, and her conflict and her tragedy are the result of this refusal. Longing for life and yet afraid of it, she refuses to admit this fear and convert the energy of the conflict into action, and so, at the centre of the play, is a mind turning upon itself in a kind of vacuum. The other plays of this group are studies of spiritual explorations, *Hedda Gabler* of a refusal to embark.

No less interesting than the relations of material and thought in these three plays are their relations as works of art. We pass from the clear, firm, almost diagrammatic structure of *The Pillars of the Community*, with its superb articulation of theme and subject, to the complex organization of *The Wild Duck*, in which Ibsen reached the height of his power as a structural artist, handling several themes and the destinies of different characters with an almost Shakespearian balance. From this we come, in *Hedda Gabler*, to the bare, economical plotting characteristic of the late plays despite their great variety of form. In the binding together of the structure, irony and humour play an increasingly subtle part. The light-hearted comedy of Lona Hessel's arrival, with the slight but regrettable confusion as to the identity of the Fallen Sisters, the neat theatrical effects of entrances that give an ironical twist to the last speaker's words, all these characteristics of the first play give place, in *The Wild Duck*, to the graver irony that dares to introduce, in the flood of Hjalmar's false and sentimental emotion, the first reference to the pistol which is to be the instrument of pathos if not of tragedy, and faintly to foreshadow the catastrophe itself. Even the unfortunate rabbits run in and out of the dialogue like a brief comic motif on the wood-wind in the final and increasingly tragic movement of a symphony.

Nor are the modifications of Ibsen's technique in the drawing of character less remarkable. It is no longer, in any of the plays, a question of skill: Ibsen is a master-craftsman before he writes *The Pillars of the Community*. But the technique varies with the nature and purpose of the play: from the deliberately clear outlining of most of the characters in the first, so that the detailed drawing of Karsten stands out from the background; to the full and profound revelation of rounded personality in *The Wild Duck*, with its subtle implication and cross-bearing; to the limpid but, at first glance, colourless technique of *Hedda Gabler*, which deliberately focuses the attention of the reader upon the inner movements of the minds.

So close and economical is the relation of theme to subject in *The Pillars of the Community* that the play appears at times almost schematic, and even the chief character, Karsten Bernick, has something of this in him. He seems perhaps, at first reading, to explain himself too much and too clearly, to border upon an analysis of a character rather than the dramatic semblance of a living man. But as we look closer we see that, though this is in some sense a necessity of the play, of a play that must convey a moral problem and elucidate it, it is at the same time psychologically sound. Ibsen has not failed as an artist; for Karsten's habit of explaining his own motives, of explaining what kind of man he is, is at once a subtle piece of self-deception and the resultant of a life-long habit of arguing with his subdued but not yet silenced conscience. He must justify himself to himself, and so he continually calls for help in that continual effort; his admiring fellow-citizens and his adoring wife repeat faithfully what he dictates to them. The more dishonest his action, the nobler are the sentiments and motives he defines, until, at the moment of his conversion in the fifth act, he speaks for the first time soberly and plainly, humbly destroying the illusion he had so strenuously created. This is a special type of character-drawing, but it is not shallow or, in the end, undramatic.

Utterly unlike this treatment is that given to the people of *The Wild Duck*. Here each in turn calls out our sympathy and each is created for us as much by what is said of him and by the characters of those who say it as by his own words. There are the masterly background studies of Werle senior and of Mrs. Sörby, of whom no one speaks well and who yet win upon us and command our respect because the cross-fire of bitter and vindictive comment subtly reveals them as better than their critics. So it is with other minor figures in the play, while in the foreground is the figure of Gina, as enigmatic in her silences as Jean Jacques Bernard's Martine. Is it impercipience, a slightly coarse-grained placidity, that gives her tolerant patience with Hjalmar's selfish egotism, or is it an almost divine, inarticulate wisdom and charity? We do not know, and she herself is the last person to tell us. But Ibsen builds this characteristic into the grouping with a delicate sense of intricate balance. Her tolerance or obtuseness seems now a factor in the destruction and disintegration of the lives about her, now a binding and redemptive power. Sometimes, as in the discussion in Act III about Werle senior, we are persuaded that she has driven Hjalmar to escape into irresponsible, falsely heroic gestures. Sometimes, when she bears with equanimity his insults and injustice, we see how this very quality helps her to hold her little society together without rebellion and without thought of her own rights. Such is the balance of character with character and of both with action throughout the play.

Different again is the function of character in *Hedda Gabler*. But how subtle is not only the final effect, but Ibsen's touch upon our sympathies, and how tightly interlocked are all these human destinies, not by action but by psychological reaction! Jörgen Tesman, the despised and unworthy husband of Hedda, is in his way as inarticulate as Gina Ekdal, but he conceals his mind not in silence but in a stream of garrulous and insignificant chatter; for all his fussy, naïvely self-important talking, he comes no nearer to expressing what is there. The devotion, the genuine humility, the good, bourgeois family affection reveal themselves as it were by accident; in spite of his words rather than through them. The most pitiless exposures of his character come not from the clever, cynical, worldly Brack or the contemptuous Hedda, but from the simple, devoted aunt who innocently believes that to collect a trunkful of notes is to be a great scholar and that the ability to sort and arrange another man's papers is proof of a master mind. Simple as he too is, Jörgen knows better; and the foolish little pedant slips suddenly into a gesture of unconscious greatness as, putting aside his own hopes and ambitions, he settles down, full of doubts and misgivings, to reconstruct the book of his dead rival. It is the ambivalent nature of the characterization in this play that links Hedda Gabler, in this aspect of its technique, with the plays of Ibsen's final period.

Ibsen, like all major dramatists, allows the differences between the mental habits of his characters to reflect themselves in their way of speech—in vocabulary, sentence structure, imagery. In *The Pillars of the Community* Aune, the shipwright, mixes plain workman's speech with the language learnt from political textbooks; Rörlund drifts into the vocabulary and rhythms of the pulpit when he becomes self-conscious, and Karsten Bernick into the language of the platform, with all its temptation to confused metaphor. In *The Wild Duck* each character speaks his own language. Gina's original illiteracy breaks through the surface of that 'education' that Hjalmar had imparted, not in moments of deep feeling, but, as might be expected, in moments of irritation or embarrassment. It is then that she misuses words that she has overheard in her husband's conversation and speaks ungrammatically. The speech of old Ekdal shows the same process working in the opposite direction: in him the speech of a gentleman has been gradually overlaid by the habits of Pettersen and his like, and when his confidence is at its lowest these show most clearly. But when he is happy and unselfconscious, showing off his rabbits, his attic and his wild duck, he tends to revert to what was native to him and the speech is that of an old-fashioned army officer. These two individual ways of speech, to go no farther, cross and recross like bells in a change and make their slight but subtle contribution to the pattern of the play. The same skill is at work in *Hedda Gabler*; each character plays its own instrument, Berte, Miss Tesman, Hedda, Brack, Thea and Eilert. Of them all, Jörgen Tesman is perhaps the most obvious, for he seems to keep about him relics of undergraduate slang, little more than half-jocular turns of phrase, which nevertheless serve to make his incessant chatter sound now pleasantly boyish now rather foolish in a man of his years, but in either case carry the merciless implication of undeveloped personality.

Beside the pattern given to the dialogue by this relation of speakers to speech, there is, in most mature plays of Ibsen, a running pattern of words that recur as imagery might do in poetic drama. It is very seldom that this recurrence can be reproduced. The sequences 'fag', 'fagmenneske', 'fagskriften', etc., can never be fully preserved without endangering the naturalness of the dialogue, but great loss is inflicted on every play by a translation that must perforce abandon some of them.

Structure, characterization and dialogue such as this are the despair of the translator, and perhaps the best justification for a translation is the hope that a proportion of its readers will think Ibsen worth the trouble of learning his language. But in order that the glass through which they see him may not be unnecessarily dimmed, I should like to explain some of the differences between his language and ours and show what lines I have tried to follow.

Some of the specific problems that trouble a translator arise at those points where one language is more precise than the other. If the facility for sharper distinction belongs to the original, it is often hard to render this in the translation; if the other way about, ambiguity which may be the source of intentional confusion is equally difficult to reproduce. An instance will make this clear. The Norwegian language, in common with many others, often uses the equivalent of the English 'thou', where modern English has lost the power of distinguishing, in everyday speech, between the singular and the plural of the second person. A translation can often avoid making any distinction, though there is always an appreciable loss when this is done, because the form 'du' conveys a certain degree of intimacy. This flavour may perhaps be conveyed by other means, but the problem becomes much more acute when the characters themselves discuss their own ways of addressing each other. In *Hedda Gabler* alone there are three such passages; in one Hedda invites Thea to use the intimate 'du' instead of the formal 'de', and in another she rebukes Eilert Lövberg for his presumption in doing so without her permission. The advocate of accurate translation will generally incorporate the actual word in the dialogue, generally in quotation marks and accompanied by a footnote, thus achieving the 'clingingly close' translation enjoyed, albeit disrespectfully, by Mark Twain. Even William Archer, to whom, for his services to Ibsen, all honour is due, could still, at the date at which he was writing, adopt some such method as this. But what would be the effect today, when prose drama is almost as widely read as the novel, if we presented Jörgen Tesman's appeal to Hedda, "Hvis du bare kunde overvinde dig til at sige "du" til hende' in the form 'If you could only bring yourself to say "du" to her'? That 'du', with its reference number above it and its footnote at the bottom of the page, would kill the dialogue for the majority of modern readers. On the stage, shorn of its footnote, it would perhaps be less obtrusive, but it would certainly be more bewildering. Today we insist that the dialogue shall run continuously without the intervention of the commentator, and the modern translator must find his way as best he may through passages that refer explicitly to ways of speech, thought or customs that have no equivalent in modern English. We perhaps do Ibsen's art more injury by checking the flow of his dialogue to explain what he is at than by substituting an inadequate translation of the original for a conscientious annotation. If we have to choose between the run of the dialogue and the accurate presentation of one of its component sentences, the interests of the dialogue as a whole must win. Drama, in this, furnishes its own special set of problems.

There are, moreover, in modern Norwegian as in modern German, several words which from time to time do the work of particles. To translate these into separate English words would overweight them, for their function is to give a slight, delicate qualification to the sentence, to throw a shimmer of meaning over it that Englishmen find it hard to imagine, much less to translate. A Greek scholar, accustomed to the habits of μεν and δε, finds himself at home in the company of *ja, jo, nej, da, naa, nu, saa, ogsaa, altsaa, alt, bare, netop*, and so forth, but even he may wish they were not so numerous. And although the word-order in a Norwegian sentence does not differ so much from the English as does that of French, German, Latin, the factor of cadence subtly modifies the lighter forms of punctuation, so that the equivalent pace and timing in emotional passages must sometimes be supplied in other ways.

A few modifications in the text here presented should perhaps be made in production. Since Ibsen carefully prescribes the setting of these plays, it is essential to produce them in the costume of the period. But because the modern reader will naturally visualize the figures in modern dress, I have once or twice altered a reference and substituted its modern equivalent. In the first act of Hedda Gabler Miss Tesman produces Jörgen's slippers from her pocket, and in the last act Thea carries the rough notes of Lövberg's book there. No modern pocket would hold either of these, and so, in order not to confuse the reader or transport him suddenly to the Victorian world, I have substituted a handbag in each case. But in a costume production the pocket will be natural, and the literal translation should replace mine. In the same way, Miss Tesman's hat should become a bonnet, the proper head-dress for a lady of her years in 1890. I have taken a perhaps less warrantable liberty with Gina Ekdal's cloak in the first stage direction of Act III of *The Wild Duck* and substituted the modern coat.

The setting for these three plays are indoors. The garden room of *The Pillars of the Community* is a characteristic feature of a Norwegian house, a large room opening on to a veranda, much used during the summer months. In the other two plays the set consists of two rooms with folding or sliding doors between; in *Hedda Gabler* the main acting area is the outer room and the inner room lies at the back throughout; in the first Act of *The Wild Duck* the audience's position is reversed, and we look through the small inner room to the larger, outer one.

MICHAEL MEYER

Introduction to The Pillars of Society

Ibsen completed *The Pillars of Society* a few months after his forty-ninth birthday; he wrote it in Munich between 1875 and 1877. Enormously successful and influential at the time of its appearance, and indeed for the next quarter of a century, it has rarely been performed during the past fifty years, having rather glibly been relegated to the category of polemical dramas that have lost their topicality. It is customarily thought of nowadays as an apprentice work of documentary rather than practical interest. In fact, however, the whole question of which plays of Ibsen are still theatrically valid is in serious need of reappraisal. Recent productions in London of *Brand* and *Little Eyolf*, which had both long been dismissed as unactable, have shown them to be full of theatrical life, and the same is probably true of *The Pillars of Society*. It is tightly plotted and beautifully characterized; and at this distance of time we can see that its true subject is not women's rights or the evil practices of nineteenth-century shipowners, but human emotions and relationships. The ending has been condemned as facilely happy, but the same accusation was, until recently, made against *Little Eyolf* and *The Lady from the Sea*, and has been proved false if the plays are capably handled. The chief obstacles to a professional production are the size of the cast and a tendency to verbosity on the part of Bernick and, more particularly, Dr. Roerlund the schoolmaster. Trim them down, and *The Pillars of Society* stands

From "Introduction to *The Pillars of Society*" by Michael Meyer from *Henrik Ibsen: The Pillars of Society*, translated from the Norwegian by Michael Meyer. Copyright © 1963 by Rupert Hart-Davis.

as an absorbing example of Ibsen in his less familiar mood of humane comedy—the mood which pervades *Love's Comedy*, *The League of Youth* and much of *Peer Gynt* and *The Wild Duck*, and of which isolated characters in his more sombre plays, such as George Tesman in *Hedda Gabler*, Ballested in *The Lady from the Sea*, and Vilhelm Foldal in *John Gabriel Borkman*, are belated manifestations.

The *Pillars of Society* is often referred to as the first of Ibsen's social prose dramas. That honour in fact belongs to *The League of Youth*, a vigorous and delightful comedy completed eight years earlier which hardly deserves the oblivion which has enveloped it. To *The League of Youth*, too, belongs the credit of being Ibsen's first attempt to write dialogue that was genuinely modern and colloquial. His earlier prose plays, such as *St. John's Even*, *Lady Inger of Oestraat*, *The Vikings at Helgeland* and *The Pretenders*, had been written in a formalized style. But *The League of Youth*, often assumed by those who have not read it to be an earnest political tract, is a loosely constructed and light-hearted frolic almost in the manner of Restoration comedy, which happens to have a pushing young politician as its chief character—"Peer Gynt as a politician," someone has described it. *The Pillars of Society* is in a much truer sense the forerunner of the eleven great plays which followed it. Apart from the tightness of its construction, it contains, as *The League of Youth* does not, the elements we commonly associate with an Ibsen play—a marriage founded on a lie, passionate women stunted and inhibited by the conventions of their time, and an arrogant man of high intellectual and practical gifts who destroys, or nearly destroys, the happiness of those nearest to him. It also exhibits, unlike his earlier plays, what Henry James admiringly described as "the operation of talent without glamour . . . the ugly interior on which his curtain inexorably rises and which, to be honest, I like for the queer associations it has taught us to respect: the hideous carpet and wallpaper (one may answer for them), the conspicuous stove, the lonely central table, the 'lamps with green shades' as in the sumptuous first act of *The Wild Duck*, the pervasive air of small interests and standards, the sign of limited local life." Above all, *The Pillars of Society* has, despite its overtones of comedy, that peculiarly Ibsenish quality of austerity; what Henry James, on another occasion, described as "the hard compulsion of his strangely inscrutable art."

It is indicative of the technical problems posed by this new form of tightly plotted social realism that *The Pillars of Society* took Ibsen longer to write than any of his other plays except the triple-length *Emperor and Galilean*. No less than five separate drafts of the first act have survived, and over a period of nearly eight years his letters are scattered with excuses for its lack of progress. He began to brood on it as early as December 1869, just after finishing *The League of Youth*. On the fourteenth of that month he wrote to his publisher Frederik Hegel: "I am planning a new and serious contemporary drama in three acts, and expect to start work on it in the immediate future." The following month (25 January 1870) he informed Hegel that he hoped to have it ready by the following October, but on 11 April he wrote: "My new play has not yet got beyond the draft, and since I have to get my travel notes into order it looks like being delayed for some time." These travel notes referred to the visit he had made to Egypt in November 1869 to attend, as official Norwegian representative, the opening of the Suez Canal.

October 1870 arrived, and so far from having the play ready he could only tell Hegel that it "has sufficiently developed in my mind for me to hope that any day now I may be able to start writing it." Two sets of notes have survived from this year which contain the first germs of the play. By now he had found a more impressive excuse than the Suez Canal: the Franco-Prussian War, which had started in July of that year. In such an atmosphere (he was living in Germany) how could he concentrate on writing a social drama set in a small Norwegian seaport? He returned instead to the broader historical canvas of *Emperor and Galilean*, on which he had been working intermittently since 1864.

It was in fact another five years before he began the actual writing of *The Pillars of Society*. Apart from completing *Emperor and Galilean*, he prepared for publication a selection of his poems covering the past twenty years; it was his deliberate farewell to poetry, the form which had been his earliest love. He explained this decision in a letter written to Edmund Gosse on 15 January 1874, shortly after the publication of *Emperor and Galilean*, and although his remarks were made with specific reference to that play, they apply even more strongly to the works which followed. I quote the passage in Gosse's own translation:

"The illusion I wanted to produce is that of reality. I wished to produce the impression on the reader that what he was reading was some-thing that had really happened. If I had employed verse, I should have coun-teracted my own intention and prevented the accomplishment of the task I had set myself. The many ordinary and insignificant characters whom I have introduced into the play would have become indistinct, and indistinguishable from one another, if I had allowed all of them to speak in one and the same rhythmical measure. We are no longer living in the age of Shakespeare. Among sculptors, there is already talk of painting statues in the natural colours. Much can be said both for and against this. I have no desire to see the Venus de Milo painted, but I would rather see the head of a negro executed in black than in white marble.

"Speaking generally, the style must conform to the degree of ideality which pervades the representation. My new drama [*Emperor and Galilean*] is no tragedy in the ancient acceptation; what I desired to depict were human beings, and therefore I would not let them talk in 'the language of the gods.'"

In the summer of 1874 Ibsen returned to Norway for the first time since he had left it ten years earlier. There the strife between the conservatives and the liberals had reached its height and, as a result of *The League of Youth*, which was an attack on the hollowness of radical politicians, Ibsen found the conservatives hailing him as their champion. He had, however, no intention of attaching himself to any political party, and when he read in the right-wing newspaper *Morgenbladet* an editorial demand that a candidate for a professorship at the University should be rejected on the grounds that he was a freethinker, Ibsen seized the opportunity to advertise his independence. He withdrew his subscription to *Morgenbladet* and changed to the left-wing newspaper *Dagbladet*. The uneasiness of the conservatives on hearing this—Ibsen was famous enough by now for the students to arrange a torchlight procession in his honour before he left—would have been considerably increased if they had known what he was preparing for them.

After two and a half months in Norway, he returned briefly to Dresden and then, the following spring (1875), he moved to Munich, a city which he found much more to his liking and where he was to spend most of the next sixteen years. At last, in the autumn of that year, nearly six years after he had first begun to brood on it, he settled down to the actual writing of *The Pillars of Society*. At first things went well. On 23 October he wrote to Hegel: "My new play is progressing swiftly; in a few days I shall have completed the first act, which I always find the most difficult part. The title will be: *The Pillars of Society*, a Play in Five [*sic*] Acts. In a way it can be regarded as a counterblast to *The League of Youth*, and will touch on several of the more important questions of our time." On 25 November he writes: "Act I of my new play is finished and *fair-copied*; I am now working on Act 2." By 10 December he is "working at it daily and am now doubly anxious to get the manuscript to you as quickly as possible." On 26 January 1876 he expects to "have it ready by May."

But now things began to go less smoothly. After 26 February, when he writes to the director of the Bergen Theatre that it "will probably be printed during the summer," there is no further mention of the play in his letters until 15 September, when he explains rather lengthily to Hegel that he has been so distracted by productions or plans for productions of his earlier plays—*The Pretenders* in Meiningen, Schwerin and Berlin, *The Vikings at Helgeland* in Munich, Leipzig, Vienna and Dresden—that he has been "compelled to postpone completion of my new play; but on my return to Munich at the beginning of next month, I intend to get it polished off." But progress continued to be slow. 1877 arrived, and on 9 February he could only tell Hegel, who must by now have been growing a little impatient: "I shall have my new play ready in the summer and will send you the manuscript as soon as possible." However, on 20 April he wrote that it "is now moving rapidly towards its conclusion," and at last, on 24 June 1877, he was able to report: "Today I take advantage of a free moment to tell you that on the 15th inst. I completed my new play and am now going ahead with the fair-copying." He posted the fair copy to Hegel in five installments between 29 July and 20 August 1877.

The Pillars of Society was published by Hegel's firm, Gyldendals of Copenhagen, on 11 October 1877, and achieved immediate and widespread success. Throughout Scandinavia, the liberals and radicals hailed it with as much delight as that with which the conservatives had greeted *The League of Youth*. The first edition of 6,000 copies sold out in seven weeks, and a further 4,000 had to be printed. It was first performed on 18 November 1877 in Copenhagen, where it was received with great enthusiasm, and it was equally acclaimed in Christiania, Stockholm and Helsinki. It also gave Ibsen his first real breakthrough in Germany. In the absence of any copyright protection, three separate German translations were published early in 1878 (one of them by a man described by Ibsen as "a frightful literary bandit"), and in February of that year it was produced at five different theatres in Berlin within a fortnight. Twenty-seven German and Austrian theatres staged it within the year. In England, William Archer, then aged twenty-two, made a "hurried translation" entitled, rather uninspiringly, *The Supports of Society;* an analysis by him of the play, with extracts from his translation, was published in the *Mirror of Literature* on 2 March 1878. Since "no publisher would look at" this version, he made another and more careful one, under the new title of *Quicksands*, and this was performed for a single matinée at the Gaiety Theatre, London, on 15 December 1880—a noteworthy occasion, for it was the first recorded performance of any Ibsen play in England. *The Pillars of Society* was not staged in America, at any rate in English—though it had been acted there in German—until 13 March 1891, when it was produced at the Lyceum Theatre, New York. In 1892 it was performed in Australia and South Africa, in 1893 in Rome; and in 1896 Lugné-Poe staged it at his Théâtre de l'Œuvre in Paris. By the end of the century, according to Archer, it had been performed no less than 1,200 times in Germany and Austria, a remarkable record for those days.

The Pillars of Society dealt with two problems of extreme topicality for the eighteen-seventies, and it is a measure of the play's emotional and dramatic content that it has retained its validity despite the fact that both issues have long since been settled. One was the question of women's rights; the other, that of "floating coffins," i.e. unseaworthy ships which were deliberately sacrificed with their crews so that their owners could claim insurance. Controversy over the former problem reached its height in Norway during the seventies. The Norwegian novelist Camilla Collett had fired a warning shot as early as 1853, with her novel *The Judge's Daughters.* In 1869 John Stuart Mill published *The Subjection of Women*, which Ibsen's friend Georg Brandes translated into Danish the same year. Matilda Schjoett's *Conversation of a Group of Ladies* about the *Subjection of Women* (published anonymously in 1871) and Camilla Collett's *Last Papers* (1872) set the issue squarely before the Norwegian public; in 1874 a Women's Reading Society was founded in Christiania, and in 1876 Asta Hanseen, a great champion of the cause, began a series of lectures on women's rights, but was so furiously assailed that in 1880 she emigrated to America. She was the original of Lona Hessel (Ibsen at first gave the character the surname of Hassel, but changed it, presumably so as to avoid too direct an identification with Hanseen). Camilla Collett exerted a direct influence on Ibsen, for he had seen a good deal of her in Dresden in 1871, and again in Munich in the spring of 1877 when he was writing the play, and when they had many arguments about marriage and other female problems. Another influence was Ibsen's wife Susannah; the subject of women's rights was one about which she had long felt strongly. Ibsen had already touched tentatively on this problem in *The League of Youth*, and he was to deal with it more minutely in his next play, *A Doll's House*. His original intention in *The Pillars of Society* was to be even more outspoken than he finally was, for in one of the preliminary drafts Dina announces her decision to go off with her lover without marrying him; but he evidently doubted whether the theatres would stage a play which suggested anything quite so daring, and legalized their relationship.

The problem of the "floating coffins" was first forced upon Ibsen's attention by an English Member of Parliament. In 1868 Samuel Plimsoll had sought in the House of Commons to have the State interfere against the cold-blooded and unscrupulous sacrifice of human life by sending men to sea in rotten ships. In 1873 he succeeded in getting a law passed to enforce seaworthiness; but this proved too slack. On 22 July 1875 he created a tremendous commotion in Parliament by a boldly outspoken attack on the people responsible for such a policy; he called the owners of such ships murderers and the politicians who supported them scoundrels. This so roused the conscience of the nation that a temporary bill went through in a few days, and its principles were made permanent by the Merchant Shipping Act of the following year. Plimsoll's protest echoed throughout the world, and in a seafaring country such as Norway it rang especially loudly. A particularly scandalous case had occurred in Christiania during Ibsen's visit there in 1874. On 2 September of that year, at the annual general meeting of the shipping insurance company Norske Veritas, questions were asked about a ship which, after having been declared seaworthy, sprang a leak while at sea and was shown to be completely rotten. At the annual general meeting a year later two similar cases were mentioned, and a storm of indignation was aroused. The matter was reported in detail in the newspapers, and Ibsen can hardly have failed to read about it.

The Pillars of Society is full of memories of Grimstad, the little port where Ibsen had spent his years as a chemist's apprentice (just as *The League of Youth* is full of memories of his birthplace, Skien). *The Palm Tree* was the name of a Grimstad ship. Touring theatrical companies played in the hall of a sailmaker named Moeller; an actress belonging to one of them had returned there after being involved in a scandal, and had tried to keep herself by taking in washing and sewing like Dina Dorf's mother, but had been shooed out of town by the local gossips. Foreign ships came in for repairs, and foreign visitors turned the place upside-down, like the crew of the *Indian Girl*. In the autumn of 1849, six months before Ibsen left for Christiania, the Socialist Marcus Thrane had arrived in Grimstad and founded a Workers' Association, like the one Aune belonged to. And the Bernicks had their origin in a family named Smith Petersen. Morten Smith Petersen, the original of Karsten Bernick, returned to Grimstad from abroad in the eighteen-forties, and ran his aged mother's business for a while, but finally had to close it down. He then started his own shipyard and an insurance company, and eventually founded the Norske Veritas company which earned the notoriety referred to above. He had died in 1872, but his sister Margrethe Petersen survived. She was an elementary schoolteacher, and was the original of Martha Bernick.

The rich quantity of notes and draft material which has been preserved enables us to plot the development of *The Pillars of Society* in some detail. His first notes, made in 1870, begin: "The main theme must be how women sit modestly in the background while the men busily pursue their petty aims with an assurance which at once infuriates and impresses." The main characters are to be an "old white-haired lady" with two sons, one a shipowner, the other a ship's officer who has been abroad for ten years on foreign service. The shipowner's wife, "a fêted beauty before she married, is full of poetry but is bitter and unsatisfied; she makes demands of life which are, or seem, excessive." In other words, Mrs. Bernick, as originally

conceived, is a forerunner of the great line of Ibsen heroines—Nora
Hellmer, Mrs. Alving, Rebecca West, Ellida Wangel, Hedda Gabler, Rita
Allmers, the Rentheim twins in *John Gabriel Borkman*, and Maja and Irene in
When We Dead Awaken. Martha, too, appears in these early notes, jotted
down five years before the play was written: "her sister, still unsure of herself;
has grown up quietly admiring the man who is absent and far away." But
although several of the characters of *The Pillars of Society* as we know it are
here, the plot as originally conceived bears little relation to that of the final
version; the naval officer falls in love with the sister (i.e., Martha), but she is
already in love with a student, and the officer's mother persuades him to give
up the girl and go away. "The greatest victory," she tells him, "is to conquer
oneself"—a kind of echo of Brand's "The victory of victories is to lose everything." There is also reference to the "foster-daughter of sixteen, sustained
by daydreams and expectations" (i.e., Dina). The play at this stage was to be
"a comedy," presumably of the same genre as *The League of Youth*.

In his next notes, made five years later, we find much more of the
play as we know it. A scenic synopsis includes the schoolmaster reading to
the assembled wives, the husbands discussing the railway, the foster-daughter
(here called Valborg) impatient and longing to get away (to her mother, who
is still alive), and Lona's arrival with the steamer; Act I ends with her
"appearing in the doorway to the garden as the curtain falls." In Act 2, "the
returned wanderers [i.e., Lona and the Captain] start turning things upside-
down in the town. Rumours about the Captain's great wealth and the earlier
scandal concerning Valborg's mother. The schoolmaster begins to think of
getting engaged to Valborg. Conflict begins between the factory-owner and
the Captain." Act 3: "News about irregularities in the repairs to the ship. The
engagement is announced and celebrated. The Captain decides to leave the
country. Fresh information from the yards. The factory-owner hesitates; for
the moment, nothing must be said." Act 4: "Secret understanding between
the Captain and Valborg. The railway project secured. Great ovations. Olaf
runs away with the Captain and Valborg. Exciting final catastrophe."

The list of characters has by now grown considerably. Apart from
Bennick [*sic*], his wife, his blind mother and his sister Margrete (Martha),
Miss "Hassel," the schoolmaster "Roerstad," Valborg (who suddenly
becomes Dina), and Captain John Tennyson (later Rawlinson), we also have
Madame Dorf, young Mrs. Bernick's father Mads Toennesen (a "shipowner
and master builder nicknamed 'The Badger'"), his other son Emil (altered to
Hilmar), and Evensen, "a supply teacher." As synopsis follows synopsis, the
list of characters changes; Aune, Sandstad and "Knap" appear, Bennick
becomes Bernick, and the whole of the older generation is removed—
Bernick's mother, Madame Dorf, Evensen the supply teacher and, eventually,

with Bjornsen, whose literary reputation actually surpassed Ibsen's during much of their careers, although there were always those who saw the large discrepancy of their talents. Ibsen's biographer, Michael Meyer, tells the possibly apocryphal story of the occasion in 1903 when Bjornsen, an inordinately vain man, went to Stockholm to receive the Nobel Prize (which Ibsen was never given). "He tried to enter the palace through a side door but found his way barred by a sentry. 'My good man,' Bjornsen informed him, 'I am Norway's greatest writer.' 'Oh,' said the sentry, making way. 'I beg your pardon, Herr Ibsen.'"

Bjornsen seems by turns to have helped Ibsen and either condescended to or reviled him. Several times he solicited financial support when Ibsen was in particularly great need, and he encouraged him with expressions of faith in his genius. But he also wrote to a mutual acquaintance when he and Ibsen were in their thirties that "as soon as Ibsen recognizes that he is a minor writer, he will at once become a charming poet," and he later said of *A Doll's House* that "it is technically excellent, but written by a vulgar and evil mind," an opinion which, it is true, was shared by many at the time. Still, Ibsen seems to have depended on the friendship more than on any other, initiating several reconciliations after fallings-out and accepting, if without overt enthusiasm, the marriage of his only child Sigurd to Bjornsen's daughter.

A man complicated beyond our usual biographical methods, Ibsen seems to have united many contrarieties in his being. He was known (and known to himself) as something of a physical coward and exhibited extreme diffidence—possibly amounting to periodic impotence—in sexual matters. Yet he possessed intellectual valor of the highest kind: courage in the face of derision and attack. He was absolutely indifferent to ordinary literary politics, yet had a hunger for ceremonial recognition; he was a great medal chaser, pursuing decorations like any official hack, at one time writing to a court functionary about a decoration he was in line for in Egypt: "This honor is highly flattering to me, and it would also be of the greatest possible advantage in establishing my literary position in Norway."

In his defense we ought to know that for years his countrymen mostly ignored him, so that among other oppressions his financial situation was for a long time nearly desperate. And in his wider defense we should know that when his fame did mount, when he became world-renowned, he was always aware of the fickleness of public taste and, more important, how little he was actually understood, how little he could count on understanding. The medals and honors (for which he sacrificed nothing in his art) then became, perversely if we need to think so, emblems of acceptance, protections against his works and name falling into oblivion.

Whatever the truth of that, he was a hero, a knight of the imagination, and not least for having tested his own honor in his works. It is another thing we find hard to connect with him, thinking him so objective, so coldly analytical and aloof, a playwriting machine. Yet late in his career he wrote that "everything that I have created has had its origin in a frame of mind and in a situation in my life. I never wrote because I had, as they say, 'found a good subject.' Everything that I have written has the closest possible connection with what I have lived through inwardly . . . In every new poem or play I have aimed at my own spiritual emancipation and purification."

His "subjects" were discovered by an extension of himself into the speech and gestures of possible surrogates. He embodied himself in his characters, as any true playwright does, except that in his case it is especially difficult to see because of those dramas—*A Doll's House, Ghosts, An Enemy of the People, Hedda Gabler, The Wild Duck*—which seem so descriptive of "others" and are the plays by which he is chiefly known.

In 1898, seventy years old, at the height of his fame and, as it turned out, with only one more play to write, he was given a testimonial banquet by the Norwegian Society for Women's Rights. With characteristic understatement he told the assembled ladies, for whom of course *A Doll's House* was the Bible, the Iliad, and *Paradise Regained* in one, that "I have been more of a poet and less of a social philosopher than people have generally been inclined to believe. I thank you for your toast but I must decline the honor of consciously having worked for women's rights. I am not even quite sure what women's rights really are. To me it has been a question of human rights."

"I have been more of a poet and less of a social philosopher . . ." Several years after Ibsen's death in 1906 Rainer Maria Rilke, who was to become one of his most fervent admirers, wrote after seeing his first Ibsen play (*The Wild Duck*) that he had discovered "a new poet, one to whom we will go by path after path, now that we know one." He saw further than Gabriele D'Annunzio, who complained to André Gide about Ibsen's "lack of beauty," or Paul Valéry, who found him "tiresome."

Rilke went on to say that Ibsen was "a man misunderstood in the midst of fame, an entirely different person from what one hears." He was obviously using the words "man" and "person" to mean artist and playwright. There is something extremely significant in this for our understanding of cultural process, specifically the manner in which works of art become anthropomorphized into extensions or equivalents of their creators. It is not a question of biography—the most abstract and impersonal works undergo the same process—but of the human need to grant personality to the inventions of the mind. For most of us Marx *is* Communism, Einstein relativity, Darwin evolution.

In the same way works of art take on their creators' names and souls. We speak of a Rembrandt and of Shakespeare when we mean either the man or the world of plays. We talk about long-dead artists "doing" or "saying" something in their work as though they were as alive as we are, the imagination making contemporaries of us all. Most importantly, we think of the works, and even find ourselves responding to them, under the simplified distinctive sign of their genius, the emblem by which to know them. Rembrandt is chiaroscuro, El Greco lightning flashes; more subtly Baudelaire is decadence, Joyce experiment. Intellectual rumor: the art of the past, and even of the present, comes to us like gossip in a salon. Criticism is, or ought to be, the action of dispelling such rumors or making them into more than phrases.

To most of us now, Ibsen comes down as narrow, programmatic, the social philosopher he knew he had never been. And the name stands between our senses and the plays. Ibsen: cold light, problems, living rooms, instruction. We can't obliterate the name; there would be nothing left by which to refer to the work. And besides that, he is the man who wrote it, though the life and the dramas neither explain nor justify one another. But they went on together, the work not representing him but rather being brought into existence to fill the moral and psychic spaces, the poetic space, between what he was and what it was possible to be.

In 1901 the nineteen-year-old James Joyce wrote a letter to the man misunderstood in the midst of fame, sending him greetings on his seventy-third birthday, in Norwegian, which he had learned in order to read the plays in the original. After telling Ibsen how he had been shouting his praises in public, Joyce went on:

> I did not tell them what bound me closest to you. I did not say how what I could discern dimly of your life was my pride to see, how your battles inspired me—not the obvious material battles but those that were fought and won behind your forehead—how your willful resolution to wrest the secret of life gave me heart, and how in your absolute indifference to public canons of art, friends and shibboleths you walked in the light of your inward heroism.

The inwardness of Ibsen's heroism, the hiddenness of his valor, was largely a matter of a temperamental inability to make himself known otherwise than in his work. The tight lips were those of a man for whom what he had fashioned spoke for itself. It was protracted work—Ibsen's career as a playwright covered half a century—and it is likely that one of the reasons he insisted so strongly at the end of his life that his plays be looked upon as parts of a whole, a single enterprise, was that he knew how long it had taken him and the shifting nature of the ruses and strategies he had had to employ. He knew, too, as many "cultured" persons do not, that to keep on writing plays, to keep on making art of any kind, is to have to learn as one goes, to wrestle with newly intractable material, to develop new strengths and modesties, to fail in the very appearance of success, but to be always engaged in a long, unbroken action whose unforeseen end lies in its beginnings.

The roots of Ibsen's dramatic art were in an exceedingly unpromising soil. Born in 1828 in the coastal town of Skien to middle-class parents (his merchant father later got into legal difficulties and fell on hard times, a circumstance which seems to have greatly affected Ibsen and may help account for the peculiar intensity of his terror of poverty in later life), he went before he was sixteen as an apothecary's assistant to another small town, Grimstad, where he remained for over six years. During this period he began to write and publish poetry and completed his first play, a rather windy and amateurish drama on Roman themes called *Catiline*. In 1850 he went to the capital city of Christiania (the modern Oslo) to prepare for his matriculation examination at the university there (he apparently intended to study medicine), and upon failing the test seems to have given up all thought of further education in favor of devoting himself entirely to writing.

But his literary work brought him next to nothing, so in 1851 he accepted a low-paying position as "dramatic author" with the Norwegian Theater of Bergen, a post whose duties entailed writing for the resident company, directing plays, and consulting on a hundred and one theatrical matters. He stayed there for over five years, then moved back to Christiania to fill a similar position with a new theater that had opened there, remaining in this job for nearly six more years. This long period of apprenticeship and immersion in practical theater undoubtedly laid a rough foundation for his future art, but the education was one he would have later to repudiate in large part. It was a bitterly frustrating time, for reasons mostly having to do with his own growing imaginative size and aspirations in relation to the low, crimped state of theatrical knowledge and practice in Norway.

Michael Meyer has described the conditions Ibsen met on his arrival in Bergen. Productions, for example, were rehearsed no more than four or five times and in performance "the normal placing of actors . . . was in a horizontal bow, with its tips in the downstage corners and everyone facing the audience, even when they were meant to be speaking to one another." Ibsen tried to do away with this convention and to move the theater generally toward more professional and intelligent practices (he had learned something about stagecraft during a short trip to Germany and Denmark, where the art was rather more advanced), but he made little headway and, what was even more discouraging, could do almost nothing with the prevailing repertoire. This was composed of pseudo-rustic folk plays, banal melodramas, historical pageants, and the most trivial of farces. During his stint at Bergen, Ibsen directed nearly 150 plays, more than half of them adaptations of light French *drames des boulevards,* twenty-one of these by Eugène Scribe.

The theater in Norway was almost wholly cut off from the stage's past. There were no worthwhile or even complete translations of the Greeks, Shakespeare, and the Elizabethans, the French tragic playwrights, or indeed any classics whatever. (Ibsen was more than once to lament his failure ever to learn English, although the likelihood is that in later life he read Shakespeare in German translations.) And there was almost no native drama, or literature of any kind for that matter.

The only dramatic writers Ibsen ever acknowledged learning from were Danish, or wrote in that language. They included the very minor Johan Ludvig Heiberg (1791–1860), who was also a poet and philosopher; Adam Oehlenschläger, a nineteenth-century poet and author of Schiller-like poetic tragedies; and Baron Ludvig Holberg, an eighteenth-century Norwegian who had lived in Denmark and written broad comedies of contemporary life in Danish. Ibsen was notoriously unwilling to admit influence, and in his case there is almost no evidence of there having been anyone from whom he learned more than some broad principles of construction, no master from whom he would have had to dissociate himself in order to strengthen a claim on originality.

It fell to him, therefore, to create a Norwegian drama, although for a time he seemed to be sharing the task with Bjornsen. His countrymen's pride in having this accomplished, their satisfaction in being brought into the wider European culture, became a chief basis for the esteem in which he later came to be held. It was a regard unaccompanied by much understanding, and it was continually under siege by an opposing attitude of resentment against him for having, as it was thought, held his fellow Norwegians up to ridicule, particularly in works like *Peer Gynt* and some of the later domestic dramas.

But even the opprobrium, with its testimony to recognition, was late in coming. In 1864, at the age of thirty-six, feeling unappreciated at home— such reputation as he possessed derived more from his poetry than his plays—and needing a wider and warmer world (he was to speak often from abroad of his countrymen's provincialism, their "cold, uncomprehending eyes"), Ibsen left Norway to begin a self-imposed exile that was to last for twenty-seven years. He had written ten plays, all but one of them historical dramas, of which many were based on the Norwegian sagas, half of them in verse and several others in a mixture of verse and formal, elevated prose.

As distinctive as these plays were by the standards of the day and place, with one exception they would have very little interest for us now were it not for their being Ibsen's, the first segment of his career's arc. Their inspiriting force is most often a nationalistic fervor (something that was to characterize Ibsen for many years and be present, though with decreasing explicitness and ardor, in a number of his later plays) whose principles and particularities are almost wholly alien to us now. Worse than that, these plays were written in a language engaged in trying to throw off the conventional attributes of "high" expression but having little else to rely on. Here is a representative passage from *The Vikings at Helgeland* (1858):

> I will follow you, in battle array, wherever you may go. Not as your wife will I go—for I have belonged to another, and the woman still lives who has lain by your side. No, not as your wife, Sigurd, but as a Valkyrie is how I will come—firing your blood to battle and great deeds, standing by your side as the sword-blows fall, shoulder to shoulder with your fighting men in storm and tempest. And when your funeral song is sung, it shall tell of Sigurd and Hjordis together!

Yet verbally stilted and physically clumsy as these plays almost wholly are, we can detect in them some faint foreshadowings of what Ibsen will come to do. The Nationalism will be modulated into a structure of values of a far less localized kind, the historical materials will give way to those of a present seen as having invisibly assimilated the past. And the language will win its freedom from culture, from what is expected of seriousness in literary expression, from the corrupted inheritance of a classic set of rubrics.

In this regard *The Pretenders*, the last play of Ibsen's Norwegian beginnings, has the most stature of all as prediction. Although it too is a historical drama, set in thirteenth-century Norway and concerned with a struggle for the throne which resulted in the nation's being unified for the first time, *The Pretenders* compels our attention precisely by its nearly modern sound, its being written in prose of a sometimes terse and colloquial kind, and its rough elements of psychological and spiritual investigation. In it Ibsen begins to reach toward his true ground. Still, there is a seemingly unaccountable leap from its many awkwardnesses and inconsistencies and its ultimate failure as original consciousness to the plays in which his genius fully manifests itself for the first time, the first he would write away from Norway.

With his wife and small son Ibsen went to Rome, a favorite city among Scandinavian expatriates. He lived there and in other places in Italy for four years, spent the next seven years in Dresden, and the following three in Munich, returned to Italy for five more years, then, in 1891, having paid only sporadic visits to his homeland during all this time, went back to Christiania for what proved to be the rest of his life.

In Italy, between 1865 and 1868, Ibsen wrote *Brand* and *Peer Gynt*. With the exception of the monumental *Emperor and Galilean*, which he began in Italy and finished nine years later in Dresden, they are physically his largest works. But while *Emperor* and *Galilean* is very seldom performed or read, *Brand* and *Peer Gynt* remain at the very center of any consideration of Ibsen and are indispensable to a full encounter with his mind and art. Everything he would write after this would in one way or another issue from their soil.

Unlike each other in subject and tone as they are, the two plays are bound in the most intimate unity, seeming to have been written in an unbroken sequence ("After *Brand*, *Peer Gynt* followed almost of itself," Ibsen later remarked). Their composition thus reflects what must have been a spontaneous movement of his imagination between the polarities he had come to understand in his own nature.

Far more directly than will be true again until the last series of spiritually autobiographical plays, *Brand* and *Peer Gynt* give us Ibsen projected on stage. They wear disguises, *Brand*'s protagonist that of an evangelical preacher, *Peer*'s of a picaresque adventurer, but internally, as moral and spiritual metaphors, they are their author's clear surrogates. And it is this movement toward the self, toward making plays out of what the self has discovered about its hungers and injuries, that becomes the basis of Ibsen's originality in these works and helps account for, though scarcely explain, the abrupt growth of his imaginative powers.

If the protagonist of *Brand* has too narrow a self, that of *Peer Gynt* has too wide a one; if *Brand* is an absolutist of the ideal, Peer is the epitome of anti-transcendence. Brand is an apostle, a man trying to serve something other and "higher" than himself; Peer is egoism incarnate, the very figure of self-regard. While Brand hunts with the hound of heaven, Peer seeks out the gross and subtle pleasures of the world.

Brand feels himself set on a prophetic mission, "born into this world to heal its sickness and its weakness." His religion is a species of newly primitive Christianity, a return to origins and sources through a faith whose central dogma, however, is that of human will and not divine mercy, and whose ruling principle is a Kierkegaardian "all or nothing." The world's illness is its spirit of compromise, its trafficking between material pleasure and metaphysical value, with a consequent softness and debility of soul. "We shall wander through the land," Brand exhorts his followers, "freeing our souls, purifying our weakness. Be men, be priests, renew God's faded image."

In his merciless pursuit of the absolute, Brand runs up against the limits of human nature, its inherent relativism, and is himself trapped in a fateful contradiction between abstract values and palpable life. To fulfill what he thinks of as his duty, he is forced to sacrifice his wife and child (a theme reminiscent of Kierkegaard's *Fear and Trembling*, which Ibsen may well have read) and he dies under an avalanche, one of those symbolic events in Ibsen which his detractors find so hard to accept. On his lips is a question to God—"If not by Will, how can man be redeemed?" to which the reply, from a voice crying "through the thunder," is: "He is the God of Love!"

While Brand incarnates will and an ideal purity whose unexpected action in the world is the destruction of the impure but living self, Peer is the embodiment of unprincipled selfhood, a representative of the search for unbounded personal fulfillment at the expense of soul and of others. To the long Western tradition of the value of knowing oneself he opposes the idea of "choosing" one's own being over all other life. The alternatives are most explicitly stated during the key scene in the hall of the mountain king: the motto is not to be "to yourself be true" but "to yourself be enough." This kind of self-sufficiency, Ibsen makes clear, is the province of animals, who have no need to work at being "true," and of that lower or animal self in man which is represented in *Peer Gynt* by the trolls, which Ibsen drew from Norwegian folklore.

The results of choosing oneself are thus to fall under the sway of one's baser part, to gain immediate satisfactions at the cost of dignity and honor, to cut oneself off from friendship and love, and so, finally, having no anchor in community and no center, to be "no one." The exact metaphor of this is the onion Peer peels off layer by layer to reach no core. "The art of daring, of courage in action," Peer says, "is to move with uncommitted feet among the tricky snares of life." But it is just this refusal to commit himself to anything that makes Peer, despite his charm and vivacity (or perhaps because of them: seductiveness is an agency of corruption), material for the Button Molder, another creature drawn from folklore whose function is to melt down such anomalous souls into a non-human substance. For, as the Button Molder tells Peer, he has not been a "serious" enough sinner for hell or "buoyant" enough for heaven. He is only spared in the end—a denouement which with some justification has been criticized as rather arbitrary—by his reunion with and acceptance of Solveig, the woman who has loved him and waited patiently for his pilgrimage of appetite to end.

From their antipodal starting points both Brand and Peer Gynt arrive at love as the power that will judge them. Nothing is clearer than that the writing of the two plays was in part an act of Ibsen's own submission to such an examination. "To live," he once wrote, "is to battle with trolls in heart and mind; to write is to sit in judgment on oneself." Another time he said that his work was concerned with the "contradiction between word and deed, between will and duty, between life and theory in general."

He knew these contradictions and antinomies in his own nature, and this is why, given the definition of writing he upheld, his work is never impersonal or narrowly objective, even when it seems to be most directly "social." He is Brand and Peer, the tragic and comic sides of his own propensities, if we want to categorize them that way. At the time, though, the plays were widely taken to be about *others*, Norwegian types who embodied national characteristics seen by an aloof ironist. *Peer Gynt* was mostly interpreted as a topical satire ("Why can't people read the thing as a work of fiction?" Ibsen protested), and *Brand*, which quickly became a rallying point for radical youth throughout Scandinavia, was often misread as a straightforward call to order, its protagonist being thought of as a kind of Promethean figure instead of as his own victim and debacle.

Ibsen's consciousness would remain rooted in these plays, which were like accusatory and cautionary fables of his own being. But the forms of his theater were about to change drastically from theirs. Both plays were written in verse and rank among the greatest poetic dramas since the Elizabethan and French classical periods. *Brand* is terser, harder, more economical and bare; in *Peer Gynt* Ibsen's style opens out into an expansiveness, flexibility, and sumptuousness it will never again attain. In both plays, though in *Peer Gynt* more freely, the unconscious issues its own images to describe its previously unreported life; the play will be the ancestor of many dramas pitched beyond rationality, among them Strindberg's dream plays and Alfred Jarry's *Ubu Roi*. But with these poetic monuments accomplished, Ibsen will appear to turn back, to reduce himself, abdicating from those verbal heights in order to gain a different kind of freedom, one he sensed was to be forbidden him there.

When *Peer Gynt* was published in Scandinavia (in accordance with contemporary practice, Ibsen's plays were published before being produced; in some cases, that of a potentially scandalous work like *Ghosts*, for example, it would be years before they saw the stage), it was extravagantly praised by some perceptive readers but more widely condemned for being ugly and "unpoetic." Ibsen's response was one of those violent, seemingly vainglorious replies to criticism which can be found throughout his career. "If my play is not poetry," he wrote to a friend, "then it will be, the definition of poetry will have to be changed in Norway to conform to my play." By poetry Ibsen meant something more than a technical category, as he knew his opponents did. For what was at stake was the definition of art itself. In that perennial finding that a new form or style of art is not art at all, the critics were rebuking *Peer Gynt* for its rough, unfamiliar energy, its unprecedentedly earthy and even vulgar language, and its wayward, "illogical" shape.

It was out of anything but a spirit of meek obedience to such judgments, then, that Ibsen now abandoned formal verse as the mode of his dramatic writing. The matter has become historical, which is to say it reaches us now with the ponderous inevitability the past forces on all its events. Ibsen changed the course of drama, theater historians tell us, because the drama was ready to be changed; modern, prosaic life was making its claims on the theatrical imagination, as on the novelistic one, and Ibsen was the first fully to respond. In this view, which is wrong only in that it misses the spirit of his action, everything personal in it, the artist is the servant of cultural destiny and originality is a question simply of foresight: the original artist is the one who does what is *supposed to come next*.

Brand and *Peer Gynt*, for all their splendors, belong to the pre-modern period, we argue now in retrospect. And whether or not we dislike this aspect of the modern in drama, whether we think that Ibsen's social period brought the theater into an ironic kind of decadence in which prosaic actuality supplanted high imagination, or that the social plays were a new species of imagination made sober and truthful, we all succumb to the sense that this was the way it had to be. Yet Ibsen was a temperament as well as a man worked on by the times; his change of tactics, so portentous for the future of the drama, was the result of a choice, which he did not have to make and which much later on he would to some degree regret.

Ibsen knew that the dispute about his art would go on to the end. But he had become aware that contemporary tastes and attitudes worked against the success on stage of verse drama, however much it might be admired as literature, as among a passionate minority *Brand* and *Peer Gynt* certainly were. The sweep and range of his imagination in these plays were obviously better served by poetry than by the narrowly colloquial language of a work like *The Pretenders*, which had in fact been mixed with a more inflated prose, a pseudo-poetry such as "serious" drama was supposed to employ. Poetry had allowed him a suppleness, a power of implication and of elision that gave the plays their literary strength but at the same time made them difficult to perform. "I don't think the play's for acting," Ibsen said to a friend about *Peer Gynt*, and in fact neither play was to be staged for many years after their publication and both remain excessively difficult to produce well today.

It was essential for Ibsen that his plays be performed or at least have the potential for being stages. More than most innovators, he felt a need to count, to be immediately effective, so that changes in the formal means of his art were seldom dissociated from his effort to win a place, a large high position within the main enterprises of European civilization in his time. And the theater was the arena where that place might be most swiftly and decisively seized. Out of this urgency and with an internal struggle to bring into coherence his public ambition and sense of aesthetic rightness, he moved after *Peer Gynt* to make his theater more available, if without illusions that it would be more truly understood.

Some time later he was to write that "I came to regard verse as wrong . . . verse has been most injurious to dramatic art. It is improbable that verse will be employed to any extent worth mentioning in the drama of the future; the aims of the dramatist of the future are almost certain to be incompatible with it." He was to be proven right, to be one of the chief agencies of the proof, but the remark about the injuriousness of verse has a ring of rationalization to it. Since nineteenth-century plays in prose had not been a bit more distinguished than those in verse, the latter could scarcely be assigned the blame for drama's low estate.

But being intent now on writing in prose, Ibsen may have feared that this would appear to be a diminution of his artistic voice, since the prestige of poetry as the proper vehicle of important drama was still high, if only as a shibboleth. He needed now what he felt to be the right voice, the necessary one for a type of drama that would move from the external spaciousness and the perennial, legendary considerations of *Brand* and *Peer Gynt* to society, cities, houses, and rooms, to men and women as they actually, recognizably lived. He needed prose, felt it to be the more "human" voice now, seeing poetry slipping away, becoming inappropriate, too grand, too lofty and literary for his purposes.

Ibsen is certainly a "realist" in the cycle of plays which begins somewhat tentatively with *The League of Youth* in 1869, is set fully going with *Pillars of Society* in 1875-7, and ends, although the dividing line is not as absolute as that, with *Hedda Gabler* in 1890. But dramatic realism is not synonymous with emphasis on social problems and Ibsen is not the limited playwright of "ideas" whose dramas, in Walter Kerr's most recent formulation of the uncomprehending critical line, are ones in which "people are digits, adding up to the correct ideological sum." Our habit of looking at Ibsen not as an artist but as a sort of grim (or splendid) fulminator, an ideologue, or, at the lowest, a designer of problematic living rooms, a theatrical upholsterer, has prevented us from seeing how in his plays specific ideas or issues conceal truer, more permanent subjects.

Ibsen's realism is in the first place a matter of having chosen paradigmatic situations from the life of contemporary society, from the newspapers in certain cases. He was a great reader and creative user of newspapers (for much of his later years he read very little else), and to this fact we owe a large element of the renewed life of the theater, for the sources of almost all other dramatic writing of the time were the artificialities and brittle inventions of the theater itself. Ibsen made his social plays out of nothing other than *what might have occurred* in what we call real life. It was a form of anti-romanticism, an outward sobriety of imagination, but it was also a specifically aesthetic repudiation of the stage as an arena for fantasy.

This realism incorporated into its enterprise what might be, and were, regarded as "issues." But it long ago became clear that we have to distinguish Ibsen's thought from the narrow and localized ideas for which he was at first wrongly praised and then wrongly blamed, the former because he was being so intellectually "advanced" and modern, the latter because he was scanting feeling and sensuousness in his work. As Eric Bentley has written, Ibsen "is far less interested in 'modern ideas' than in certain ideas that go behind them. In Ibsen one must always look for the idea behind the idea."

One must also look for the poetry behind the prose. In giving up formal verse Ibsen remained a poet in the sense in which he had earlier defined it: as the man who sees. The apparent prosiness of the social plays was a mask for poetry of the most subtle, hitherto-unfamiliar kind. To achieve a drama of contemporary life, one whose language would be other than that of literature, conceived of as elevated expression, Ibsen rooted his methods in a lyricism that was informal, hidden, a matter of textures and relationships, implications and elisions, a prose-poetry which at first glance seemed only to be prose. Driven down into the depths, beyond the audience's immediate ear, it lay out of the grasp of paraphrase and socially exploitable meanings; the conscious, public, quickly assimilable events of the plays, their ostensible subjects, would make for those things.

What were those subjects, those purported themes which in Ibsen's own time caused so much scandal and uproar and in ours are grounds for thinking him invalidated by history? Consider the three plays for which he is probably best known. *A Doll's House* was and is held to be about women's rights; *Ghosts* about sexual morality and immorality or, more subtly, about moral continuity, how the sins of the parents are visited upon the children; *Hedda Gabler* about sexual frustration or neurosis among the upper class or the tensions of caste, or all three. We have seen how Ibsen repudiated that reading of *A Doll's House*; he never spoke about the widespread misinterpretations of the others, but if he had ever decided to, he surely would have issued the same sort of laconic, devastating corrections.

In his remarks to the feminists about *A Doll's House* Ibsen had said that to him it had been a question of "human rights." The clear implication is that the play is really about human appetites for power and exploitation and the corollary victimization of those who are not so driven. Beneath the appearances—a husband who patronizes, a wife who at first submits and then rebels—patronization, submission, and rebellion are themselves on exhibition; something more than sociological data is making itself known.

Historically, *A Doll's House* stirred or shocked most of its audiences or readers on circumscribed political or ethical grounds; married women ought not be the slaves of their husbands; married women ought to obey and defer to their husbands, etc. Yet the play's movement goes well past such limited meanings and arguments, so that when all the images and verbal intensities have crystallized in our memories, the work seems to point to something quite different from what we have supposed.

In its central movement *A Doll's House* is a drama of preparation, pitched beyond sexual difference, a play of encounter with the obstacles—in this exemplary case the institution of marriage—that act to prevent us from knowing ourselves and the world. "I must stand on my own feet if I am to find out the truth about myself and about life," Nora says, and when Thorwald replies that "first and foremost you are a wife and mother," her rejoinder—a statement that lifts the play wholly past ideology—is "I don't believe that any longer. I believe that I am a human being first and foremost . . . or . . . that I must try to become one."

Thorwald's very diction is that of someone for whom existence is organized into categories and whose feelings are shaped according to received ideas of fitness and acceptability. In Nora's speech we can detect the initial stages of a repudiation of such a "civilized" process, and this rejection, going so much deeper than a refusal of matrimonial responsibility, is what most profoundly, if subliminally, shocked the bourgeois audiences of the time. If *A Doll's House* now has a certain thinness, if it seems to us somewhat attenuated, this is not due to its being a play of narrow theoretical issues but to the thinness of the ice on which Ibsen was skating, to the fact that he did not yet quite have the artistic weapons to deal with so dangerous a subject.

The subject of *Ghosts* was also dangerous and so was partially concealed. It was surely not the "rigidity of middle-class Norwegian morality," as one recent critic has argued, but something far less fettered to a social proposition of that kind. *Ghosts* is "about" the rigidities, the fatal, blind movements of ideals and abstractions in a universe of fact, and about the status of the mind and will as prisoners of a tyrannical, invisibly operating past.

Morality, sexual or otherwise, is simply one strand of the web of self-deception and ignorance in which Mrs. Alving is caught. The "ghosts" that haunt her refer much more significantly to the complex of inherited, unexamined ideas and values which rule her as they do us all than to the specific forms of her moral and physical past. The evil she has done is ontological: she has failed to think for herself, to be herself. She has acted in bad faith, and the physical disaster that follows on this—Oswald's sickness and implied death—is a demonstration of her faithlessness, its "objective correlative." The reason why the discovery of penicillin did not invalidate *Ghosts*, as has so often and so seriously been argued, is that venereal disease was never the problem; it was simply an instance.

Hedda Gabler, the last and poetically richest of the social plays, is also the most mysterious. It was surely possible at the time and remains possible to think of Hedda as a decadent aristocrat chafing under the pettiness of her bourgeois marriage and surroundings, or as a deeply neurotic woman whose sexual aggressiveness masks a radical frigidity. When Bernard Shaw wrote that the trouble with such women is that they *don't* ordinarily kill themselves, he was of course partly subscribing to a view of the play as a sociological character study. Yet beneath its surface, under the mercilessly accurate portraits and the exact iconography of domestic crisis, Ibsen was trying to fashion something else: a new kind of tragi-comedy, more metaphysical than it is comfortable for us to think, whose elements are energy turned in on itself and being wrestling with its tendency to dissolution.

On one level Hedda is indeed a frustrated woman and the play does offer a cold view of specifically bourgeois existence. Yet it is a mistake to stop there. For there is not the slightest indication in the play that a change of circumstances would have saved Hedda, that she is suffering a local, socially engendered fate. Her revenge upon Loevborg, the destruction of his manuscript (a murder of the "child" she cannot have) and then of herself, are actions in a dimension beyond technical or scientifically identifiable pathology. Hedda is unable to *live*. At the deepest level of Ibsen's vision she is caught not so much in a particular set of determining circumstances—these make up the dramatic occasion, providing the details by which the dramatic vision is made palpable—as in human circumstance itself. She is a victim of the way things are, a fish in Ibsen's great polluted boiling sea where ill-adapted creatures struggle to know what to do.

Loevborg swims alongside her, even blinder, more powerless and unhappy. He is the self-destructive creator, the one who, inadequate to the richness of his own intellect, turns his violence inward in an effort to escape responsibility. If he doesn't kill himself but dies in a ludicrous accident, it is because he is morally less than Hedda, not as brave; for her, suicide is an act out of a steely recognition that an intolerable point has been reached, that nothing outside herself will give way. Thus the sound of the pistol going off is an announcement that there is at least that strange sort of courage in the world which can cut through such impasses. It is left to the "dull" ordinary personages of the drama, Thea and Tesman, to go on, devoted, staying within human bounds, working away at Loevborg's manuscript, generous as Hedda in her anguish and deeper, fatal vision cannot be. *Hedda Gabler* is one of the greatest anti-romantic plays we possess, for its perception is of what remains possible after the outcries and seductive whispers of our own impossible cravings have faded.

It was Henry James who in Ibsen's lifetime saw most clearly the nature of his genius, grasping with great perspicacity the true imaginative action of the social plays. On the surface Ibsen was "massively common and middle-class," but James could see past that to his "independence, his intensity, his vividness, the hard compulsions of his strangely inscrutable art." That the art should be "strangely" inscrutable was due to just that discrepancy which was pointed out before between the plays' objective events, their stories or plots, and their hidden values or meanings. An art depicting society should be entirely available; if Ibsen's was all politics and moral study, if its energies were essentially forensic, why should it resist analysis so obdurately?

Ibsen's subject, James went on to say, "is always, like the subjects of all first-rate men, primarily an idea," and his chief idea is the "individual caught in the fact." The barest of propositions, the most abstract of critical formulations, but in its light everything puzzling and deceptive in Ibsen yields something to our understanding. Mysteries will remain, as they should. But we can see now what kind of dramas are being staged: enactments of the self versus the structure of experience, of personal being opposed by the hard details, outside and beyond the values we may place on them, of things as they are. Ibsen had spoken of his plays as dealing with contradictions, most widely that between "life and theory in general." One of his greatest artistic achievements was to have imagined the individual as a kind of theorem, something asserted but not proven; life, facticity, would provide the test, and the testing was the drama.

To accomplish this kind of philosophically oriented dramatic creation within the realistic mode he had chosen was Ibsen's unprecedented problem. In this regard nothing in the history of the modern theater has been more exhaustively studied than the question of his relationship to the French well-made play, the dominant theatrical genre during his apprenticeship and afterward.

The place to begin is in metaphysics, not stagecraft. For the well-made play was pre-eminently a bourgeois mode in having been designed for the amusement and edification of an affluent, newly cultured class and in reflecting that class's values and self-estimation, its sense of the world. The Russian theologian and critic Nicolas Berdyaev, citing the thought of Charles Péguy, once characterized what he called the "bourgeois mind" as "idolatrous" in so far as it invariably preferred the "visible to the invisible." Berdyaev was describing a predilection consistent with but going beyond economic materialism, and his terms are particularly applicable to matters of art.

The well-made play was one of almost entire visibility, which is to say it possessed almost no dimension beyond what was literally placed before the audience's eyes and ears; figures of inflated physical and deprived moral or spiritual status, at their extreme points the stock personages of melodrama and farce, its characters moved through dramas whose values were wholly corporeal, or else abstractions for corporeality—myths of love, power, social prowess, etc.—which its audiences uncritically accepted as the reflected truths of their own lives.

"The Ego against the Ego . . . the Soul against the Soul," James had said of the human encounters in Ibsen's plays and had gone on to describe them, in a wonderful and mysterious phrase, as "thinkable things." The very notions of ego—selfhood—and soul were what were missing from the French *pièces à bien faites.* Ibsen took over the apparatus of the genre and by infusing it with self and spirit put it to unheard-of intellectual and imaginative uses. By compelling the past to reveal its tyranny over the present and abstractions over palpable life, he gave to the well-made structure a depth of conflict that radically exposed the superficiality of the kinds of contests—immediate, mechanical, effortlessly assimilable—which were its stock in trade.

In doing this he changed the nature of dramatic plot, or at least the premises from which it proceeded in the well-made play. For the bourgeois audiences of the period (as for their counterparts today) plots were physically eventful stories mirroring the logical, unmysterious ways in which their own lives were presumed to move. Or else they were fanciful tales, logical and transparent in their own manner, that grafted comfortingly romantic inventions onto otherwise prosaic existence and provided it with solacing endings.

Ibsen's plots were instrumentalities of spiritual and moral revelation, seeking to work against the process of replication of ordinary life or that of its romantic enhancement. They did this through the presence of poetic implication and statement beneath the realistic surfaces and in the interstices of the story's physical events, constituting what we would now call the "subtext." Unlike the plots of Scribe, for example, to whom story was every-thing ("When my story is right, when I have the events of my play firmly in hand," he once said, "I could have my janitor write it"), Ibsen's plots were in part *pretexts*, traps for the attention of the audience, which was then led, if it was willing to follow, toward his deeper subject.

Yet as time went on Ibsen grew more and more aware of the constric-tions on the imagination that lay in even a strategic obedience to the tenets of the well-constructed plot. Had he been a novelist he would have been able to make use of those integumentary and aesthetically environing elements, that atmosphere of reflection, opinion, point of view, and so on which the writer of fiction brings into being in order to give his characters richer and more complex destinies than their literal actions can amass. Under the surfaces of Ibsen's social plays are present elements of a far-reaching tragi-comic vision, yet this vision is continually impeded by the literalness of the narrative. Moral quests spread past the incidents devised for their unfolding; metaphysical actions take place in imperfect collaboration, sometimes in acute disharmony, with the physical details of their stage life, obliged as the latter are to provide recognizable portraits.

Most noticeably in plays like *Pillars of Society*, *A Doll's House* and *Ghosts*, but also in more complex works like *Rosmersholm* and *Hedda Gabler*, the machinery of plot works logically to establish necessary physical connections, more or less narrow sequences of cause and effect which propel the action forward but at the expense of a fullness of poetic significance. The poetry survives—it is what keeps the plays alive for our pleasure—but it is hemmed in, cramped; the trouble we have with these plays is that their plots keep crowding out their perceptions.

In the end their denouements have issued from mechanical rather than organically imaginative progressions, from an inevitability of physical causa-tion resembling that which we illusorily feel in "real" life. The famous letter in *A Doll's House*, the father's pipe in *Ghosts*, Loevborg's manuscript in *Hedda Gabler*—quintessential objects of the well-made plot—have the effect of imposing on the plays a stringency, an inevitability of a smaller, more limited kind than Ibsen's imagination had conceived.

There has been little room for choice, the movement by which a char-acter is shown to elect his or her own fate, the way Oedipus and Macbeth do, as a consequence of his own nature and existential situation and as an image of these things, instead of having a destiny thrust on him by a logic of happenstance. However much these events strive to attain the condition of fatality, they remain incommensurable with the characters, too local, specific, and literal to contain all their meanings and significances or to support fully their stature as freely imagined beings. Thus once the letter is in the box

Nora is compelled by the logic of the plot-as-fate to act on the coercive knowledge of the effect its discovery will have on her husband; once Rosmer has learned of Rebecca West's machinations he is propelled by that knowledge to a death intended partly to atone for her acts and on that account smaller in implication and metaphoric density than the one Ibsen was trying to create for him.

In the same way, once Hedda has destroyed Loevborg's manuscript, which has itself come down to her through a chain of plotted, charted circumstances, she is led to destroy herself, having literally burned her bridges behind her. Or rather it is the plot that has burned them for her; and thus we feel a discrepancy, an uneasy space, between its inexorable physical action and the realities of her nature. The violent circumstances may be physical or objective indications of her moral and psychic being, but they are by no means equivalent to it, so that what she incarnates is reflected in the events of the play like a face overflowing a small mirror held too close. The miracle is that Ibsen has been able to make her fate, with its implications of a disorder at the heart of existence itself and not merely in a particular social or psychopathological modality, as convincing as he has.

With *The Master Builder* in 1892 Ibsen entered his last phase, the so-called "symbolic" period. At the age of sixty-four, unquestionably the world's most famous playwright, he set out once again to alter his methods, one result being to disconcert all those who thought that they had finally come to grasp what he was about. The undertaking is an exemplary instance of the subtle relationships between psychic reality and aesthetic forms. Pressures within his sense of self now compelled Ibsen toward the creation of new dramatic styles, new structures of consciousness, for the awarenesses he now possessed could no longer be contained within the forms he had been working with, the tightly organized, logically proceeding, objective-looking drama which he had strategically employed and compromised with for so long.

If psychological criticism scants formal values for the sake of clinical findings, pure textual criticism proceeds as though the art had been created in an inhuman zone of aesthetic autonomy. Much of the criticism of Ibsen's last plays is psychological rather than textual, and much of it has a negative cast. The plays are most often seen as problematic documents of embattled old age, with a subplot concerning the risks of being an artist; what is sometimes ignored is that they are also problematic exercises in dramatic technique, experiments in the working out of forms that will be the aesthetic equivalents of the playwright's experiences. Ibsen's internal life had entered a new, beleaguered stage. Realizations he had been holding at arm's length had come steadily closer, crowding his self-knowledge; he is growing old, the stern and amazingly disciplined practice of his art (for nearly thirty years he had written at the rate of a play every two years or so) has cost him human warmth, a fullness of actual life.

In the summer of 1889 at Gossensass in the Tyrol, he had met an eighteen-year-old girl, Emilie Bardach, who seems to have fallen in love with him, a feeling he reciprocated but kept severely under control, so that apparently nothing was consummated. In time he cut off their correspondence, but she, and several other young women he was to meet in the next few years, remained in his sentiments, poignant reminders of what he had missed and would not now have.

The question of Ibsen's emotional and sexual life, particularly as it concerns his wife of nearly fifty years, has been much debated. Michael Meyer's biography tries hard to do justice to the matter, in the face of the lack of any real evidence, and concludes that the marriage, while clearly lacking in passion, was solid and harmonious. Yet Meyer prints testimony of an opposite kind, excerpts from a diary (which was to remain unpublished for seventy-five years) kept by one Martin Schneekloth, a young Danish acquaintance of the Ibsens in Rome around the time of the writing of *Peer Gynt*:

Ibsen, Schneekloth wrote,

> took [his wife] from her father's house, led her out into the strange world, and instead of devoting his life to finding some form of reconciliation he gives all of his mind and passion to a demonic pursuit of literary fame. It is disturbing to hear him describe his plans to send his wife and child home so that he may work in peace abroad. He lacks the courage to pursue his career without abandoning his domestic responsibilities, to face up to the consequences of his ambition, to work incessantly to give her life fulfilment, to suffer and strive to educate his son. Thus he, who so loudly and brilliantly condemns the cravenness of our age, who in mighty poems proclaims the strength of human will, is himself a craven, a vacillating weakling.

We cannot know the truth of these charges. But what is important is that Ibsen came to convert into art the substance of the debate and the dilemma. By the time of *The Master Builder* he had become acutely aware of the dangerous ambiguities of consciousness itself, the relationship of artistic sensibility to wider human experience, to put it most flatly, the effect of being an artist on being a man. Once again we are reminded of Kierkegaard, in this case of *Either/Or* with its posing of the aesthetic/spiritual antithesis, and we think too of Yeats' dictum of the intellect having to choose "perfection of the life or of the work." In his last four plays Ibsen was to initiate, as nearly as such matters can be chronologically placed, the long contemporary process of the artist's questioning of his art.

His task in these plays was the nearly unprecedented one of making art out of the ambiguities and contradictions, the "inhumaneness" of the aesthetic mode of life itself. A half century later Thomas Mann would compose the definitive work of this kind, the novel *Doctor Faustus*, which a critic described as Mann's "eloquent compromise with silence." For Ibsen to speak or to be silent were never the alternatives; he would go on writing to the end. But from now on he would make the costs of writing, of living in and through language and ideality, his subject.

At first glance *The Master Builder*'s structure and procedures seem to be as before. Contemporary characters act in a sequential way within a recognizable social milieu, events concatenate and issue in a violent denouement. An aging architect or "builder," as he calls himself, forges a relationship with a young, intellectually and physically seductive girl (the original for whom was undoubtedly Emilie Bardach) who presses and inspires him to attempt a "dizzying" feat which brings about his death. In the course of this narrative, themes emerge which have to do with the pressure of youth upon age and the profound hostility between the life and commitments of art and the demands of the domestic and social. Yet we quickly become aware of a change in something beyond subject.

Ibsen's art has undergone a transformation into a suggestive indefiniteness, a mysterious transcendence of era and place. *The Master Builder* attains a more complete and self-contained metaphorical existence than has been possible for Ibsen to achieve as long as he was under the exigencies of his intricate entente with the realistic theater and its methods. His meanings and implications, the images and vocabularies from which they radiate, the objectifications of his intuitions, all exist now within an aesthetic environment less bound to historical time. His imagination functions more freely as a bestower of metaphor; he enters more completely into his creation, whose principles are now more consistent with his own nature and needs; and plot, the soul of the tragedy in Aristotle's definition, makes fewer concessions to the fixed, mechanical movements of a well-fashioned body.

As in the earlier social plays, the action begins in a long history anterior to the drama's physical events. Even more completely than is true of

Ibsen's earlier protagonists, Solness, the master builder, is already almost wholly what he is going to be in the play, which is to say the latter's events do not so much create his character as reveal it.

This character, moreover, is not fixed, waiting to be exhibited through the stresses of the plot, nor is it representative of what we call "themes"; Solness is less an agent of meaning than a locus of ideas and intuitions brought together in an active, a dramatic *instancing*. The problem for Ibsen was how to make these ideas and intuitions, these experiences halfway between actuality and art, issue in a work that would transcend personal, limited fate to be exemplary of a condition of existence and not a mere career. It was the problem of how to make fate universal and perennial in an age in which the only publicly accepted fatalities were social and what we might call technical, questions of success or failure within a realm of palpable values.

In the way in which what is necessary and inevitable works itself out lies the subtly radical change from the previous plays. Nothing better illustrates this than the matter of the crack in the chimney. When Solness tells Hilde about the fire which had destroyed his house and led to the deaths of his children, he prepares the audience for causation within the canons of melodrama and the well-made play. Yet he quickly reveals that the crack he had failed to repair had had nothing whatever to do with the fire; it has continued to operate as an element in his awareness of mysterious spiritual connections among material phenomena, and his revelation of the part it did not play in the fire is an oblique declaration by Ibsen that there are going to be no more causal sequences of the earlier mechanical kind.

The Master Builder thus expands the space available to its protagonist for the discovery and assumption of his destiny by converting much of the machinery of plot from the order of physical contingency and necessity to that of ontological urgency and spiritual choice. Solness is not free to evade his fate—that he has one means that the work exists dramatically—but he is free within the dramatic narrative to choose the events that will reveal and constitute it. For the tyranny of the past is no longer absolute; it will not act now as a remorseless sequence of cause and effect. Nothing Solness does issues from the past like a time bomb going off; nothing has to happen simply because something else has happened earlier.

The "cause" of the culminating action of *The Master Builder* is an effect of choice, not the result of a coercion by a logic of physical event. When Solness climbs up the tower for the traditional wreathing ceremony, he has willed to do something he can repudiate at any time. That we feel his decision to be inevitable is not the result of his having been caught by circumstances, hooked in the mouth by plot, but of Ibsen's successful creation of a world of imaginative necessity. Solness is acting out of his creator's intuitions about the greatness and futility of art, about the terrible burdens it lays on the artist's ordinary life and the doubts it perpetually raises about its agency in the world.

Along with this awareness of art as the necessary but disastrous "dream of the impossible" is consciousness of another and related realm of besieged being: human existence in time, the tyranny of age and the loss of the self through the depletions brought about by the very choices we make in the belief they will carry us into "fullness." These two recognitions of finiteness work inexorably, as poetic potencies and dramatic energies, toward the tragic attempt at reversal, the leap to overcome the laws of time and physical being, by which Solness is made into a legend and the play crystallized into an irreducible image.

Unlike any of the social plays' protagonists, Solness has gone to the end of his possibilities with internal assent if not with full consciousness, and above all with freedom from mechanical pressure. His decision to climb the tower in the face of his tendency toward vertigo has arisen from his original promise to Hilde of a "kingdom," a promise which, since he had made it as nothing more than a flirtatious utterance to an enchanting child, puts him outside any rigorous moral or social obligation to fulfill. Yet he will give her her kingdom, for only this way can he assume his destiny.

Not since *Brand* and *Peer Gynt* has Ibsen made such complex and resourceful use of a controlling image. Beginning with its narrower function as a figure for romantic aspiration generally and for sexual promise, the notion of kingdom is steadily developed into a resonant metaphor for the life of art and, beyond that, for the ways in which existence presses toward its limits and discovers them in a dialectic of necessity and disaster. In the end the idea of kingdom has been modulated, after an intricate interchange in which Solness and Hilde swiftly uncover all the meanings and implications of their relationship, into that of "a castle in the air," one built, as Solness says, "on a true foundation." No more suggestive image for the nature and location of art in relation to life has ever been offered us.

When Hilde, in "quiet, crazed triumph," cries out at the moment of Solness's death that she has heard "harps in the air" and apostrophizes him as "*my—my* master builder!" she gives a home in consciousness to his lucid act of overreaching, one that contains all the splendor and dementedness of man's effort at transcendence. Solness has gone too far, which means he has reached a tragic condition, something that for a dozen plays Ibsen has been unable to achieve for his protagonists. But he has been able to achieve it for this one only as the outcome of a major shift in dramaturgical procedure and not as the simple result of a change of values or cultural ambition or experience.

Ibsen's last three plays are filled with even greater anguish than *The Master Builder*, yet they are even more minimal in style and architectonics, more sparing of means and less dependent on narrative structure and sequential action. Among them *Little Eyolf* stands somewhat apart, in its morale if not dramaturgically. In this play the extreme moral vision which it shares with the others is meliorated by an acceptance short of fatality, a narrow, immensely austere awareness of corrupted moral being which may still however be redeemed. But like the protagonists of the two plays to follow, as well as of *The Master Builder*, its central character is an artist, or artist-type, and its chief preoccupation is with the losses inflicted on others by the devotion to abstractions, to surrogate experience and ideal truth, which being an artist can entail and which by extension is a temptation in every life.

For *Little Eyolf* and even more for the plays which came after it, Ibsen reached a condition of lyric expressiveness that sharply reduced his reliance on linear movement, a progression of linked events. The great image of Borkman, the "sick wolf" perpetually pacing his room, is the type of Ibsen's utterance in these works. In all of them the decisive physical events issue from a generating environment of poetic feeling, not from a tightly knit narrative structure.

This is one of the reasons why so many critics have found the last plays inferior, thinking them, as Mary McCarthy once wrote, "inflated" and "grandiose." In this view Ibsen is supposed to have lost his way, gone artistically soft. The charge does gain a degree of plausibility from the fact that Ibsen was not able fully to solve the nearly unprecedented problem he faced: how to write directly about himself, about his moral and existential turbulence, within the rubrics and expectations of a dramatic method that contained no provision for this kind of writing to be conceived, let alone undertaken. As a result, the pure lyrical impulse is not always secure, assured of its rights. Still, the plays are not pretentious or self-indulgent or vague; incompletions, perhaps, partial failures at the extreme edge of ambition, they testify to the most unaccommodating and indestructible integrity.

John Gabriel Borkman and *When We Dead Awaken* are especially static creations, informed by the most radical moral and ontological perceptions and intuitions, and what is needed for their dramatic vitality is a form extensively different from anything Ibsen had thus far been able to control. He would not of course have called it "spatial form," that recent intellectual construct, but the terms suggests what he was seeking. For the fact that almost all the crucial physical action of the plays has been completed before the stage life is set in motion, the two protagonists moving toward their deaths not as a result of traditional dramatic development but out of recognitions that have been almost wholly present throughout, means that development will have to take place in some other fashion. Something other than a chain of causally connected events will have to generate the ongoing movement, the suspense- fulness without which no drama can be said to exist.

The suspensefulness is created by the poetry, by what we might call the gathering evidence of the condition of feeling in which the works will end, the almost intolerable recognitions the tension of whose presentation consists in our being led by them step by step past our ordinary vision and into a change of sight. It is a poetry of accumulating discovery and lamenta- tion, of cold acceptance that the cost of wanting everything is everything, and of dark crystallizations of the sense and emotions of finality, of the irre- versibility of the self's catastrophic ambitions. It has been argued that in these last plays Ibsen was repudiating his own career as an artist. This may be so, but it is important to remember that the repudiation took place within art itself; it is as if Ibsen was establishing once again that only the imagination can teach us about the imagination's own afflictions.

The two protagonists, Borkman and Rubek, have "sold" love and human connection for power over the earth and over experience, Rubek through art and Borkman through an aesthetically informed dream of an Alexander-like conquest of physical nature. They have thought of themselves as benefactors, but they have been monsters of self-regard. Their deaths, even more explicitly than that of Solness, are demonstrations of their having crossed a boundary line; they are punishments in the moral order, but beyond that are culminating actions in newly shaped artistic creations, legends of morality as the process of discovering the ruin our ambitions will always incur.

Yet the poetry of this had still to have a base. For dramaturgical coher- ence and dramatic momentum, the problem was to make things "happen" within a structure of plausibility such as Ibsen's temperament and training as a playwright required but that could scarcely be sustained now by the replicas of stories from the self-dramatizing world outside the formal stage that he had been forced to devise and that had been barely adequate to his purposes even so. His main instrument, the past, is no longer a principle of active dramatic pressure, one that brings about revelations and denouements of the plays as physical consequences of moral realities or, as in *The Master Builder*, as spiritual ones in a sequential line. For both Borkman and Rubek already possess the attributes of their ultimate condition, and the plays, instead of being the unfolding processes by which that condition is reached, are its swift flowerings.

In a brilliant stroke Ibsen anticipated and partly inspired an entire genre of plays to come by describing his protagonists as already "dead," as they are told by others, already, that is to say, in the condition to which ordinary drama, and life of course as well, must lead with its parade of events. As far as he was able in these plays, Ibsen took the drama out of what Ionesco was fifty years later to call the line of the "detective story," the statement, development, and resolution or solution of one or another kind of human problem, tracked from beginning to end.

But he was unable to go the whole way. What marks *Borkman* and even more *When We Dead Awaken* as transitional plays (although no less wonderful for that; Joyce thought *When We Dead Awaken* Ibsen's greatest work) and brings down upon the accusation of being damagingly "symbolic" are, even more than their language, their settings, the world of mysterious rooms, snow, storms, mountains, and avalanches, within which the true poetic bodies of the play form themselves. It may seem strange to say, but the real work of both plays is complete without those external elements, the consciousness is present apart from them.

Ibsen nevertheless brought into both plays this apparatus of external scene and suggestive setting partly in order physically to accomplish the deaths of his protagonists, but more subtly because he could not yet imagine how a play whose ambition was nothing less than to exist immediately, all at once, causing itself and not being instigated by anything outside itself, by anything from the world of "nature," and therefore existing as a poem does whose passage through time is a concession to physical laws but whose end is really in its beginning—how such a play could be written and staged.

And yet, great mind and tireless spirit that he was, he remarked after writing *When We Dead Awaken*, which he had called a "dramatic epilogue," that now that he was finished with this long segment of his career he might very well return to the "battlefields" but with "new weapons and new equipment." Not long after that he fell victim to a stroke. He lived on, increasingly debilitated, for five years, writing nothing more before his death in 1906. Passers-by and would-be visitors used to see him sitting stiffly in a chair by his window, gazing with his badger's eyes at the life of the streets, as he had once gazed at the living forms of the sea.

SVERRE ARESTAD

The Ibsen Hero

The subject of Ibsen's hero is so very nearly synonymous with the totality of his production that a consideration of all his protagonists would seem to be in order. Since this task obviously presents insurmountable obstacles, certain characters will have to be selected to represent the several kinds of heroes that Ibsen depicted. The selection cannot be arbitrary, for it is essential to choose the most representative one from each of three categories. When this has been accomplished, the discussion of Ibsen's hero can proceed. This matter is a bit complicated because two of the heroes to be discussed, Brand and Solness, are quite alike, and they therefore constitute one category, while Peer Gynt and Mrs. Alving represent two categories of the Ibsen hero.

Two matters need to be set forth as a preliminary to the whole complex problem of Ibsen's hero. First of all, I must state that I have worked with the Ibsen hero, directly and indirectly, for a number of years and have, from time to time, made public certain views concerning this topic. I now find myself drawing upon some of those views, and, consequently, I am consciously placing myself in a position that Peer Gynt, unknown to himself, was guilty of when he drew upon the whole repository of secular lore and of biblical tradition to prove a point and, finding these inadequate to his purposes, resorted to quoting himself. In the second instance, I want to acknowledge a

From "The Ibsen Hero" by Sverre Arestad from *The Hero in Scandinavian Literature from Peer Gynt to the Present*, eds. John M. Weinstock and Robert T. Rovinsky. Copyright © 1975 by the University of Texas Press. By permission of the author.

115

debt to numerous students, both undergraduate and graduate, who, over the years, have wrestled with me on the problem of the Ibsen hero, and I want to get that acknowledgment in before any of them begin to accuse me of plagiarism.

I believe it was Paul Valéry who once cited the mathematician Gauss's observation that one must put a problem in such a form that it can be solved. When a poet must cite a mathematician, there may be trouble for the lesser man who attempts to emulate the admonition. It is reassuring therefore to draw upon the more comforting formula of the philosopher. As Bertrand Russell stated in his essay "On Scientific Method in Philosophy," the discovery that a question is unanswerable is as complete an answer as can possibly be obtained. My task, therefore, will be to state the question and attempt an answer; Ibsen himself would hardly have demanded more.

If one asks the simple question, "What is a hero?" in the present context, the problem is immediately complicated, because forthwith one must pose the ancillary questions of "What is an Ibsen hero?" and "What is *the* Ibsen hero?" There are thus three aspects to the question, which is proper, because there are actually three different kinds of hero in Ibsen's plays: the literary hero, the modern hero, and *the* Ibsen hero. It is the final definition that will present the greatest difficulty, because a formulation of it involves a subjective, a value, judgment, but it is the hero image of central concern.

There can be no doubt that some of Ibsen's heroes reflect prototypes from earlier literature, from Shakespeare for instance, and some reflect features from sources other than drama or belles-lettres, like the Bible or Kierkegaard. These heroes I call literary heroes. Now these questions must be asked: Are, in fact, any of Ibsen's heroes commensurate in stature with the most notable of those in Greek drama? In Shakespearean drama? In the tragedies of Racine? I should answer all three questions in the affirmative, although I have ringing in my ears Butcher's admonition to all Ibsen admirers that he was limited and provincial and that, although he achieved intensity, he failed to achieve greatness as a writer of tragic drama and, consequently, as a creator of heroes of tragic stature. It is comforting to have on one's side in this debate several astute students of Ibsen who are also sensitive interpreters of tragedy.

I shall refrain from involving T. S. Eliot in my discussion of Ibsen's hero, except to cite his view that the mirror of wholeness or completeness had been shattered into a thousand pieces by the time of Shakespeare and that one would have to go back to Dante for a valid portrait of the whole man—the Renaissance Man—and, consequently, for an acceptable basis for the true tragic hero. It follows from the above that I regard Ibsen's hero to be essentially tragic, and that I shall discuss his hero from a more traditional point of view than that proposed by T. S. Eliot.

The question now arises of the nature of an Ibsen hero. Is the Ibsen hero a universal, timeless abstraction that can readily be equated with the classical hero of earlier literature, or is it identifiably Ibsen's own? Moreover, does Ibsen's concept of the hero shift with time and still retain its validity? Finally, does Ibsen's idea of the hero evolve from an earlier concept, then change, and finally revert to the original one?

My discussion will begin with *Brand* and will continue with *Peer Gynt*, Mrs. Alving of *Ghosts*, and Solness of *The Master Builder*. I must, however, make a few remarks concerning earlier Ibsen protagonists before proceeding to Brand.

The key to Ibsen's hero lies in his understanding of man's tragedy. Ibsen's concept of tragedy centers on the question of whether or not man is free to order his life as he chooses, a question that he tested against both the conventions of the early nineteenth century and the naturalism of the 1870's and 1880's. The three tragic heroes chosen to be discussed are markedly different, although there is a much closer relationship between Brand and master builder Solness than there is between either of these two protagonists and Mrs. Alving. This is due to the fact that Ibsen conceived of *Brand* as high tragedy, that he abandoned high tragedy in middle career, when he wrote *Ghosts*, and that he restored high tragedy in his last period, when he wrote *The Master Builder*. Peer Gynt is not mentioned here, but he will be considered in due time.

The tragedies of Ibsen's first period—from *Lady Inger of Østrât* (1854) to *Emperor and Galilean* (1873)—revolve around the broad theme of *idealism*. *Brand*, written in the midst of this protracted speculation on the nature of individual freedom of choice and action, became Ibsen's most profound tragedy.

It will be profitable to look briefly at the manner in which Ibsen evolved and extended the character of Brand. At the end of *Love's Comedy* (1862), the poet Falk assumes a position that can loosely be called idealistic. He has freed himself—so he thinks—from the "manacle of slavery" (tradition), and he can now carry on the war against the lie: social hypocricy. But there is no assurance that he will succeed, because he relies on Svanhild's belief in his mission rather than on his own. The idealist Falk, who goes forth to do battle on borrowed good, becomes the doubter and the procrastinator Skule of *The Pretenders*. Skule demonstrates that one cannot live for another's view; the best he can do is to die for it. Although Skule is one of Ibsen's finest tragic heroes, he falls far short of being the Ibsen hero. Another hero in *The Pretenders*, King Håkon. bears a curious relationship to Brand. Håkon had complete faith in God's support of his endeavors, but his faith was based on arrogant presumption. He is finally made to realize this after he has condemned Skule to death; Håkon says: "God, God—why have you stricken me so sorely, when I have not sinned?" (act 3). Brand has the same view, perhaps as naive as Håkon's, that his idea of his mission has God's sanction. But he is made to realize that it may be beyond man's ability to know absolutely what his fate or destiny is and therefore what his limitations as a mortal may be.

If this relationship is continued further into *Peer Gynt* and *Emperor and Galilean*, numerous facets of the character of Brand will emerge; Brand's character as hero will presently be considered in detail. *Brand* and *Peer Gynt* represent two aspects of the Kierkegaardian syndrome. Kierkegaard provided for three stages in man's moral, intellectual, and spiritual life: the aesthetic, the ethical, and the religious. These Kierkegaardian categories contain complete, complex analyses of three divergent views of life, but Ibsen has employed only one principle from two of them, the aesthetic and the ethical. Brand as an ethical character has assumed full responsibility for his decisions and resulting actions, while Peer as an aesthetic character has not committed himself to any such irrevocable responsibility. While an individual may rise or fall on Kierkegaard's scale, a character within the compass of a play cannot pass from one stage to another. The moment the hero did that, the play would have to end.

As an ethical character, Brand must constantly call upon all his powers to refuse compromise of any kind. He must adhere to the principle that to will a thing and fail is forgivable, but to refuse to will even the impossible and therefore not attempt it is not only unforgivable but also contemptible. Peer, as an aesthetic character, is the opposite of Brand. One's first impression of Peer might well be that he is an irresolute egoist, a fraud, a failure, a completely negative character, who never reaches a decision, never fulfills a promise, never attains a goal. But Peer cannot be dismissed so cavalierly, as a further comparison with Brand will show. Brand displays an inflexible adherence to principle, an inability to compromise, an absolute assurance of the correctness of his view of life, and a willful determination to achieve an ultimate goal. Peer, on the other hand, shows a seemingly casual disregard of principle, an unwillingness to commit himself fully when he cannot obtain absolute proof of the correctness of a tenet, and an inability to base his actions upon a view of life whose validity may not be questioned but must be accepted on faith. Brand bases his whole course of action upon the assumption that his particular view of life is infallible. Peer, however, tentatively tests the value of each principle of life, without finding any of them tenable. In a real sense, Peer's search for the meaning of existence and man's role in the world is much more sophisticated than Brand's.

Brand has assumed responsibility for his actions, but he at no time questions whether those actions result from his own decisions or whether the actions are dictated for him. Peer evades the problem. Julian, in *Emperor and Galilean*, however, comes to direct grips with the issue, and he rejects the condition, that is, "freedom under necessity," by which man is forced to assume responsibilities for actions that he does not himself choose. If Brand had questioned what he was asked to assume in the way of obligations, as Julian did, he never would have undertaken his mission. I conclude, therefore, that Julian also is a more sophisticated character than Brand.

I come now to a brief consideration of the nature of the hero Brand. Brand is an uncompromising idealist who has determined to fulfill his mission as an agent of God by bringing to the people the desire to live a Christ-like life and, by steeling their wills, the means to achieve that desire. He has married Agnes, a woman of as great a spirit as his own, compassionate, forgiving, considerate, aware of the weaknesses and limitations of man and willing to compromise with those weaknesses and limitations but forced to accede to Brand's inhuman demand for no compromise. He has assumed the family guilt, as a result of which he refuses to give his mother the last sacrament unless she will give up all her worldly possessions. When it is feared that his child will die unless he is removed from the damp climate of the cramped valley, Brand only for a moment wavers in his resolve to consider no obstacle too great if one but wills to overcome it. But when the doctor observes that it is strange that Brand should yield when his own son's life is in jeopardy, though he will not do so under any other considerations, Brand reverses his impulsive decision and declines to move away, and as a result his son dies.

Agnes must willingly give up all physical mementos of her son—a lock of hair, a cap—she must not look upon her son's grave; she must, in fact, divest her mind and soul of any remembrance of him whatever, and she must do this willingly and gladly, for such are the demands of God. Being inadequate to these demands, Agnes dies. Brand, without realizing it, has lost the one person who sustained him in his mission.

Alone at the end, Brand gives voice to his utter despair at the state of man.

> God, I plunge into death's night,—
> Shall they wholly miss thy Light
> Who unto man's utmost might
> Will'd—? (act 5)

Brand's greatness lies in his unyielding and inflexible urge to attain the unattainable even after the impossibility of successful achievement has been inexorably demonstrated. Even in defeat, Brand leaves one with the optimistic, encouraging, and germinating idea that, although it has been demonstrated through him that he cannot attain the ideal, he will not admit that he cannot. In a very real sense, Brand's words, "But the path of yearning's left," are the most magnificent words that Ibsen ever penned.

The tragedy of *Brand*, then, is that of a man who, in attempting to live according to the ideal and demanding that others do likewise, realizes that his ideal is false because it is based on will and not on love, a realization that renders him incapable of fulfilling his mission.

Brand had voluntarily accepted responsibility for his actions, but he had not inquired whether his choice was free or whether it was predetermined. He failed to consider whether what he chose to do was what God had decreed that he should do. Ibsen clarified this aspect of Brand's character by presenting an opposite nature in the person of Julian in *Emperor and Galilean*.

Julian's task in *Emperor and Galilean* was to attain harmony of being by uniting in himself the forces of the flesh and of the spirit, whereupon he could proceed to effect a synthesis of the classical and the Christian traditions, that is, to institute harmony in his world. The Oracle had informed him that he was a chosen man under necessity, that is, the necessity of doing God's bidding, all the while assuming full responsibility for his actions. Julian refused to subordinate himself to a higher authority, for he would not accept any limitations on his freedom of choice and action. He rejected the formula "to will under necessity," and, in denying necessity and thereby a higher power, he discovered that what he struggled for he failed to achieve and what he struggled against he served to promote. The paradox is that, in refusing to will what he must, Julian willed what he wanted, only to discover, as Brand did, that that was what he was all along destined to do. These early Ibsen heroes are thus compulsive but, in actuality, not free individuals.

While Peer may well be Ibsen's most beloved character, and his search for the meaning of the self may perhaps be Ibsen's most sophisticated treatment of this central theme in all his works, Ibsen could not have condoned Peer's life style, although he tolerated it. Peer, therefore, falls short of Ibsen's ideal.

Peer Gynt is so great a drama that one feels apologetic about devoting only a few lines to it. In many ways it is as profound a work as has ever been written. One intriguing thing about *Peer Gynt* is its ability to arouse young people. They ask: How do I know what course to take? With every decision I make, I get into a mold. Do I know that I am proceeding in the right direction? What evidence do I have that what I am now doing is best for me?

Where do my decisions lead? The basic element of *Peer Gynt*, as seen by the young, was well expressed by Kierkegaard, who said that life can only be understood backwards, but it must be lived forwards.

I have already commented on *Peer Gynt* in relation to *Brand*, and I need not repeat those observations. It only needs to be emphasized here that the negative aspects of *Peer Gynt* that were presented in the comparison are quite widely held, but they do not correspond to my view of *Peer Gynt* at all.

Although Peer may appear to be evasive and dilatory, he is so only because he acts according to a certain axiom: he will proceed only so far as empirical evidence of the validity of the tenets of life will carry him. The Button Molder's ultimate challenge to Peer, in act 5, is that, if he doesn't know God's purpose with him, he must divine it. Peer rejects this absurd demand, and rightly so. Two predecessors of Peer Gynt, the young King Håkon of *The Pretenders* and Brand, are relevant here. When Håkon's mother is performing the ordeal by fire on his behalf, an aide says to him, "Pray to the Lord, thy God." Håkon replies, "That is not necessary, I'm sure of him." Early in the play, Brand says, "I am on the mission of a great man. His name is God!" It is obvious how far off the mark these two characters were. Peer Gynt, in the opening scene, is asked by his mother to swear that what he is saying is true. Peer answers with a question: "Why swear?" That is, why commit yourself when you don't know what the score is? So, while Brand discovered that his protracted mission was based on a false assumption, which was his infallible belief that he had been chosen by God to play a specific role, Peer decided to find out something about this world we inhabit before he committed himself.

Peer's pilgrimage through life is known to everyone, so it does not have to be repeated here. Although he lived most of his life on the principle "*To thyself be—enough*," he ultimately realized that this attitude toward life left one unfulfilled and that this view of life, moreover, deprived others of their share of life's rewards. While he was active, Peer drifted along on the currents of materialistic existence, but, when he had become sated with that life style, he paused to reflect. As Housman expressed it: "Some men think by fits and starts / and when they do, they fasten their hands upon their hearts." This is what Peer did. He succeeded ultimately in divesting himself of the Gyntian Self, but, as usual in an Ibsen play, there is a question of whether he realized his true self, that is, the recognition of what the self constitutes in the life of man. However one wishes to interpret the conclusion of *Peer Gynt*—whether he is saved or not; the skeptical will say no, the strong of faith will say yes—he nevertheless succeeded in demonstrating that man's knowledge of the world is insufficient to his needs. A faith of some kind is essential to survival, if not to triumph.

I want only to suggest here that critics, reading *Peer Gynt* in casual fashion, have found Peer to be the progenitor of Hjalmar Ekdal, in *The Wild Duck*, and Dr. Stockman, in *An Enemy of the People*. These suggestions, in a sense, are not invalid, but I doubt that Peer Gynt would ever have recognized Hjalmar Ekdal or, for that matter, Dr. Stockman. The matter of influence completely baffles me, but I should not think it unlikely that, fed by critical suggestions, subsequent authors may have seen in Peer Gynt the genesis of the antihero. If so, Ibsen would share with Dostoievski the distinction of introducing the antihero into literature, the latter's *Notes from the Underground* (1864) usually thought of as originating that concept.

Since Ibsen is the ideological forerunner of much of subsequent drama, one looks to him for the genesis of the modern tragic hero. Classical drama affords a wide range of protagonists, the few who are truly great and the many who are of lesser stature. The latter are called diminished protagonists. Ibsen has some of each of these, but he also has an entirely new hero—the modern hero—who, though of smaller stature, cannot be understood in terms of the diminished hero of classical tragedy. I shall give only one example, Mrs. Alving of *Ghosts*. In today's increasingly democratic orientation, Willy Loman, for example, has come to be accepted as a tragic figure, a protagonist who has his origin in Ibsen. It took Arthur Miller ten years, with fits and starts, to evolve a concept of modern tragedy that would include Willy Loman, the substance of which was that intent is primary and performance secondary. In other words, if a character in a modern play commits himself wholeheartedly to his goal, though because of almost total deficiencies he fails, he must nevertheless be considered a tragic figure. Ibsen would have agreed to this formulation of the modern tragic hero.

Ibsen's concept of the tragedy of modern man is nowhere more forcefully represented than in *Ghosts*. Mrs. Alving is a noble personality and a remarkable woman. She is thus, actually, a diminished protagonist in terms of the classical hero, but she inhabits a naturalistic world, and the tragedy therefore becomes a "mixed" tragedy, as I have called it elsewhere. Ibsen's intent in Ghosts is to demonstrate how meaningless existence becomes for an idealist who must seek to surmount the jungle of a mechanistic order.

Whether one reads or sees *Ghosts*, one leaves the reading or the performance with the feeling that this is one of the most powerful dramas that Ibsen has ever written. Mrs. Alving was conceived by Ibsen as a heroic personality, with diminished protagonist status, whose mission was to attain an idealistic goal: to create the basis for an environment that would make possible the achievement of the "joy of life." Far from being a cliché, the "joy of life" lies at the very center of Ibsen's concern in *Ghosts*. It is fundamental to an understanding of *Ghosts*, and to an appreciation of its tragedy, that Mrs.

Alving be thought of as an unusual personality, a heroic or perhaps semi-heroic character. But she is caught up in a nonidealistic situation, in which any choices she makes become meaningless because her choices are predicated on an idealistic view of life, while her environment is nonidealistic. Her efforts toward achievement are therefore totally ineffectual, and she becomes the victim of the circumstances she endeavored to overcome.

The feeling the spectator has in viewing *Ghosts* is that nowhere has he been elevated by a gigantic contest, because all efforts are doomed through negation rather than through meaningful struggle and conflict; and at the end one has a feeling of debility without any realization of compensation for the horrible fate that has befallen Mrs. Alving and her son. There is no rising to heights of emotion at the prospect of any notable achievement, and there is no possibility of accepting things as they are at the end, for they are too horrible even to contemplate. Leaving the theater after viewing *Ghosts*, one walks on shoes of lead.

Thus, if one looks for the elements of the classic formula of awe, catharsis, and the reestablishment of emotional equilibrium, one does not find them in *Ghosts*. They are absent because Ibsen substituted a naturalistic for a moral universe. *Ghosts*, despite all, is a remarkable play; the tragedy is undeniably powerful, but it must be considered on another basis than that of high tragedy, despite the presence of a protagonist of at least semiheroic proportions. And *Ghosts* is not a tragedy of character in the sense in which this term would apply to Ibsen's earlier tragedies, nor is it a tragedy of personal psychology, such as one finds in Strindberg's *Miss Julie*. It is the tragedy of situation or circumstances in which an individual of noble aspirations must contend, always ineffectually, against a hostile, nonidealistic environment.

A distinction must be made, finally, between a hero in an Ibsen play and *the* Ibsen hero. After three examples of the former, I can now formulate what to me, with perhaps some modifications, constitutes the Ibsen hero. I believe it to be Solness of *The Master Builder*. I do not make this commitment because I believe that *The Master Builder* is largely an autobiographical work. On the contrary, I hold that, despite certain resemblances to Ibsen's own life, *The Master Builder* is an objective consideration of the nature of the artist. After all, the stages in Solness's life parallel those of every individual. This play considers the demands he makes upon life; his choices, whose consequences are ultimately apparent to him; the question of guilt, or conscience; and, finally, what measure of freedom the artist has.

During his fifty years as a dramatist, Ibsen was concerned with only a few fundamental problems, namely, the will, love, man's calling, and the question of man's freedom of choice. All four of these are included to a greater or lesser extent in *The Master Builder*, but choice is predominant. This is by no means the first time Ibsen emphasized the problem of choice in his characters—in Brand, Emperor Julian, Consul Bernick, Mrs. Alving, among others—but in a real sense it is the most significant. This will become clear from a study of Ibsen's portrayal of the artist.

Ibsen portrays characters from many walks of life: churchmen, kings and emperors, politicians, doctors, lawyers, businessmen and entrepreneurs, and artists. Numerous callings and professions are thus represented in his gallery of portraits. He never consciously sought, however, to present a psychological delineation of a king or a churchman or a politician. In Ibsen's great historical drama, *The Pretenders*, there is no hint of the myth of kingship nor any attempt to understand a king as king. Ibsen's politicians in *The League of Youth* are at best stereotypes, and the bear little resemblance to the masterful portrait of the politician that Bjørnson created in *Paul Lang og Tora Parsberg*. Of Pastor Manders in *Ghosts* the best that can be said is that he is a flat character, but his is not a psychological portrait of a man of the cloth; at most, he is possibly emerging into the round. Referring to Brand, Ibsen dispels any notion that he ever attempted the portrait of a man of the church; he remarks: "I just happened to make Brand a minister: I could equally well have made him a member of any other calling." More important in this connection, however, is the fact that Ibsen did not, and, indeed, could not have said the same thing about his entrepreneur- and artist-protagonists— Bernick, Solness, Borkman, and Rubek.

Though a weak character, Falk of *Love's Comedy* is portrayed as an artist per se. His is really the portrait of an early-nineteenth-century youth with some poetic pretensions, romanticized and idealized by others but cut to ribbons by Ibsen. While it is only a cameo portrait, Ibsen's portrayal of Jatgeir Skald in *The Pretenders* is one of his most brilliant achievements. Here is a true romantic poet, but somehow he does not seem to be Ibsen's ideal. Another artist in Ibsen's plays who displays the proper sense of independence is Oswald of *Ghosts*, but his destiny is determined by extraneous forces exclusively, so he cannot be considered. The self-declared artists in *The Lady from the Sea* and the unbalanced Eilert Løvborg in *Hedda Gabler* could hardly represent the Ibsen hero, even if he has to be sought among the artists.

All artists prior to Solness have been briefly considered and simultaneously rejected as possible candidates for *the* Ibsen hero. Why is Solness so special? The answer to that question lies in the exploration of two matters that become curiously interrelated for the first time in *The Master Builder*. The first is Ibsen's portrayal of an artist of stature, and the second is the question of freedom of choice.

I have already indicated who Ibsen's artists are. It remains only to

reemphasize that Ibsen's preoccupation with the artist-protagonist intensi-
fied during his later years and to state that the artist and the entrepreneur
(Solness and Rubek, Bernick and Borkman, respectively) are the only characters Ibsen drew who are to be understood in terms of their calling. In other
words, these four characters are psychological portraits of the artist and the
entrepreneur. While Ibsen could say of Brand that he just happened to make
him a minister, but that he could equally well have made him a representative of any other calling, he could not have said that of the two artists and the
two entrepreneurs whom I have mentioned. Moreover, Ibsen could not,
except through complete and almost unrecognizable modification, have
made Brand an artist. It has been suggested by a Norwegian critic that
Emperor Julian, whose conflict arises by virtue of the "freedom under necessity" syndrome, could be equated with Ibsen's artists, namely with Solness
and his *non serviam* view. This position is hardly defensible.

There is a very close affinity between Ibsen's two principal artist-
protagonists—Solness and Rubek—and his two entrepreneurs—Bernick and
Borkman. The latter I have called nonartistic creative personalities. Implicit
in this designation are two important differences between the artist and the
entrepreneur. The first lies in the different nature of their respect endeavors:
the one creates poetry, music, sculpture; the other creates vast industrial
empires. The urges, drives, compulsions of each are similar, and the goals
(i.e., the achievements are identical, but the end product is dissimilar. The
artist, according to Ibsen, because of his special endowments, has an obligation to his fellowmen, but this obligation becomes effective only after the
artist has performed according to his own satisfaction. The artist does not
curry the favor of the public but does find a modicum of reward if his efforts
are recognized. The entrepreneur, on the other hand, needs and curries
public acclamation for his good works. It is sufficient here to note John
Gabriel Borkman's procession down the street in top hat and a handsome
carriage, drawn by a span of four splendid horses, acknowledging the acclaim
of the public: King John. Ibsen's artist and Ibsen himself were above this sort
of thing. This seems to me a strong argument in favor of Solness, rather than
Bernick or Borkman, as *the* Ibsen hero.

Until *The Master Builder*, Ibsen had often considered the problem of
man's freedom of choice. If other men are not free to choose, Ibsen said,
perhaps the artist—who withdraws from repressive conventions and traditions, establishes his own set of values, and goes it alone—is free. In *The
Master Builder* he set about to consider this matter. While Ibsen restored in
this play the conditions for high tragedy—the artist's challenge to God to be
permitted to do in his sphere what God did in his—his protagonist, Solness,
obviously failed because he could not compete on equal terms, given his limi-

tations, against a universal force. But Ibsen's insistence that genius, at least, be free to choose goes by the board. *The Master Builder* represents a valiant attempt on the part of a select individual to gain complete freedom of action. Unfortunately, this freedom is not available to man, but the effort he makes to attain it in the character of Solness is Ibsen's supreme attempt to establish mortal man's demand of any and all forces that he be completely free to choose and do what he desires. There is, however, another aspect to this theme, because the artist has been endowed with certain gifts that drive him toward certain goals: he has creative urges over which he has no control. How free then can any man be? Perhaps he can achieve only a limited freedom.

Of course, this urge to be free—to be one's own man—is a universal quest for all except dolts. For Ibsen it became the most important of all human problems. And that is the reason I have chosen Solness as *the* Ibsen hero: he represents most clearly the force of this urge and displays the greatest effort toward noble achievement among all of Ibsen's heroes.

It has been suggested that Brand may have had a measure of the will to power, and that pride (hubris) may also have been a part of his nature. I doubt this. I should, moreover, like to make it abundantly clear that I do not agree with the usual interpretation of Bernick of *Pillars of Society* or, especially, with that of John Gabriel Borkman, who is supposedly a Napoleon, a man hungry for power, a "superman" who disdains ordinary man's morality. This is a popularized, though mistaken, Nietzschean concept. I hold that Ibsen does something with Borkman, a man of great talent and ability, who needs to find outlet for his talent and ability in order to realize his potential. Borkman is not seeking power for its own sake, but personal fulfillment through accomplishing what he can do and *must* do. Bernick, in effect, expresses this very well to Lona Hessel, saying that if he is restricted in his activities, he might as well be dead—as, in fact, Borkman is.

It should be emphasized that *the* Ibsen hero, Solness, is not motivated by a will to power. The source of his ultimate choice and resulting actions is not willed by him but dictated to him by the need to give expression to his creative talent. Will is, of course, operative and so is hubris, but I think Ibsen is subtly suggesting that an individual like an artist, a genius who tells society, tradition, or convention to go hang, is actually no more—and he may, in fact, be less—free than some more ordinary mortals who demand less from life.

My reason for choosing Solness as *the* Ibsen hero will become even clearer when I briefly refer to Rubek of *When We Dead Awaken*, an artist and another likely candidate for heroic stature. Although Rubek throws additional light on the artist as Ibsen ultimately came to see him, I think his apologetic tone is hardly commensurate with Ibsen's view of the hero. There is a note of resignation or reconciliation in the later or last works of other writers, Shakespeare or Racine, for example, as Tillyard has so succinctly pointed out with reference to Shakespeare. This same note in Ibsen permits the protagonist, Rubek in *When We Dead Awaken*, in this instance, to reduce his sights, acknowledge his limitations, and quit beating his head against a stone wall. Rubek speaks several times of the fact that his fate—because of his gifts as creative artist—is to go on creating one work after another until his dying day. This really is not freedom in the absolute sense that Ibsen conceived it, but it is a belated recognition, on Ibsen's part, of the human condition, at whatever level of human endeavor. The only consolation to be found here is that given by Niels Bohr after he had renounced any possibility of arriving at a complete understanding of the physical universe, namely, his *Komplementaritetsphilosophie*, which is the idea of complementarity. This simply means that by universal physical law, as at present understood, man is cast in a mold, but, aside from the predetermined restrictions, he has freedom of choice. I rather think that Ibsen recognized this principle in *When We Dead Awaken*, but that he would have looked back fondly and nostalgically to a man who had not yet accepted so sophisticated a view of the world that we inhabit, a view that, in a sense, makes us lesser men than we would like to think ourselves capable of being.

In a magnificent poem, "Timann skrid undan" [The hours flit by], Olav Nygaard reflects the ultimate in man's desire to be free from the constraining forces of universal law that curb his freedom of action or his desire for peace. Ibsen would have reveled in these sentiments. Nygaard, in effect, asks if there is nowhere in space a spot, hidden in dreams, beyond all man's fate, where he can sleep while galaxy after galaxy is extinguished, where he can rock and heal his searing wounds.

The Ibsen hero is an individual who demonstrates through action a professed belief in complete freedom of choice. But the triumph of the individual over circumstances or forces is not thereby assured, for his life appears to be predetermined. In spite of this, the Ibsen hero repeatedly refuses to accept the conditions that make him a subordinate individual, and, consequently, he openly opposes the forces, the circumstances, or the predetermined plan that prevents him from ordering his life as he chooses. In the resulting struggle values obtain, but there can be no absolute certainty; yet no Ibsen hero can find comforting assurance in a cynical rejection of the universal plan of which he is both product and victim. Ibsen's heroes reflect the noblest expression of the terror and the glory of life, and they make one sensitive to man's tragic fate. In spite of their imperfectibility, one comes to admire their struggle toward the achievement of complete freedom of choice and of action against the powers and the forces of a baffling and perplexing world.

Two matters remain to be explored briefly: Ibsen's supposed indebtedness to Nietzsche and the seemingly appalling seriousness of my discourse, which gives the impression that there is neither humor nor comedy in Ibsen.

Ibsen and Nietzsche were acquainted with one another's works and thought. Nietzsche went so far as to call Ibsen an "old maid." Why? Ibsen was soft on the woman question. This issue aside, there are numerous correspondences between the two. While Nietzsche may have reinforced Ibsen's concept of the artist-hero, there is no evidence that he led Ibsen to his view of him. Born in 1844, Nietzsche published his *The Birth of Tragedy* in 1872. This was just a year before Ibsen completed his first cycle of plays, ending with *Emperor and Galilean*, the first notations to which had been made eleven years earlier.

A few quotations from three Ibsen plays previous to Nietzsche's *The Genealogy of Morals* (1887) will be briefly considered. In *The Pretenders* (1864), Bishop Nicholas, having returned from the nether kingdom, encounters King Skule on his way to his death. He states:

> While to their life-work Norsemen set out
> Will-lessly wavering, daunted with doubt,
> While hearts are shrunken, minds helplessly shivering,
> Weak as a willow-wand wind-swept and quivering—
> While about one thing alone they're united,
> Namely, that greatness be stoned and despited,
> When they seek honour in fleeing and falling
> Under the banner of baseness unfurled—,
> Then Bishop Nicholas 'tends to his calling,
> The Bagler-Bishop's at work in the world! (act 5)

At the conclusion of *The Wild Duck*, Dr. Relling says to Gregers Werle: "Oh, life would be quite tolerable, after all, if only we could be rid of the confounded duns that keep on pestering us, in our poverty, with the claim of the ideal" (act 5). Ulrik Brendel, returning to the house of Rosmer after his failure as a lecturer—he found himself bankrupt—speaks of Mortensgaard, who is in the ascendancy in the community, in undoubtedly the most discouraging passage in the idealist Ibsen's production:

> Hush, hush, hush! Peter Mortensgaard is the lord and leader of
> the future. Never have I stood in a more august presence. Peter

Mortensgaard has the secret of omnipotence. He can do whatever he wills. ("Oh, don't believe that," says Rosmer.) Yes, my boy! For Peter Mortensgaard never wills more than he can do. Peter Mortensgaard is capable of living his life without ideals. And that, do you see—that is just the mighty secret of action and of victory. It is the sum of the whole world's wisdom. Basta! (act 4)

In his *Genealogy of Morals*, the following year, Nietzsche wrote;

Here I want to give vent to a sigh and last hope. Exactly what is it that I, especially, find intolerable; that I am unable to cope with; that asphyxiates me? A bad smell. The smell of failure, of a soul that has gone stale. God knows it is possible to endure all kinds of misery—vile weather, sickness, trouble, isolation. All this can be coped with, if one is born to a life of anonymity and battle. There will always be moments of re-emergence into the light, when one tastes the golden hour of victory and once again stands foursquare, unshakable, ready to face even harder things, like a bowstring drawn taut against new perils. But, you divine patronesses—if there are any such in the realm beyond good and evil—grant me now and again the sight of something perfect, wholly achieved, happy, magnificently triumphant, something still capable of inspiring fear! Of a man who will justify the existence of mankind, for whose sake one may continue to believe in mankind! We no longer see anything these days that aspires to grow greater; instead, we have a suspicion that things will continue to go downhill, becoming ever thinner, more placid, smarter, cosier, more ordinary, more indifferent, more Chinese, more Christian—without doubt man is getting "better" all the time . . . This is Europe's true predicament: together with the fear of man we have also lost the love of man, reverence for man, confidence in man, indeed the *will of man*. Now the sight of man makes us despond. What is nihilism today if not that?

These quotations need no comment, except that one would like to echo Kierkegaard: The times are not evil; they are contemptible, because they lack passion.

Having treated Ibsen in deadly serious fashion, how am I to relieve the tragic tension? Simply by indicating that comedy and tragedy are closely intertwined in Ibsen's entire production. *The Master Builder*, however, from which I have selected the Ibsen hero, is almost devoid of comedy—there are only two instances of it. However, as in all of Ibsen's plays, there is in *The Master Builder* an abundance of irony—a saving grace in all his work

In his early plays, particularly in *The Pretenders*, Ibsen used Shakespearean comic relief. But in a later play, *Brand*, though the tragic tone is predominant, comedy is nevertheless ubiquitous. In *Peer Gynt* comedy pervades, but the tragic element rises up, on occasion, through the comic surface. I recall that Friedrich Dürrenmatt said, when asked why he wrote *The Physicists* as a comedy, that a subject so serious could not be treated as a tragedy. The paramount example of this concept in Ibsen is *The Wild Duck*. Here, as in *Peer Gynt*, the tragedy rises inexorably (as in *The Physicists*) through the comic overlayer. Ibsen's great achievement in *The Wild Duck* can be all the more appreciated when one considers how inferior this play would have been if it had not been conceived as a comedy on man's foibles. Perhaps Chekhov could have written a tragedy on the subject, but not Ibsen. So, while one thinks of Ibsen's hero in terms of tragedy, it should not be lost from view that this treatment of man by Ibsen would not have been endurable and it would not have been viable without the relief of a rich comic component.

Having dealt briefly with Ibsen's use of comedy, I should also indicate that, while I considered almost exclusively his unusual personalities, Ibsen did not neglect ordinary man, for his plays are peopled with individuals from all walks of life. A consideration of a single group of these, extending from *Brand* to *When We Dead Awaken*, will suggest the wealth of material that Ibsen included in his dramas to support the main action and, moreover, confirm the view that all mankind was his province. There is a peculiar fascination in a number of these minor characters, and in a real sense they serve to illuminate the nature of Ibsen's hero.

In almost every Ibsen play there is represented a male character of middle age or older, who is either a remnant of former greatness and glory, like old Ekdal of *The Wild Duck*, or a complete bankrupt, like Ulrik Brendel of *Rosmersholm*, one of Ibsen's most tragic figures. Sometimes these human wrecks are saved from complete destruction by varying agencies. Thus Krogstad of *A Doll's House* is rehabilitated through the regenerative power of love, as is Ulfheim of *When We Dead Awaken*, while Engstrand of *Ghosts* keeps his miserable head above water through blackmail, a means of survival that Krogstad, to his everlasting glory, has abandoned. There are instances, too, in which men must accept compromise in order to survive, as does Aune of *Pillars of Society*. Life on the level represented by these characters can in turn be harsh, cruel, ugly, debasing, and degrading, but, as Dr. Rank of *A*

Doll's House observed, they all regard the business of living to be excessively important, even for them.

In many respects old Foldal of *John Gabriel Borkman* most clearly illuminates these pathetic older men in Ibsen, and he most aptly illustrates their relationship with the chief protagonists. Like his counterparts in all the other Ibsen dramas, old Foldal serves a dual purpose. He is employed as a dramatic device to aid in the exploration of the character of Borkman, against whom he is pitted in the most unequal struggle conceivable, while he simultaneously serves as a commentary on that multitude who in one way or another fail of achievement or succumb to the adversities of fortune. Looking back over the road traveled, which is literally strewn with human wreckage, one discovers how well old Foldal symbolizes the destinies and summarizes the failures of those losers in the battle of life. Superficially, old Foldal's relationship to Borkman appears to be almost identical with old Ekdal's relationship to the elder Werle of *The Wild Duck*. However, as Borkman is a continuation of the study of Consul Bernick of *Pillars of Society*, so old Foldal has a closer psychological affinity with Aune, the shipbuilder of the same play, than he has with old Ekdal.

Ibsen's elder male characters, who play subordinate roles to the chief protagonists, are perhaps not very significant as individuals, but taken as a group they open up in vast perspective the author's brooding upon the human condition in general. Through these widely different secondary male characters, who dogged Ibsen for the greater part of his productive life, he reveals one aspect of the tragedy of man. Usually the hero is considered to be the sole tragic figure, and his destiny is set forth in what is called high tragedy. Ibsen was well aware that the noble protagonist was not present in naturalistic tragedy, but he also knew that there were tragic implications in the lives of any and all unfortunate human beings under any kind of order. Therefore, the most obscure person, for example the man in *Brand* who has strangled his starving child and is now clutching it in his arms and calling on the devil for deliverance, may reveal elements of tragedy and of suffering of the same degree and of the same kind as do the lesser characters of the naturalistic plays. Rosmer of *Rosmersholm* may well be Ibsen's paramount example of the tragedy of the disintegration of personality, and, while he is a significant personage, several of the lesser characters share with him the same tragic fate. Through the minor characters one thus gains greater insight into Ibsen's unusual personalities.

ROBERT BRUSTEIN

The Fate of Ibsenism

Whenever groups of people join together to pay homage to the achievements of some literary artist, I cannot help thinking of what T. S. Eliot wrote about the reputation of Ben Jonson: "To be universally accepted; to be damned by the praise that quenches all desire to read the book; to be afflicted by the imputation of virtues which excite the least pleasure; and to be read only by historians and antiquaries—this is the most personal conspiracy of approval."

The celebration of the 150th anniversary of Ibsen's birth has made us conscious that his reputation is considerably more muscular than that. After all, he is being read by other than antiquaries and historians—by those of us who teach him, for example, and by the students of those of us who teach. But I cannot throw off the suspicion that, like Ben Jonson, Henrik Ibsen may have become something of an academic icon, who has entered our libraries without finding a place in our minds, a familiar figure in our classroom, but a relative stranger to our stage. It is true that the Ibsen Sesquicentennial is at present inspiring productions here and there in various parts of the country, as did the Pirandello Centennial some years ago. But if the productions of *Henry IV* and *Right You Are* in 1967 are any guide, the performances today of *Peer Gynt* and *The Wild Duck* and *A Doll's House* will not be followed by much in the way of further celebration, once the candles on the cake have been

From "The Fate of Ibsenism" by Robert Brustein from *Critical Moments: Reflections on Theatre and Society 1973–1979* by Robert Brustein. Copyright © 1978 by Robert Brustein.

extinguished and the birthday party is over. For Ibsen is now beginning to suffer the deadly fate of the classic author—to be included in the anthologies and excluded from the imaginative life of the people, to be universally accepted without being much liked or understood.

I can think of two reasons for this unfortunate condition, one being formal, the other philosophical. Certainly, the stylistic breakthroughs of the modern Ibsen have been achieved at a high price, for his decision to subordinate his expansive poetic imagination, fully expressed in such dramatic poems as *Brand* and *Peer Gynt*, to prose stories about contemporary life, in such plays as *Ghosts* and *Hedda Gabler*, resulted in a severe restriction of creative freedom, at least on the surface of his work. The landscape of theatrical realism, once so novel and vital, now tends to seem stale and unconvincing, particularly since the invention of motion-picture photography. And Ibsen's decision to set his scene in the contemporary drawing room, piled high with bourgeois upholstery, where the action is continually being punctuated by interludes over herring salad and Tokay wine, made it likely that the attention of the audience would be distracted by contemporary details, that the eye would make listless the mind and the imagination. Ibsen embraces these scenic limitations for the sake of establishing a deceptive surface, which he hoped to penetrate through revelation and exposure— as if to say, the reality you perceive is an illusion or chimera, with as much fidelity to the truth as matter has to Plato's Idea. Ibsen believed that the poet's task is "not to reflect but to *see*." By this he meant, to see through the appearances of the surface to the deeper truths beneath.

For such a strategy, as I said, he paid a price. By developing the style called realism, by inhabiting his role as "father of the modern drama," Ibsen became imprisoned, against his will, in what Henry James would later term the "tasteless parlor." And generation after generation of admirers and enemies alike, of both readers and audiences, would begin to consider Ibsen as the playwright of everyday life—"The chosen author," as W. B. Yeats called him, "of very clever young journalists," describing reality, to recall Synge's scornful phrases, "in joyless and pallid words." And what of his characters? Fat belching burghers in three-piece suits, emancipated women slamming doors on unfeeling husbands, an adolescent girl blinking away her growing blindness, a drunken doctoral student leaving his manuscript to be thrown in the fire, an aging architect falling off a tower to impress his young admirer, a bankrupt industrialist pacing back and forth upstairs while the women below discuss his life. A menagerie of domestic animals, desperately trying to get some edge on their teeth, some point on their claws, some sheen to their fur, but ultimately too tame to do more than evacuate their energy in long expository barks and growls.

It goes without saying that such a perception of Ibsen is both false and misleading; and a generation of excellent critics, analysts, and biographers have devoted themselves to exposing the injustice and superficiality of such conclusions. Nevertheless, the perception persists in the general mind, and it is usually consolidated in the theatre, on the few occasions when plays by Ibsen are staged. We know that, even at his most apparently prosaic, Ibsen remained a great poet, but the Ibsen who is most immediately recognized by the public is a crude psychologist of the conscious mind, and a clumsy set designer who tries to create living spaces out of canvas and glue, with doors that wiggle on their frames, and windows that look out on painted views of fjords. Ibsen could not have foreseen the advent of motion pictures, though he does tantalize us, in *The Wild Duck*, over some revolutionary invention in photography that Hjalmar Ekdal pretends to be working on. But the movies have had the effect of rendering many of Ibsen's stage devices unworkable. For it can be argued that the theatre is no longer able to compete with the film medium in creating a realistic environment. We are much too familiar with close-up reality now to be charmed by theatrical simulations, no matter how much verisimilitude the designer can devise. After the authentic locations seen on the screen, it is unlikely that fake environments of the stage can persuade us, any longer, to suspend our disbelief, no matter how artfully they may be constructed.

By the same token, those middle-class men and women whom Frank Wedekind contemptuously called *Haustier*—continually turning gas lamps on and off to suggest their enlightened or benighted states—are now as recognizable to us as our own brothers and sisters, but, alas, as predictable too. Instead of astonishing us, as they astonished Ibsen's contemporaries, instead of appearing as a new stage species, they are now all too familiar from continual repetition in countless post-Ibsen plays; and Ibsen, the enemy of all that is conventional, is ironically suffering the fate of being identified with the conventional, of being held accountable for much that is stale and stodgy on our contemporary stage. The theatrical revolution that Ibsen helped to initiate has been so successful that today it informs our establishment acting-training, directing techniques, and design strategies, which now constitute the conventional modes against which a new breed of theatrical revolutionaries are defining themselves. Brecht, who once declared Ibsen obsolete, said it was the theatre artist's obligation to make the familiar strange, and the strange familiar; after Brecht, it soon became common to charge Ibsen with encouraging the familiar onstage, and not only the familiar, but the safe, the comfortable, the culinary.

Those of us in the theatre who love Ibsen, therefore, have an obligation to rescue him from such misapprehensions and misconceptions, first by rediscovering the heroic dimension of Ibsen's characters, and secondly, by excavating the poem that always lies half-buried in Ibsen's prose mechanisms. We know that even toward the end of his career, Ibsen always claimed to have remained a poet, not a social thinker; we are also aware that he always created his work out of a powerful and textured poetic imagination, even though he made a conscious, painful decision to dispense with verse. As he told Lucie Wolf in a famous letter, "During the last seven or eight years, I have hardly written a single verse, devoting myself exclusively to the very much more difficult art of writing the straightforward, plain language spoken in daily life." What he didn't say was that this language only *seemed* plain and straightforward, that it was pulsing with ambiguity, and that, underneath the deceptively simple surface, lay an elusive nexus of images, symbols, and metaphors.

That hidden poetry is the reality of Ibsen, not the illusion of surfaces. And it is the duty of directors, actors, and designers alike, at this moment in theatrical history, to explore that poetic reality, even if this means rejecting physical verisimilitude altogether. For if it is the poet's task to *see*, then nothing has prevented us from seeing what Ibsen saw more than the clumsy machinery of realism that informs his plays both in the study and on the stage. It is our duty to explore the visionary side of Ibsen by looking below the comfortable and familiar images of everyday life. The place to find this visionary quality is in the text itself, for that is where Ibsen hid it. Anyone who has ever worked carefully on an Ibsen play, either for the sake of analyzing. teaching, or directing it, knows that everything is there for a purpose, including a complicated apparatus of clues and hints about his interior meanings. What is true of Shakespeare is just as true of Ibsen—namely, that a thorough understanding of the text will always yield a fresh and original interpretation, just as a stale production is always the result of superficial reading and received ideas.

Let me frame my remarks in the form of an exhortation to future Ibsen directors and readers: Find the poem inside the play, and you will have found the play. And permit me to advise all future Ibsen actors to imagine they are performing not in *All My Sons* and *The Hot l Baltimore*, but rather in *Othello* and *King Lear.* For characters in Ibsen owe more to Shakespeare than they do to Hebbel or Scribe; they are heroic creations, despite their bourgeois origins. The spirit of Brand lives in Gregers Werle, just as the spirit of *Peer Gynt* lives in Hjalmar Ekdal; the Vikings and trolls of Ibsen's earlier drama lurk behind every door and window of *The Wild Duck* and *The Master Builder.* What is buttoned-up and commonplace about the characters of Ibsen's modern plays is not what they are, but rather what they have been forced to become; and it is the banalizing condition of modern life that constitutes

Ibsen's central theme. In developing an Ibsen character, the modern actor must show us both what the character is and what he might have been, the essential creature of nature and how this natural creature has been forced to adapt for the sake of survival in society.

I am suggesting, in other words, that Ibsen, like every great writer, must be rediscovered by every new generation, and this means going beyond what is known to what is still there to be unearthed. But there is another great area of rediscovery for Americans, and that is the nature of Ibsenism itself. By this I mean the content of Ibsen's thought, insofar as that can be gleaned from his letters, speeches, and plays.

I am, of course, well aware that Ibsen himself was always afraid of being institutionalized, and that the ideology called Ibsenism, as defined by such well-intentioned followers as Bernard Shaw, is hardly a satisfactory way to approach a complicated artist, no matter how valuable it might have been in defining Bernard Shaw. As we know, Ibsen always thought himself, with considerable justice, to be moving away from any fixed position, engaged as he was in a continual process of intellectual and creative evolution that made it impossible for anyone to establish a quintessence of Ibsenism. "I maintain," he wrote in a letter to Georg Brandes, "that a fighter in the intellectual vanguard cannot possibly gather a majority . . . The majority, the mass, the mob will never catch up with him, and he can never have the majority with him. As regards myself at least, I am quite aware of such unceasing progress. At the point where I stood when I wrote each of my books there now stands a tolerably compact crowd; but I myself am no longer there. I am elsewhere; farther ahead, I hope."

Well, here we stand, all of us, a tolerably compact crowd around each of Ibsen's books; and he still stands elsewhere, considerably farther ahead. And none of us would have it otherwise, for if we ever assimilate Ibsen, if we ever "understand" him completely, then he will have become a domesticated animal, too, having lost that untamed, evasive quality that attracted us to him in the first place. Still, I do believe it is possible to catch this wild bird in flight, just for a moment as in a freeze frame—not to define his dogma, since he possessed none, but rather to identify the posture with which he gracefully avoided being fixed in dogma. It is this posture that, with some hesitation, I would call Ibsenism; and it is this posture which keeps him engaged in his "unceasing progress," always farther ahead than the tolerably compact crowd.

The task is necessary, I believe, because Ibsenism has still failed to leave its mark on us. It is a remarkable fact, considering Ibsen's fame, that for all the influence he has had on the social and intellectual life of Americans, he might just as well have never written a word. If you doubt this, just think of what he would have said, had he had the opportunity to observe our mores and behavior as he once observed those of his own countrymen. What would Ibsen have said, for example, of a nation dedicated to forcing democracy into every area of endeavor except the one for which it was originally designed, namely, political and economic equality? What would he have thought about our intellectual life, where scholars popularize their learning and critics swallow their standards to reach a wider market? How would he have regarded our educational system, which has installed mediocrity as a national norm in the face of pressures from administrators, students, and parents alike? What would he have said about our obsessive concern for material comforts and our sacrifice of the spirit? How would he have regarded the way we manipulate language to alter reality and retouch the truth? With what scorn would he have greeted the loss of individualism in our society, and the way in which majority and minority groups coerce dissenting opinion? What would he have said of our liberal press, our conservative politics, our Watergates and Vietnams, our commodity theatre, our system of rewards and prizes, our corporate-controlled media, our industrial poisons, our endless daily conflicts between men and women, parents and children, blacks and whites, employers and unions, gays and straights, Jews and Gentiles, city-dwellers and farmers?

We already know what Ibsen would say because he has said it; and the fact that he said it so well, and that we have not herd it, is bound to create a little disenchantment with the idea of human progress. Yet perhaps it might be valuable to listen to Ibsen on these subjects again, if only to demonstrate the remarkable cogency and prescience with which he analyzed our problems, a hundred years before we were in a position to suffer them.

Among the major political issues being debated today is the responsibility of the individual to the state, for involved in this issue is the whole question of equal rights, not to mention the relationship between the artist and the citizen, and how much private freedom should be sacrificed to the needs of the larger group. This is one of the things Ibsen had to say (in a letter to Brandes) about the whole political process. "As to liberty, I take it that our disagreement is a disagreement about words. I shall never agree to making liberty synonymous with political liberty. What you call liberty, I call liberties; and what I call the struggle for liberty is nothing but the steady, vital growth and pursuit of the very conception of liberty. He who possesses liberty as something already achieved possesses it dead and soulless; for the essence of the idea of liberty is that it continue to develop steadily as men pursue it and make it part of their being. Anyone who stops in the middle and says, 'Now I have it,' shows that he has lost it. It is exactly this tendency to stop dead when a certain amount of liberty has been acquired that is characteristic of the political state—and it is this that I said was not good. Of course it is a benefit to possess the right to vote, the right of self-taxation, etc. But who benefits? The citizen, not the individual. Now there is absolutely no logical necessity for the individual to become a citizen. On the contrary [his favorite phrase], the state is the curse of the individual. . . . The state must be abolished! In that revolution I will take part. Undermine the idea of the state; make willingness and spiritual kinship the only essentials for union—and you have the beginning of a liberty that is of some value. Changing one form of government for another is merely a matter of toying with various degrees of the same thing—a little more or a little less. Folly, all of it. Yes, dear friend, the great thing is not to allow oneself to be frightened by the venerableness of institutions. The state has its roots in time; it will reach its height in time."

I have quoted at such length from this letter because it contains, I think, the taproot of Ibsenism, and its appropriateness to our time; just consider Ibsen's remarks in relation to that most pressing contemporary American issue, feminism and women's rights. Ibsen has been expropriated by the women's movement—today, as in his own era—as an ally in the fight for female liberation, because of such plays as *A Doll's House* and *Lady from the Sea*, but such specific designations always confused him, given his concern for humankind in general. Addressing the Norwegian League for Women's Rights, he had this to say: "I am not a member of the Women's Rights League. Whatever I have written has been written without any conscious thought of making propaganda. I have been more the poet and less the social philosopher than people generally seem inclined to believe. I thank you for the toast, but must disclaim the honor of having consciously worked for the women's rights movement. I am not even quite clear as to just what this women's rights movement really is. To me it has seemed a problem of mankind in general. . . . True enough, it is desirable to solve the woman problem, along with all the others; but that has not been the whole purpose. My task has been the *description of humanity*."

This is the answer Ibsen gave to every group that tried to expropriate him for its cause: "My task has been the description of humanity." Even more, he might have said, "My task has been the description of the *struggle* of humanity," for it was the sense of continuing struggle, of process, of movement, of change that obsessed him, rather than the accumulation and consolidation of special liberties for special-interest groups. "All development hitherto has been nothing more than a stumbling from one mistake into another," he wrote. "But the struggle itself is good, wholesome, invigorating." Or as his hero, Brand, discovered, "Man must struggle till he dies"—it is the struggle, not the goal, that mattered most. Why so much emphasis on struggle? Because that is what keeps the human animal alive. It was the struggle against both external and internal enemies—the forces in society that would tame and domesticate you, and the forces in the self that would have you settle for half. "What I recommend for you," he advised Brandes, "is a thorough-going, full-blooded egoism . . . There is no way you can benefit society more than by coining the metal you have in yourself."

By egoism, Ibsen did not mean narcissism, which is how we have translated his meaning into our own self-indulgent tongue. He recognized that there was an artist or genius in every self which was almost another self— another persona within us—to be nurtured and cared for, as we would nurture and care for a child. He meant that the writer's talent was not there to advance the writer; it was a means to advance the writer's art. He meant that the actor's gifts were designed not for preening and strutting, but rather for the service of something higher than the attainment of celebrity. Self-realization, not self-promotion; loving the art in yourself rather than yourself in art. "I have been a poor caretaker of my talent," Scott Fitzgerald complained toward the end of his life. Ibsen's demand on us was that we be good caretakers of our talent, for this talent was a loan or gift that we held without possessing, something we could either develop or destroy.

A thorough-going, full-blooded egoism, then, did not mean creating an Empire of Self, as Peer Gynt learned to his regret; one discovered the self only by slaying the self. What Ibsen is describing is the development of moral character through the exercise of the will. This sort of thing admittedly falls strangely on the ears of our time, but it is the essential component of Ibsenism, and the basis for the only kind of human supremacy that Ibsen recognized. For Ibsen did not believe that anyone could lay claim to superiority in consequence of being male or female, black or white, rich or poor, or even on the basis of inherited gifts. The aristocracy he called for was an aristocracy of character, will, and spirit; the nobility he described was a natural nobility that transcended class and inheritance, that distinguished the individual from the state, and the artist from the citizen.

For Ibsen believed that the artist and the political animal were unalterably opposed, indeed, were incapable of occupying the same space. "For every statesman who crops up there," he wrote, "an artist will be ruined. And the glorious longing for liberty—that is at an end now. Yes—I for one must confess that the only thing I love about liberty is the struggle for it; I care nothing for the possession of it . . . How the old ideas will come tumbling about our ears! And high time they did. Up till now we have been living on nothing but crumbs from the revolutionary table of the last century, and I think we have been chewing on that stuff long enough. The old terms must be reinvested with new meaning, and given new explanations. Liberty, Equality, and Fraternity are no longer what they were in the days of the late-lamented guillotine. That is what politicians will not understand; and that is why I hate them. They want only their own special revolutions—external revolutions, political revolutions, etc. But that is only dabbling. What is really needed is a revolution of the human spirit."

A revolution of the human spirit! With this, Ibsen makes his break with contemporary materialistic thought, and reveals his secret messianic ambitions. For Ibsen conceived his own mission to be a spiritual one, his role as an artist to provide the modern religion that would replace the worn-out creeds of Caesarism and Christianity, of the secular state and the spiritual hierarchy. This ambition—dramatized in *Brand* and codified in *Emperor and Galilean*—explains Ibsen's indifference to political revolution and social advance, for it was to be realized through culture, art, and education. As Ibsen conceived his "Third Empire," it was to be a synthesis of Roman self-assertion and Christian self-abnegation; today, it looks to us more like an extension of Protestantism, with its demand that each man be his own church, even his own God. But as always with Ibsen, the end result was less important than the struggle toward that end, the actual content of his messianic doctrine of less significance than the process through which it was to be achieved.

And more important than both was the perception that inspired them: Ibsen's belief that what is commonly called progress is simply a disguised form of further disintegration that will eventually leave us stranded on the shoals of false ideals. "There are actually moments," he wrote, "when the whole history of the world reminds one of a sinking ship; the only thing to do is save oneself. Nothing will come of special reforms. The whole human race is on the wrong track." The passage reverberates with Doctor Stockmann's discovery that "he is the strongest who stands alone," and reminds us that, however honored and bemedaled Ibsen became toward the conclusion of his career, for most of his life he stood alone. Having chosen exile, he suffered for it, with a crushing loneliness and sense of alienation, as he confided to a group of university students bent on paying him homage: "He who wins a home for himself in foreign lands—in his inmost soul he scarcely feels at home anywhere—even in the country of his birth." But such was his temperament that he also found such isolation bracing. The advice he gives to Brandes, suffering a similar kind of ostracism, shows the posture he has adopted for himself. "You say that every voice in the faculty of philosophy is against you. Dear Brandes, how else would you want it: Are you not fighting against the philosophy of the faculty? . . . If they did not lock you out, it would show they are not afraid of you . . . To me your revolt is a great, emancipating outbreak of genius. . . . I hear you have organized a society. Do not rely implicitly upon everyone who joins you. With an adherent, everything

depends upon the reasons for his adherence. Whether you may be strength-
ening your position or not, I cannot tell. To me it appears that the man who
stands alone is the strongest."

How strangely, how chillingly such words fall upon the ears of twentieth-century America, where the terror of aloneness is so pervasive that a
whole technology has been devised to defend us against a single moment of
solitude. What does Ibsen have to communicate to a people who, if they
desire a transcendent life at all, seek it at mass rallies in Yankee Stadium, or
in the spiritual barbiturates of the Reverend Moon and the Mahatma Ji, or
in the totalitarian seances of *est* and encounter sessions? How does an intelligent student stand alone against the passionate collectivity of the young?
How does an independent black stand alone against the racial orthodoxies of
Black Power? How does a clear-headed woman stand alone against the
remorseless sexual categorizing of Women's Liberation? How does an American Jew stand alone against the narrow stances of nationalistic Jewish
groups? How does an American novelist establish his independence of the
National Book Association, or an American actor of Equity, or an American
trucker of the Teamsters' Union? How does a member of the philosophy
faculty declare his opposition to the philosophy of the faculty? How does a
conservationist express his conviction that the air and oceans are being
poisoned in the face of expensive promotional campaigns by wealthy industrial corporations? And finally, how does a solitary American preserve his
autonomy within a government of agencies devoted to manipulating and
controlling his destiny?

Clearly, the United States today is a massive conglomerate of pressure
groups and political lobbies and liberation fronts and committees—a huge
magnetic force which yanks every particle into its orbit—where nothing can
be heard or accomplished until it is first monitored, scanned, blipped, and X-
rayed by a vast bureaucratic mechanism. For those who no longer find
Ibsen's choice of exile possible, the remaining options are silence and
cunning, or conformity, or the gradual obliteration of the moral will by the
mad intellect of democracy.

The impact of Ibsenism on our time, then, has been minimal, and
Ibsen's skepticism about progress is daily being confirmed. Along with many
of the other major thinkers of his century—Nietzsche and Kierkegaard and
Emerson, for example—and many of those of ours—such as Freud and
Santayana and Ortega y Gasset—he has been drowned out by a clamorous
chorus of self-interested collectives, bent on shaping all art and thought to
their specific prejudices. But Ibsen foresaw even this, and he gave us both the
means to combat it and the courage to confront it when he told the guests at
a Stockholm banquet: "It has been said of me on different occasions that I am

a pessimist. And so I am insofar as I do not believe in the everlastingness of human ideals. But I am also an optimist insofar as I firmly believe in the capacity for the propagation and development of ideals . . . Therefore, permit me to drink a toast to the future—to that which is to come." Let us, who honor Ibsen, offer a toast to this seminal intellect, this prodigious artist, this prodigal individual. For by honoring him in our own bad times, we keep faith with the future as well.

INGA-STINA EWBANK

Brand: *The Play and the Translation*

The Play

The long poem that constitutes the play *Brand*—nearly 6,000 lines in Ibsen's original text, more than 5,000 in Geoffrey Hill's version—presents us with a peculiar, and peculiarly intense, fusion of life and art. "Don't forget," says Brand to the young aesthete Einar as, at the end of Act I, he is about to descend from the high mountains to begin his messianic mission, "life's the real work of art." Four acts later he looks back over his life and sees that it has been "the Sinai-slate / on which the hand of God could write." What God, or his own will, has written is a spiritual demand for "All or Nothing"; and in human terms he seems to have sacrificed all and gained nothing. His mission has kept him from his mother's deathbed and has cost the lives of his child and his wife. His parishioners—those whom he had wanted to lead up into the mountains to a rebirth of the spirit—have stoned and abandoned him. Now, in the Ice Church, utterly alienated from the human community and accompanied only by the mad girl Gerd, half seer half troll, he has passed through a crisis of the soul to a moment when, at last, he can weep, cathartically. It looks like a moment of recognition and reversal. "Radiant and as if reborn," he looks into a future

From "*Brand*: The Play and the Translation" by Inga-Stina Ewbank from *Ibsen*: Brand: *A Version for the Stage* by Geoffrey Hill. Copyright © 1981 by the University of Minnesota Press.

where "the poem of my life (*mit Livsensdigt*) / shall surge warm and rich."
But the reversal proves as illusory as King Lear's hopes for himself and
Cordelia as "God's spies," and the new "poem" is cut short by the avalanche
that buries Brand and fills the whole valley.

Brand has *lived* a work of art, a poem; and Henrik Ibsen has (as he was
to put it later) "lived through," imaginatively, the Brand experience; and the
resultant poem-play was not only a kind of crossroads in his art but was also
to change his whole life. As we approach the play from the outside, this last
point is perhaps the one that strikes us first. The writing of *Brand*, in the
summer and autumn of 1865, and its publication, in March 1866, form a
watershed in Ibsen's career. The editor of *Brand* in the great Norwegian
Centenary Edition speaks of the play as "a volcanic eruption" in Ibsen's life,
with a national impact like that of "a bomb exploding in our spiritual life."
As a dramatist, Ibsen had found a voice—"the voice of Savonarola," as
Strindberg was to call it when trying to define the electrifying effect it had
on a whole generation of young Scandinavians. As a person, he had found a
new identity: when he wrote *Brand* he was a thirty-seven-year-old provincial
dramatist and poet with a patchy career in Norwegian theaters and some
eight or nine plays, of varied and at most local success behind him. But no
sooner had the play been published, and sold far beyond the expectations of
its Danish publisher, than Ibsen was a celebrity, a recognized intellectual
force, and a man able to live by his pen—indeed, in comparison with his
earlier penury, a relatively wealthy man. At last he was able to eat well, to lay
in drawersfull of shirts and socks, and to develop the solemnly neat sartorial
style he was to keep till the end of his life. Ironically Brand, the greatest rebel
of them all, opened for Ibsen the way to middle-class respectability. He
trimmed his wild black beard into the whiskers so well known from portraits
and went so far as to change his handwriting, from an inspired scrawl to the
precise upright calligraphy of the manuscripts he was so careful to preserve
for posterity.

But, if "life's the real work of art," Ibsen's real life—not to be
confounded with external life-style—was at the level where *Brand* confirmed
his single-minded dedication of his life to art: to writing drama that would
be a criticism of life. In his last play, *When We Dead Awaken* (1899), in which
his sculptor hero, Rubek, is also swallowed up by an avalanche at the end, he
was to look back on such dedication and count its cost: "When we dead
awaken . . . we see that we have never lived." In *Brand* the cost of an absolute
commitment, a "calling," is also counted—and Ibsen was later to stress that
this, and not Brand's priestly vocation as such, was what mattered. "The
syllogism would apply as well if he were a sculptor, or a politician," he wrote
to the Danish critic Georg Brandes in 1869. But here the cost is matched by

a celebration of the greatness and energy of the hero's commitment, his holy wrath at "the spirit of compromise," and his capacity for suffering. "Brand," Ibsen wrote, "is myself in my best moments."

When Ibsen said that *Brand* represented "something lived through" (*noget gjennemlevet*), he was referring to his own intense revulsion from the moral half-heartedness and spiritual flaccidness (the virtually untranslatable adjective "*slapp*" and its cognate noun "*Slapphed*" are thematic words of abuse in *Brand* as in other Ibsen plays) which he saw as characterizing his fellow countrymen. Indeed, he found the spirit of compromise wherever social good was put before moral absolutes, and so much of the western world was included in his condemnation. Soon after finishing *Brand* he wrote from his self-imposed exile in Rome to his mother-in-law in Norway to explain why he did not want to return home. His own son, he wrote, "shall never, if I can help it, belong to a people whose aim is to be Englishmen rather than human beings." And Englishmen—"the soulless dwarfs who made / an empire quarrying men's greed"—receive their lash of the whip in Brand's attack on the soul-sickness of "this hideous Age" in Act V. But, as in this relentless monologue, it is Norway and the Norwegians that are the main targets of his wrath—and Ibsen's, as he responded to what Hamlet calls the "form and pressure of the times." Ibsen had always been sensitive to this pressure, and his first play, *Catiline*, was in historical guise his response to the year of revolutions in Europe, 1848. *Brand*, set in his contemporary Norway, grew from a complex of emotions brought to definition and articulation by what Ibsen saw as Norway's and Sweden's betrayal of Denmark in the Danish-German war of 1864.

Ibsen had set out on his freedom journey, financed by a puny government grant, in April 1864, at the very same time as Prussian and Austrian troops marched onto Danish territory, and as the other two Scandinavian nations were finding diplomatic reasons to remain passive, despite earlier assurances of eternal brotherhood in need. He was in Copenhagen when the fortress of Dybbøl fell and in Berlin when the cannons from that fortress were being dragged in triumph through the streets, the populace spitting into their mouths. "In those days," he wrote later, "*Brand* began to grow like a foetus inside me." But the *Brand* thus conceived, out of shame and anger, eventually began to show signs of being stillborn, its potential life strangled by an uncongenial and inadequate art form. Known now as "the epic *Brand*," it was a satirical narrative poem written in regular iambic pentameters, divided into eight-line stanzas—a genre and form for which Ibsen found a model in the Danish poet Paludan-Müller's *Adam Homo*. Ibsen's anger and sense of betrayal, bitterly expressed at much the same time in his poem on "The Death of Abraham Lincoln," carried him through the opening section,

"To the Accomplices," and through sections on the childhood and development of the Brand figure, until he assumes his calling (i.e., roughly the equivalent of the beginning of Act II of the play). There the poem stuck: the medium was too "*slapp*" for the message. It was not so much rescued as newly conceived in an epiphanic moment, in July 1865, under the dome of St. Peter's. "All at once," Ibsen wrote to his fellow playwright Bjørnson, "there appeared to me a clear and strong form for what I had to say."

Although the "epic" *Brand* fragment had taken a whole year, he wrote the five acts of the play in a white heat of inspiration between July and October, not only incredibly fast and in a release of the poison of anger, emblematized by the live scorpion that he kept in a glass on his desk, but also with more sheer joy in the act of creation than he had ever before experienced, or was ever to experience again. Ibsen's letters from this period tell us how—like so many other North European and American writers, including Henry James, whose first meeting with Rome took place only a few years after Ibsen's epiphany—he derived inspiration from the warmth, the benevolent nature, and above all the art of Italy. The creative force that went into *Brand*, as into the statues of that other fictive hero, Roderick Hudson, was a transmutation of the strength—even the sheer size—of the art of the High Renaissance and the Baroque, of Michaelangelo and Bernini. Not for Ibsen the cold aestheticism, as he saw it, of the ancient Greek statues, or of any form of classical art. Although the landscape of *Brand* is the icy mountains and sunless fjords of Norway, the hero, like Christ in the Sistine Chapel, is "the new Adam" and his God is "young like Hercules." The energies of North and South meet in a huge vertical poem on the thrust and power of the human will to perfection, and the satirical mode of the "epic" Brand is replaced by a tragic vision of the defeat (or is it?) of that will by the mere fact that it is human.

Although the "clear and strong form" that appeared to Ibsen was dramatic, he did not intend it for the stage. If he thought in terms of antecedents for Brand, they are more likely to have been in the Romantic tradition of ideological dramatic poems—Goethe's *Faust*, Shelley's *Prometheus Unbound*, or Scandinavian offsprings of these, such as Paludan-Müller's *Ahasverus*. But, as it slowly acquired a stage history, it also proved to be a touchstone for its audiences, in more senses than one. Initially it was mainly an endurance test. The first ever performance of *Brand*, apart from sporadic productions in Norway of Act IV only, was in Sweden, where the pioneering director Ludvig Josephson mounted it at the Nya Teatern, Stockholm, in March 1885—a marathon effort which lasted six and a half hours. Ibsen was luckier when he first saw the play, as part of his seventieth birthday celebrations, at the Dagmar Theatre in Copenhagen, in April 1898; for, though the author failed to notice it, the director had cut about a third of the play. In Norway, *Brand* was first staged at the National Theatre in Christiania (Oslo) in 1904, and an extraordinary continuity developed. When the play was done there in 1922, and again for the Ibsen Centenary in 1928, it still had much the same cast, including Egil Eide as Brand and the great Johanne Dybwad as Gerd. She appeared yet again, though now as Brand's mother, on the same stage in 1942—in a theater taken over by the Nazis and boycotted by the public. During the war years, the play itself had become an image of national will and feeling in Norway, much as the Moscow Art Theatre production in 1907 had, apparently, reflected a longing for freedom from oppression. In Moscow, as Brand threw the keys of the new church into the fjord and led his flock into the mountains, the audience stood up in rapt attention. But, as the political and social climate changes, so the theatrical image of Brand changes. For a time after the second World War the Norwegian Brand was a dangerous fanatic, a type of Hitler. Yet the program for the 1966 production at the Oslo National Theatre refers to the play as "a challenge to a generation anaesthetized by welfare and mass media." This swing of the pendulum indicates, more than anything, the dialectical nature of Ibsen's art—an aspect that has never endeared the play to the English theater-going public. When the National Theatre staged Geoffrey Hill's version in London, in April 1978, the *Daily Telegraph*'s critic saw it, perhaps predictably, as a tract for the "*slapp*" times we live in, and he admired "the stern idealist slamming wily politicians." But he went on to lament that it is never "quite clear whether the play is intended to exalt its uncompromising hero or condemn him for his lack of Christian charity." Brand's refusal to compromise, or in Ibsen's words "to be an Englishman," makes his territory steep and alien; and Ibsen refuses us a safe guide.

And there, perhaps, is the essence of this play and—had not Shaw given that phrase his particular connotation—the quintessence of Ibsenism. No other playwright makes his art out of such all-embracing and uncompromising questioning of how one should live, of how to write what Brand calls his "*Livsensdigt.*" Brand's will to turn his life into "the real work of art" is extreme, but it is neither new nor unique in Ibsen's work. The conflict between calling and human happiness is the source of dramatic tension in *Catiline* as much as in *Brand*; the ravages of the pursuit of calling at the expense of life are as central in the play about the sculptor Rubek as in that about the Lutheran pastor. *Brand* may be Ibsen's most direct onslaught on the spirit of compromise, but in one way or another all his twenty-five plays, from *Catiline* (1849) to *When We Dead Awaken* (1899) explore the central characters' vision of their own selves by testing the strength of their calling. Sometimes the test is negative, as when Brand's anti-type Peer Gynt—in the

play written, almost as the second panel of a diptych, in the year after
Brand—literally manages to make of his life, in the final reckoning, only a
photographic negative, and that half-erased by his tendency to "go round
about." Sometimes, as in the case of Nora in *A Doll's House*, it is only beginning when the play ends. Nearly always it is fatal, for the world of an Ibsen
play—whether "realistically" or "symbolically" presented—is a dangerous
one. It is also a vertical one, structured on a scale of "up" and "down."
Perhaps we see this most clearly by comparing him to Chekhov, whose characters long to be other than they are, or elsewhere (and often, as in *Three
Sisters*, the two longings are the same). In Ibsen, characters strive to be themselves, which means striving to fulfill what they see as their *highest* possibilities. From the first words of *Catiline*, in Ibsen's first play,

> I must! I must! thus bids me a voice
> In the depths of my soul—and I will follow it.
> Strength have I, and courage, for something better,
> For something higher than this life,

to the last lines of Irene, in his last,

> Yes, through all the mist. And then right up to the
> very top of the tower, lit by the rising sun,

they are driven by a vertical urge. Again, in Chekhov characters try to
avoid, to step sideways from, the shattering experience of self-confronta-
tion. Ibsen's characters, on the other hand, spend much of their time in an
activity that, in play after play, he defines by the verb "*grunne til bunns*"
(literally, "thinking through to the bottom of things")—i.e., trying to find
out who they are and why they are as they are. Their forward movement in
dramatic time cries out to be seen, in space, as a vertical thrust: upward, to
the heights to which they aspire, and downward, into the abysses to whose
"*bunn*" they wish to penetrate.

So, the "clear and strong form" of *Brand* crystallized much that Ibsen
had already been working toward and is also in many ways a paradigm for his
later plays. Those ways have to do with the deeper, rather than the surface or
external, structure of his drama. His "realistic"—or, as he preferred to call
them, his "contemporary"—prose plays tend toward an analytical structure.
From *Pillars of the Community* (1877) onward, and notably in plays like *Ghosts*
(1881) and *Rosmersholm* (1886), the action mainly consists of an unraveling of
the past. The action occupies at most a day or two, during which past and
present intensely, and usually fatally, interact—most intensely, perhaps, in

John Gabriel Borkman (1896), where the action extends over just as much time as it takes to see the play. In contrast, the action of Brand covers at least a few years. It does not, as in *Peer Gynt*, encompass its hero's whole adult life-time; but in both these plays the external structure is determined by the hero's progress, in the sense that we speak of Pilgrim's or the Rake's Progress. In Act I he demonstrates his attitude toward life and makes a choice which is then illustrated through the subsequent four acts, ending in his death. This progress has some support from a linear plot: Brand meets Agnes in Act I; wins her love and acquires a parish in Act II; has a child by Act III and stands to lose him if he does not leave his parish; has lost the child by Act IV and stands to lose Agnes; is widowed by the opening of Act V and, through conflict with society and organized religion, ends up an outcast and a victim of natural (or divine?) forces. But the play's action is manifested not so much by a plot as by the inner life of the hero, as it is revealed in soliloquies and in confrontations with other characters. Brand, in one of the most physically demanding parts world drama has to offer an actor, is on stage virtually the whole time. Other parts—whether small, like the Peasant's at the beginning of the play or the starving villagers' at the opening of Act II, or lengthy, like the Mayor's and the Dean's—are outlined with a clarity often amounting to caricature. In performance they may take on a life of their own, but their function in the play as a whole is, unmistakably, to serve as foils for Brand to sharpen and define his attitude against. Brand thinks of "the curse of heredity" as the one bar to being "what in truth I am"; and at once that curse materializes, in the shape of his mother. Gerd appears just when she is needed to provoke or clinch a choice, at the ends of Acts I, III, and V. Agnes is an exception in that she has visions of her own which affect Brand's, and in Act IV she is developed so far as to have soliloquies of her own. But even she makes no exception from the rule that the dramatic situations are chosen so as to form confrontations: in each Brand has to make a choice or confirm a choice already made.

Obviously there are external ideologies behind this stark, Morality-like structure. Brand's strenuousness of commitment owes a great deal to the Danish philosopher and theologian Søren Kierkegaard. No doubt the character was partly modeled on the young Kierkegaardian, Christopher Bruun, a theology graduate whom Ibsen met in Rome in the autumn of 1864. His moral ardor, and his refusal to join the established church, would have impressed Ibsen—and would have stirred his deepest feelings of guilt, too, for Bruun, true to his demand that ideology and deed must be one, had joined the Danish forces and fought at Dybbøl. The "epic" *Brand*, in which the figure of Einar was more fully developed as an antithesis to Brand, draws on Kierkegaard's *Either/Or* in its contrasting of the aesthetic and the ethical mode of life. The contrast is still there in the play, though less central now; and the hint at a reconciliation in the transcendence of religion which is contained in the closing words of the play, "He is the God of Love," are similarly Kierkegaardian. So are the series of existential choices that link the inner and outer life of Brand and make up the action of the play. But the wholeness and consistency of this as a *dramatic* dynamism is all Ibsen's own. What is more, in its thrust between the abyss and the heights, the bottom of the fjord and the icy peaks, it remains the dynamism of his later plays.

The setting of *Brand* is an essential part of this dynamism. The action takes place in western Norway, a part of the country that Ibsen (himself brought up in the relatively lowland landscape and moderate climate of Skien and Grimstad) had visited on a walking tour, to gather folklore, in the summer of 1862. Some of his experience of this wilder and remoter area went straight into *Brand*: the sense of the smallness of humanity when viewed from the peaks, the sight of cottages sheltering under overhanging cliffs, safe from avalanches but shut off from the rays of the sun. The action feeds on the geography and the climate; the treacherous glacier that tests all the characters in Act I; the storm in which Brand proves himself a true Man of God in Act II; the sunless priest's house that costs the lives of Alf and Agnes in Acts III and IV; and the avalanche that engulfs Brand, Gerd, and the Ice Church in Act V. All these features are in a sense naturalistic, and the language helps to give them a local habitation and a name, as the translator knows only too well from struggling to think of English equivalents for the varieties of crags and crevasses, tarns and becks, contained in the dialogue. In another sense they are metaphorical. We need only ask why little Alf could not have been taken by some kindly relation to a sunnier climate, or why no crag sheltered Brand against the avalanche, to see that ultimately the geography of the play is absolute and spiritual rather than Norwegian and physical. But it will not do simply to dismiss it as "symbolical." Of course there are symbols in *Brand*, such as the hawk that crazy (and knowing) Gerd is always hunting and finally brings down, transformed into a "silver-white ice-dove" and an avalanche. Meanings hover around it—is it the spirit of compromise? or "is" it anything other than itself?—and all we can say for certain is that it is far less capable of being translated into an abstract concept than, say, the polluted bathwater in *An Enemy of the People* or the rotten ships in *Pillars of the Community*. Similarly, the physical geography in Brand embodies the spiritual action, rather than merely accompanying it, on the one hand, or allegorically "standing for it" (as in *Pilgrim's Progress*), on the other. Furthermore, just as all of Ibsen's later plays, with the single exception of the "world-historical drama" of *Emperor and Galilean* (1873), are set in Norway, so they all share the geography of mind so clearly mapped out in *Brand*. The icy mountain surfaces as a dramatic setting in his last play and in the last act of his penultimate play, *John Gabriel Borkman*; but the *Brand* geography is never far from the indoor settings of the intervening plays, either. It is not just that it can sometimes be seen from the windows of parlors or garden rooms (as in the ending of *Ghosts*), but that it informs and underpins the action and language throughout. The "storm" that Gunhild Borkman says "comes drifting over" her, to "engulf" her and her belief in her son's "high" mission, is no less real in the world of her play than is the storm in Act II of *Brand*. The mystery of the depths of the sea ("*havsens bunn*") in *The Wild Duck* is felt no more acutely than that of the depths ("*bunnen*") of Rebekka West's mind, in *Rosmersholm*, or the depths—literal and metaphorical—that yawn under the hero and his family in *Pillars of the Community*. In these plays it is often difficult, not to say useless, to try to say when Ibsen is being "symbolical" and when "realistic," to tell whether his characters are speaking literally or metaphorically. Are the heights and the depths in the mind, or in the mountains and seas of Norway? More often than not, the answer is "both." The sense of an actual vertical landscape is never absent from the prose plays. It spills over not only into metaphors, explicit or submerged, but also into the ordinary verbs and adverbs of the dialogue, as characters act, think, and feel in terms of "up" and "down." Coherences like these make nonsense of the view of Ibsen's plays as prosaic structures decorated with poetic symbols; they point to an extraordinary wholeness of imaginative conception in Ibsen's plays as prosaic structures decorated with poetic symbols; they point to an extraordinary wholeness of imaginative conception in Ibsen's theater poetry—one that he seems to have apprehended most clearly and strongly in that moment in St. Peter's when *Brand*, as we know it, was conceived.

Does Ibsen then (remembering the *Daily Telegraph* critic's worries, which have been shared by many) "exalt" or "condemn" Brand? Some moments in the play offer no problem: he is clearly behind Brand in the satirical exchanges with the Mayor and the Dean, and with him in the diatribes against sentimental Norwegians worshiping a heroic past (some of which, their sting lost with their topicality, have been omitted in Geoffrey Hill's version). But what overall response does he demand? What does he want us to feel about Brand's demand for "All or Nothing"? Again the question can best be answered by reference also to his other plays. There can be no doubt that the vertical structure exalts: it intensely communicates the protagonist's viewpoint on the world and is, as such, crucial in our experience of an Ibsen play. It explains why we could never simply condemn Brand for his "lack of Christian charity," or merely see Borkman as a self-deluded embezzler, or find Hedda Gabler just neurotic and trivial. It brings home the heroism of the lonely striving for fulfillment. But, at the same time as this viewpoint is impressed on our imaginations, it is also modified, or corrected. An Ibsen play always knows more than its protagonist and keeps telling us so, by various means. Most directly, we are kept aware how they—from Catiline, to Brand, to Rubek—in pursuing their own vertical trajectories, slice through and wreck other lives. Even Nora, in this way, provokes ambivalent feelings at the end of *A Doll's House*. Brand literally wastes the ones he loves most, and Borkman has laid waste the very ability to love and be loved in Ella Rentheim. Ibsen knew the admiration—whether Romantic or Nietzschean—of the great individual; but he also knew as much about the fatal danger of self-centeredness as any English nineteenth-century novelist. Only, unlike for example George Eliot, he lets us work it out for ourselves *and* makes us weigh it against the sheer power of a self committed to a calling. This is why reading or watching one of his plays tends to be a strenuous experience; we have, ourselves, to do the work of assessing the sincerity, the greatness, and the degree of delusion, in the protagonist's vision. Even at the end of his plays he is intent on leaving us in a state of suspended judgment. Not for him the cathartic "calm of mind, all passion spent" or the Shakespearean gathering together of survivors, leaving us with a sense that suffering has been vindicated and that life will go on. Most of Ibsen's plays end, like *Brand*, with the shock of the protagonist's death and with little or no help to us to absorb it. When the mysterious voice, "*through the noise of thunder*," calls "He is the God of Love," we do not know whether it tells us to exalt or condemn Brand. All we know is that it signals not so much the end of the play's action as the beginning of its after-effects on us. "I do but ask," Ibsen said, "my call is not to answer." In the end, that would seem to be exactly the function of "the real work of art" which is the life of Brand.

The form for *Brand* that came to Ibsen in St. Peter's involved not only a dramatic structure but also a new rhythm and language. The pentameters of the "epic" *Brand* were shortened to tetrameters—iambic and trochaic— and the stanzas were dissolved into continuous verse, rhyming mainly in couplets but occasionally in other patterns. The shorter lines demanded a starker language—shorter words and tauter formulations; in combination with the rhyme scheme they pushed the style of the play toward symmetry and parallelisms in expression, toward a verbal texture that is lucid and yet dense with antitheses, aphorisms, and proverbial wisdom. Ibsen's choice of words is often guided by both rhythm and rhyme, to the despair of *Brand* translators who constantly run the risk of losing the spirit of a speech by following its letter. To take just one example, Brand, in setting out in a boat across the stormy fjord to bring solace to a dying man who has killed his own child, flings a couplet at the bystanders' fears:

En Syndersjael, sin Domsstund naer,
ej venter efter Vind og Vejr!

(literally: A sinner's soul, to his
hour of judgment close,
Does not wait for wind and weather.)

In the original, the matter-of-factness of the second line clashes ironically with the solemnity of the first, Brand is administering one of his many shock effects, clinching it by the rhyme of *"naer"* / *"Vejr."* The *Oxford Ibsen* is faithful to the letter of the lines;

A sinner's immortal soul, so close to perdition,
Cannot wait upon wind and weather.

Geoffrey Hill's rendering is apparently freer:

A soul facing its doom
can't linger till it's calm.

But its half-rhyme preserves the shock of the original, the absurdity of measuring endless "doom" against temporary and local "calm"; and the rhythm and diction mirror the characteristic Brand impatience. It would seem that this version is more faithful to the spirit of Brand as it is embodied in the idiom of the play.

    This is not to say that the whole of *Brand* uses an identical idiom. There is a wide range of modes—lyrical, narrative, satirical, vituperative, etc.—and of voices. Indeed the drama tends to lie more in the clashes of styles—the head-on collision of two kinds of rhetoric, like Brand's and the Mayor's, or the sudden transition from the colloquial to the prophetic in some of Brand's speeches—than in action or character change. But insofar as the hero dominates the play, he also sets its verbal tone: one of trenchant statements rather than analytical searching, of language handled as a weapon rather than a means of two-way communication. Even then the reach is wide, from disarming simplicities to visionary passages where the syntax goes cryptic and the vocabulary reaches out to unexpected compounds—as if Brand's will was bending and hammering language itself into his service. In an uncanny way Ibsen managed at one and the same time to draw on the natural strengths of his Danish-Norwegian language and to coin a dramatic language that reflected the uncompromising vision of his hero. This is why productions of the play have to concentrate on the spoken word, and why the

Leeds University Workshop production of Geoffrey Hill's text, in December 1979, provided a more authentic experience than the visually more elaborate performances at the National Theatre.

Looking at the language and style of the play inevitably raises the question of translation: and before moving to Geoffrey Hill's version I wish to suggest something of how Ibsen's verbal imagination works in the play and what problems it raises for the translator. Such questions can be asked only through particulars, and the particular passage that would seem to illuminate them is Brand's speech when, in Act II, he emerges from the house of the man who, maddened by starvation, killed his baby. It is typical—for this is how Brand deals with all that happens—in that it moves from the most searing realization of the specific situation to the most far-reaching generalization: in this case, from "*Det var Døden*" ("So this was death") to the condition of all human life. The closing lines lament the irony that not one in a thousand sees the "*Skyldberg*" ("mountain of guilt") which rises from the one small word "at leve" ("to live"). The 55 lines of trochaic tetrameter in the original repeat, in small, the structure of the play as a whole: a thrust downward, to the "*Svimmeldybe Nattegaade*" ("dizzy-deep night-riddle") which no one can guess. The upward thrust in the closing lines is a cruel climax: the multitudes are dancing on "*Avgrundsbredden*" ("the edge of the abyss"), not heeding that above them, above all who live, rises the mountain of hereditary guilt. The speech expresses part of the tragic vision of *Brand*, and of Ibsen's other plays: that no one can be free of the past.

In doing so, it may seem to work like a Shakespearean tragic soliloquy where—as in "To be, or not to be," or "If it were done when 'tis done"—the hero thinks in metaphors and the structure of the speech is formed by a chain of images, each growing out of the one before and each not only reflecting the speaker's thought but also modifying it, so that the end finds him in a different position from the beginning. But this is not Brand's, or Ibsen's, way with language. Brand's speech is not a growing-point but a flash-point; its argument is the ineluctable connection of life-guilt-death which he presses home throughout the play, only here it is proved on our pulses by being drawn, through staccato statements and rhetorical questions, from the "real" event just off-stage. His images do not analyze, they simply intensify the situation and so the argument. We see this most clearly, perhaps, in the central section of the speech where Brand thinks of the cruel contrast between the peaceful death of the father and the lives yet to be lived by the two surviving children—the little ones who, crouching in the chimney-corner, had to watch the unspeakable deeds and who now carry a burden of guilt which they will pass on, from generation to generation. He introduces "*de to*" ("those two") as a subject in line 13, but then makes a syntactic loop, picking up the sentence again only in line 29, where "those two" are transformed into the object of their father's inability to recognize his real guilt. The fifteen intervening lines—the loop—describe the children and how their lives will be affected, as in the following:

> . . . .
>
> *de,* hvis Livsens-Elv skal rinde
> ud fra dette stygge Minde,—
> *de,* som nu skal gro i Lys
> af hans nattegjernings Gys,—
> *de,* som aldrig ud kan braende
> denne Tankes Aadselbaal,—
>
>
> . . . .
>
> (Those whose life-river will run
> Out of this ugly memory, . . .
> Those who now will grow in the light
> Of his night-deed's horror, . . .
> Those who will never be able to burn out
> This thought's carrion-fire, . . .)

Image by image the significance of the situation is, as the punctuation shows, torn out of Brand's consciousness; and the pattern of syntactic repetition turns the lines into a litany of the horrors of heredity.

Translators into English have dealt with this passage in various ways. One way has been, like Michael Meyer's, to omit it altogether. Another has been to build a pentameter verse paragraph, as exemplified by the *Oxford Ibsen*:

> (Nay, not even in their bent and white-haired age)
> Will they from whose contaminated memories
> The river of their lives must flow, illumined
> By the ghastly flare of one night's horrifying hell,
> Will they have burned away to ashes of oblivion
> This foul carcase of their father's twisted mind.

Brand's staccato syntax and fragmented imagery have been transformed into a coherent and flowing sentence where the images are carefully interwoven, and the result is a very acceptable post-Shakespearean, post-Romantic blank verse. But, to achieve this, the translator has obviously had to sacrifice any attempt to "sound like" Ibsen, or Ibsen's Brand. The change in rhythm and verse structure gives us a less abrupt and more contemplative and analytical Brand. It becomes natural and necessary to rely on adjectives ("ghastly," "horrifying," "foul," "twisted"), whereas Ibsen's lines have only one ("*stygge*," which does not carry the moral evaluation of "contaminated") and put all their imaginative force into the verbs and the nouns. It becomes necessary to use Latinate expansions—"burned away to ashes of oblivion" for Ibsen's "*ud . . . braende*"—where Ibsen relies on the strength of brief—monosyllabic or disyllabic—Germanic words. Throughout his works Ibsen draws heavily on the facility for making compounds that Norwegian shares with the other Germanic languages. He hammers together two words into a new one that is more than the sum of its parts and that, like a metaphor, often conveys something of the shock of the unfamiliar. Often, too, such a compound will be a thematic nexus for the play where it occurs, like "*lysraed*" ("afraid of the light") in *Ghosts* or "hjertekulden" ("the coldness of heart") in *John Gabriel Borkman*. Brand is particularly given to compound-making, and each pair of the six lines we are examining pivots on such a word (as shown by the hyphenated terms in the literal translation). Almost inevitably, in the cause of good English, the concentrated impact of the original has to be dissolved into a paraphrase—as when in the *Oxford Ibsen* Brand's vision of the load on the children's minds as an "*Aadselbaal*" ("carrion-fire") has to be spread over two lines, or when, a few lines later in the same speech, the hint at a cruel divine joke that is contained in the phrase "*Hule Afgrundssvar*" ("hollow abyss-answer") has to be diluted into "The answer, like an echo's / Hollow mockery, reverberates from the abyss." In the original, the bottom of Brand's abyss is reached—or, rather, not reached—in one line of four beats, made up entirely of two compounds: "*Svimmeldybe Nattegaade*" ("dizzy-deep night riddle"). The Oxford translation's solution—"O riddle, / Lost immeasurably deep within eternity's long night"—suggests that the verse of Brand translates only too readily into a cross between Carlyle and Longfellow.

I do not wish, by these comparisons, to belittle the *Oxford Ibsen*, which is a monumental achievement, and to whose editor, Professor McFarlane, all students of Ibsen must be indebted. I merely wish to indicate some of the almost insoluble problems—not to say the untranslatability—of Ibsen's style in *Brand*. What Geoffrey Hill's version of the speech I have been discussing suggests is that, if there is a solution, it lies not in a lexical faithfulness to the original and a transposition of the verse into an existing English poetic mode, but in a re-creation of crucial qualities of the original into a new mode. He has dealt quite freely with the speech, shortening it from 55 lines to 38 and jettisoning both the "night-riddle" and the "mountain of guilt." Yet his short lines, of three or four beats, and his scheme of rhymes and assonances would seem to render Brand's argument *and* follow the curve of his experience with remarkable precision. Though he is no purist, he reflects Ibsen's dependence on simple words in significant patterns: in repetitions

He knew as much of his own crime
as his tongue fumbled at to name,
as his stained hands could bear to touch,
as his poor brain could grope to reach—

or variations

When the Day of Judgment comes
every soul shall stand accused,
shall be condemned as it condemns,
shall curse, knowing itself accursed.

As in the original, there is no emotional rhetoric as such; the language base is colloquial and ordinary verbs and nouns are made to convey feeling:

So now it's finished. Death's quiet hand
has smoothed away his grin of dread
and wiped the terror from his mind.

Adjectives draw strength from their context, as in the concatenation of "burgeon," "glare," and "sickly-white"/"sickly" in the following lines:

Condemned to burgeon in the glare
of that one awful, endless sight
like leaves in darkness, sickly-white,
growing more sickly as they grow.

As here, Geoffrey Hill has translated the emotional impact, rather than the precise wording and order of Ibsen's images. This is true for the dreaded compounds as well. Brand's tone of resentment mixed with horrified irony is caught without any fuss in "What answer blares from the abyss?" and the tone is carried into the final couplet:

There'll be no mercy for the plea
"forgive us our heredity"!

However free as a translation, this version has found "a clear and strong form" for what Ibsen had to say.

The Translation

I come to introduce Geoffrey Hill's version, not to praise it. Hence the task that remains is to explain how it came into being and what features reflect its genesis. Geoffrey Hill has always stressed that it is not a translation but a "version for the English stage of a poetic drama which was not intended for the stage," and this must be our starting point.

The real starting point of this *Brand* was the National Theatre which in the mid-1970s had become something of a translator's theater, commissioning new translations of old plays, in a laudable urge both to return to original texts and to find idioms in which those texts could be made to speak to modern audiences. The begetters were the National's Director, Sir Peter Hall, who wanted to put on *Brand,* and one of its Artistic Directors, Professor John Russell Brown, who was a long-standing admirer of Geoffrey Hill's work and intuited that he was the poet for *Brand.* Geoffrey knew no Norwegian, but, as I had just been collaborating with Sir Peter on a translation of *John Gabriel Borkman,* the idea arose that I would supply Geoffrey with a literal translation from which he would create his own version of *Brand.* In the late autumn of 1975 the four of us met, in the yet unfinished theater building on the South Bank, to discuss the idea—which did not yet seem very tempting to Geoffrey. He had reservations about Ibsen's language as he knew it through earlier translations, and above all about the possibility of finding an English equivalent of Ibsen's tetrameter. A specimen passage of "literal" had only confirmed his suspicion that the play could sound like 6,000 lines of *Hiawatha.* In retrospect he claims that what made him change his mind, to the point of seeing exciting possibilities in the project, was a combination of comments: first, Sir Peter's "Why don't you try some shorter metre?"; second, Ibsen's own remarks on having wanted a meter in which he could "ride barebacked" and so deal with both the sublime and the ridiculous; and third, some notes of mine on the style of the play, particularly on its tendency to compress and condense meanings, rather like Blake's *Proverbs of Hell.*

Once the problem of a meter had been solved, Geoffrey began—like Ibsen when he had found the form for *Brand*—to work remarkably fast. Initially we had envisaged our collaboration as stretching over several years; in the end it lasted for about eighteen months, from early 1976 until the late summer of 1977. We were both busy academics, somewhat bemused to find that *Brand* demanded, even in this way, all or nothing. For myself, what I had thought would be a weekly, Friday night, relaxation from departmental and domestic chores became a continuous struggle to keep up with letters from Leeds imploring me for more "literal." I say this not by way of complaint but in admiration of Geoffrey's sustained inspiration and of the stamina that carried him through the apparently endless lines, and problems, of the "literal." What I sent him, piece by piece, was a text of mainly quite unspeakable English that attempted to communicate to him, as accurately as possible, what appears in the Norwegian text. It followed Ibsen's verse phrase by phrase and line by line, and on every page there were footnotes to explain what could not be rendered by translation: connotations and associations of words and images, effects of rhythm, rhyme and sound, features of grammar and syntax, etc. These notes, it seemed, were often more useful than the literal text itself.

The effect of Geoffrey's discovery of a shorter line for his version of *Brand*—largely three-beat verse, though this is frequently "syncopated" with two-beat and four-beat verse—needs no expounding. The crispness and directness achieved will be obvious to the reader. But it may be pointed out how pliable and capable of variations, in tune with Ibsen's original, it is. For an example one may turn to pages 38-42 where Brand passes from his dialogue with the Spokesman for those who want him to become their pastor, to a soliloquy on these people as fallen Adams; then to a visionary dialogue with Agnes, which is not so much a dialogue as two epiphanies side by side, in which he glimpses the new Adam; and finally to the very concrete vision of his Mother trudging up the hill toward him. Each mood and state has its own rhythm, perhaps none more remarkable than Agnes's vision. After we had finished our collaboration, Geoffrey showed me a letter I had written in March 1977—the usual hasty note to accompany an installment of "literal"—in which he had marked a sentence where I said how interesting I had found this piece, "both patterned and varied, and with Agnes as a sibyl in a passage of strange, short lines." Whether or not this was, as he claims, what helped him to come to terms with the scene, it is true that he has entirely avoided the pre-Raphaelite vagueness that tends to hang about it in translations. His lines for Agnes have a beauty that is both precise and unearthly:

> I feel within me, here
> in my heart and my soul,
> the things that I foretell;
> all births, all destinies.
> Everything that is
> awaits its hour,
> and the time is near.
> Already, from above,
> He gazes down

with infinite love;
and already the crown
of infinite sorrow
pierces His brow.
And a voice cries
through the dawn-wilderness:
"creator and creature
of your own nature,
Adam, come forth
to life or death!

Agnes's sibylline ecstacy is dramatically effective, too, in marking this as a true turning-point in the play. For once, Ibsen took pains to point out, Brand is "carried away" (as Ibsen's stage-direction has it) by someone else's vision. And as he turns away from his world-wide mission to an "inner" heroism, Geoffrey makes him speak in Agnes's language and rhythm:

The new Adam, yes!
We in him, he in us.
Truth at the heart's core,
our rightful sphere,
our destiny, the abode
of our selfhood-in-God.

After the intense inwardness of the previous speech, there is in Geoffrey's text (as in Ibsen's) a sharp contrast when Brand's Mother arrives. Ibsen changes here from trochaic to iambic tetrameter; Geoffrey makes his short rhythms colloquial, even abusive. The dialogue between mother and son is a prime example of how a main problem in translating *Brand* is to keep the English terse enough. In my notes I had to point out that "the Mother is very monosyllabic, and so her lines are far shorter than I can make them here," and that the Mother's language is "tersely . . . dialectal." Geoffrey had already used dialect (mainly Yorkshire) vocabulary and turns of phrase for other characters, such as the Peasant in the opening scene; and in creating the Mother he made the English language seem naturally monosyllabic:

Ay, you grow a thick skin
there; like an icicle-man
stuck in a waterfall.
Do what you like,
skin gets that thick,

you're safe from hell,
you'll never burn.
Daresay hell-blaze
itself would freeze.

I use the word "creating" advisedly, for a comparison with more traditionally
faithful translations would suggest that Geoffrey had been very free here; and
yet it is entirely in the spirit of Ibsen's Mother that he catches, in this
woman's language, her self-righteousness *and* its oneness with the climate
and landscape. He claims to have seized on my footnote to the effect that
"the Mother is obviously a Morality figure of Avarice"; but from it he created
a speaker who takes it for granted that people and possessions are all one:

That madness on the fjord,
d'you think I'd not heard?
It's all they'll talk about
back there, you and that boat.
What happens if you drown,
eh? I'm robbed by my own
son, that's what. Ay, a thief,
that's what you'd be! My life
you're fooling with. I gave
you it, didn't I? I've
got first claim on what's mine.
You're not just flesh and blood.
You're roof-beam, corner-post,
the nails, the wood,
every plank, every joist
I've spliced into a house
for nobody but us.

Within this dialogue there is, as a kind of set-piece, Brand's account of
his childhood memory of seeing his mother rifle his father's dead and laid-
out body for any money left about it. Other translators have encountered the
words here very competently; but what Geoffrey does is to re-create the
emotional complexes in, and the impulses behind, the story Brand tells. I
doubt if he needed my footnote telling him that the passage differs in diction,
syntax, and rhythm from every other Brand mode of speech. In his
rendering, the lines are again shortened to a trimeter, and their is a pulse
beating through them, recognizable as Brand's "family theme" and trans-
posed into words as "the scar / of an early fear." The feelings of fear in the

boy are invoked in images that (the purist would point out) are not in Ibsen's original: the narrator, across the years, looks back on his boyhood elf, "like a little owl," but soon identifies himself with the boy's wondering "why his hands were claw-like / and yet so paper-thin." He turns to the present tense, as Ibsen's narrator doesn't, to achieve immediacy, as Ibsen does; and, as in Ibsen, there is in the speech as a whole a strange tension between the detached irony of a cautionary tale, on the one hand, and the pain of remembered suffering, on the other. My footnote had told Geoffrey of the irony of Brand introducing this memory as an "*Eventyr*," meaning both "adventure" and "children's story," or "fairy-tale"; and from beginning to end he keeps the awareness that Brand is telling his mother a story, only too hideously true. When, finally, he expands Ibsen's image of the Mother as a bird of prey

> Her shadow swoops; it looks
> like a swooping hawk's.
> She tears open a purse
> as a hawk rips a mouse—

then he is both true to the spirit of the speech and the play—where, after all, a hawk is going to swoop at the end—and writing remarkable English verse.

This sequence of examples from Act II should have shown something of how Geoffrey Hill's version of Brand realizes the potentials of the idiom and verse of the original and, in so doing, reveals new potentials in English. A few examples from other parts of the play will indicate—though not exhaust—his range. First, a moment in Act III: Brand, refusing to go to his mother's deathbed unless she gives up all her worldly goods, responds to Agnes's questioning of his demand for "All or Nothing" with a rare confession of weakness and an even rarer attempt at self-analysis. His speech begins on the peremptory note that we think of as his own. In Ibsen's text he simply has an axiomatic, rhyming couplet; Geoffrey dissolves this into four short lines subtly hinting at rhymes:

> Lose all if you would gain
> all. Out of the depths men
> scale even the precipice
> of their own fall from grace.

Then there is a hiatus: the original has the stage direction "*is silent for a moment; his voice changes.*" Across this, Brand modulates into what could very easily translate as sentimentality—a version of "this hurts me more than it hurts them." Geoffrey's lines, while keeping Ibsen's key image, that of a castaway, have a stark simplicity that gives them the effect of being wrung out of Brand, almost against his will:

> Everything that I speak
> is spoken in agony.
> I'm like a castaway
> crying in vain among
> the spars of a great wreck.
> I could bite out my tongue
> that must rage and chastise
> and with its prophecies
> strike terror where I crave
> the touch of human love.

At this point, the emotional curve bends naturally to tenderness before the child:

> Watch over our child,
> Agnes. In a radiant dream
> his spirit lies so calm
> like water that is stilled,
> like a mountain-tarn
> silent under the sun.
> Sometimes his mother's face
> hovers over that hushed place,
> is received, is given back,
> as beautifully as a bird
> hovers, and hovering, is mirror'd
> in the depths of the lake.

In a sense this is a self-contained lyric, its rhythms and sounds—including the mirroring effect in the rhyme of "face"/"place"—enacting the meaning and creating a rare moment of loveliness in the play. In another sense, in relation to the dramatic context—both to the particular fate that is about to overtake the child and to the general world of the play, where the elements perform exactly as they do *not* in this passage—it is as dramatically functional as the calm at the center of a hurricane.

Second, in contrast and as examples from the opposite end of the emotional range, one may refer to the gibing satire of the interchanges between Brand and the Mayor. The National Theatre audiences found the Mayor very funny; their laughter suggested that he released their objections to Brand's form of idealism:

> Chewing on the Ideal
> won't get you a square meal.

They clearly saw in his pragmatism a kind of practical lovableness:

> The birth-rate has increased
> due to my zeal and zest
> on vital matters;

and that they did so had a great deal to do with Geoffrey's ability to make him not just a cliché-speaking caricature. His opportunism, as manifested in sheer verbal inventiveness, is positively Falstaffian. It mixes condolence with glee at the thought of "all that lovely loot"—

> As soon as that old girl
> (God rest her soul)
> is laid in Mother Earth,
> just think what you'll be worth!
> You've struck it rich; you're made,
> young fellow-me-lad.
> You'll be saying good-bye
> to this out-of-the-way
> little place, anyhow.
> The world's your oyster
> from now on, Pastor.
> Believe me, I know—

and it enables his clichés to turn the crowd from the pursuit of heroic sacrifice to going after a shoal of fish in the fjord (the news of the shoal itself a lie: "I just opened my mouth / and bingo! out it came."):

> Don't question your luck; it's
> silly to tempt fate. Why
> waste your energy?
> It's time for you to learn
> what things to leave alone
> and where to stake your claim.
> Fare forth, my friends, bring home
> the Bounty of the Deep.

No need for 'blood and sweat',
no need at all. Let's keep
'sacrifice' out of it.

Geoffrey's inventiveness has made poetry out of the very clichés of the
Mayor:

We're tillers of the soil,
we're toilers of the sea.

It is only fair to point out, lest he be accused of being of the Mayor's party
without knowing it, that the same kind of wit gives Brand the last word on
the perniciousness of the Mayors of this world:

There goes a stalwart democrat,
filled with the democratic urge,
the proper sentiments at heart;
Agh, what a scourge!
No avalanche or hurricane
has done the damage he has done
with a good conscience all these years.
How many smiles he's turned to tears!

Brand's wit, freed from the turgidness of translatorese and laid bare by
the short lines of Geoffrey Hill's version, is also the subject of my last
example. The practical and emotional implications of the demand for "All or
Nothing" are made particularly vivid in the scene where messengers arrive
from the Mother's deathbed, each bringing a new and higher figure of
what—short of All—she is prepared to give up to have Brand come and bring
the sacrament. There is something ineluctably comic about the repeated
bargaining, and at the same time Brand's responses are ineluctably cruel.
Geoffrey catches both impulses in the way he reduces the colloquial and
simple to an almost lapidary relentlessness:

Then take her my reply:
'No bread, no wine,
no comfort, none.'

Ibsen compresses the ethics of Brand's religion into a rhyming couplet:

Sig, at mindste Guldkalvstump

er lige fuldt en Afgudsklump.

(Say that the smallest Golden-Calf-piece
Is just as much an idol-lump.)

Geoffrey has turned this into three and a half short lines:

    One piece
struck from the Golden Calf
is an idol, no less
than the beast itself.

Truly, the verse rides barebacked, balancing on the edge between the admirable and the absurd, carrying both the sublime and the ridiculous.

There is much in this version that I have not pointed to: the eeriness of Gerd, the troll-girl; Agnes's agony over the last little garments of Alf; the devastating words of The Choir of Invisibles; and so on. But I would only be keeping readers from the excitement of finding for themselves "the real work of art." They will find an authentic imaginative creation by an English poet, conceived and executed in the spirit of Brand and Ibsen. There is no question here, as with William Archer at the first-ever performance of an Ibsen play in England, of the translator taking the bow for the author. The work now before the reader is the greater for it.

BARBARA FASS LEAVY

Hedda Gabler and the Huldre

In his introduction to *Hedda Gabler*, Michael Meyer contends that the play's chronological place between *The Lady from the Sea* and *The Master Builder* lends it a "curious, almost anachronistic position in the Ibsen cycle." He argues that to date it from internal evidence would be to place it ten years earlier with *A Doll's House, Ghosts*, and *An Enemy of the People*. Like these earlier plays, argues Meyer, we feel that *Hedda* is written "simply and directly," from "within an illuminated circle and not, as in the plays of his final period from *The Lady from the Sea* onwards, that he is exploring the darkness outside that circle." This is an ironic view, given that among Hedda's first words in act I are "Ugh . . . the maid's been and opened the verandah door. The place is flooded with sunlight" (7: 180). Moreover, in his working notes, Ibsen began to develop the image that would later dominate *John Gabriel Borkman*, that of the dark mines which depict the "subterranean forces and powers" of the human mind. "Women as mine-workers, Nihilism . . . the subterranean revolution in woman's thoughts. Outwardly, the slave-fear of the external world" (7:488). Both internal and external evidence indicate that *Hedda* belongs just where it is, that the folklore themes and images in the two plays that preceded it are continued in the later play. But whereas the mermaid that characterizes Rebecca and Ellida is well known in world literature, *Hedda Gabler* demands a somewhat more esoteric knowledge, that

From "Hedda Gabler and the *Huldre*" by Barbara Fass Leavy from *Ibsen's Forsaken Merman: Folklore in the Late Plays* by Per Schelde Jacobsen and Barbara Fass Leavy. Copyright © 1988 by New York University Press.

of the specifically Norwegian version of the fairy temptresses, the *huldre* with her characterizing feature, a hidden cow's tail.

Critics have intuitively turned to folklore and mythology to describe Hedda's demonic character. She is thus a "Valkyrie in a corset," or comparable to Faustina or Mesaline, a "human beast domesticated, socialized, and cowed into submission," like Rebecca but without Rebecca's enthusiasm or idealism. McFarlane is more generous, describing Hedda as a "pagan priestess, driven by a vision of Dionysian beauty, whispering of vine-leaves in the hair and the thrill of beautiful death" (7: 14). Put together, these critical comments indicate that like *Rosmersholm* and *The Lady from the Sea*, *Hedda Gabler* shows Ibsen working with the story of a marriage between an ordinary man from the real world and an extraordinary, perhaps demonic woman from another realm of existence.

According to Reidar T. Christiansen, such marriages are the subject of the second most popular folktale group in Norway. In his *Migratory Legends*, the story of the man "Married to a Fairy Woman" occupies many pages needed to describe variants. Furthermore, in a comparative study of European stories, Norway occupies first place with regard to the popularity of narratives about supernatural or enchanted wives, such tales occurring there "twice as often as those about a supernatural or enchanted husband." The fairy wife in Norwegian folklore usually belongs to a group known as the *huldre*-folk, and two descriptions of them indicate why they would prove symbolically significant for the creator of Hedda Gabler. *Huldre*-folk "generally live at the fringe of an area inhabited by human beings," and the *huldre* woman figures in many traditions "about her marital and other relations to human males." The fairy woman's greatest desire "was to achieve equality with human beings," and the "*huldre* girls tried desperately to marry ordinary men, often flinging themselves at them in the most immodest way." This desire for a mortal husband placed men in a dangerous position. "If a man was unwise enough to jilt a *huldre* she was ruthless in pursuing and punishing him."

It might be going too far to claim that in these descriptions can be found an outline for Ibsen's play, but the *huldre* had filled his imagination from the time of his earliest plays. The *huldre* provides *Olaf Liljekrans* with some of its imagery, and in *Midsummer Night*, as Jacobsen has noted, the *huldre* is a symbol of Norwegian nationalism. And what I have already cited with regard to *The Lady from the Sea* can be extended to *Hedda Gabler*: in *The Feast at Solhaug*, Margit, whose marriage to Bengt can be compared to Hedda's to Tesman, imagines herself a *huldre* capable of escaping her miserable union. Hedda herself contrasts her dreary marriage to Tesman with the "fairy story" that supposedly describes how it occurred. Furthermore, her rival, Thea Elvsted (altered from the earlier, more explicit, Elvstad), is named a lady from fairyland. Nineteenth-century Europe had split the image of the fairy mistress, as I will show, and Norway had followed suit with regard to its *huldre*. Hedda and Thea represent this division. That is, whereas Rebecca and Ellida each embodies within herself both amoral mermaid and ethical human, these qualities have been divided (although, typical of Ibsen, not simply) and assigned to Hedda and Thea respectively.

Thea's married name is, of course, ironic, involving the same inverted perspective that Ibsen had already employed in *Rosmersholm*. Citizen John Rosmer would appear to be the antithesis of Rosmer Havmand and Mr. Elvsted—according to Thea's description a more unpleasant John Rosmer—offers his wife an existence quite different from what his name would seem to imply. To extend the comparison, Thea can be said in one respect to be a successful Rebecca, having married the man in whose house she worked after his wife died. Critics who compare Hedda to Rebecca have slighted this comparison to Thea, another woman from an ironically conceived of fairyland who must achieve her humanity in a man. Names are, again, very important in Ibsen's plays. Ibsen's use of "Elvsted" is a clue to his audiences and readers that has not received due attention.

In an earlier conception of *Hedda Gabler*, Ibsen named his heroine Hedda Römer, a variant of Rosmer (7:273). As the daughter of Rosmer, Hedda could be placed directly in the tradition of the demonic *havfru* who lures men to their doom. Therefore it is worth pursuing the possible connection between the names "Hedda" and *huldre*. From Grimm's *Teutonic Mythology*, Ibsen would have found a connection between the Goddess Holda and the Norwegian *huldre*. Hilde Wangel, minor character in *The Lady from the Sea* and major one in *The Master Builder* may perhaps be added to this group. Meyer points out that before *The Master Builder* (which follows *Hedda*) was written, Ibsen had entered into one of those significant relationships with a young girl that marked his late years. This was Hildur Andersen, and Meyer proposes that it was her name that reminded him of Hilde in *The Lady from the Sea* and inspired him to retrieve her from the earlier play to make her a major character in the later one. "Hildur, the Queen of the Elves," it may be noted, is the title of one of Arnason's Icelandic tales, and thus Ibsen might have had another reason to link Hildur to both the *huldre* and Hilde, the Icelandic story one that is both striking and ambiguous in its rendering of the fairy woman as both demon and penitent. To this account it is possible to add that some variation of the name *Hilde* is often taken by the *huldre* after her marriage to a mortal and conversion to Christianity. *Hilde* is also the name of a saga heroine who appears unnamed in the ballad "Kappan Ilugen" in Landstad's colleciton. Finally, Hilde is also a variant form of

Hillelil, the name sometimes given to the "Demeter" and sometimes to the "Proserpine" figure in the Rosmer ballads. In any event, the resemblance among a series of names becomes striking to contemplate: Huldre, Holda, Hildur, Hilde, Hillelil, Hedda. Christiansen has noted that *huldre* is the most general term used for the Norwegian supernatural folk. If Hedda were originally thought of as Hedda Römer, then her name, again, reinforces her connection with the supernatural world.

Two aspects of the *huldre* stories prove significant in *Hedda Gabler*. The first has to do with what would appear to be as insignificant a reference in *Hedda* as the sealskin trunk is in *Rosmersholm*. But to catch its significance, it is necessary to recognize how important in the folklore is the mark of the beast that characterizes the *huldre*, who is very beautiful, but possesses a repellant physical characteristic that renders her identifiable: a cow's tail that can often be spied beneath her long skirt. McFarlane has noted, and Jacobsen has already elaborated upon, the ironic tension that rises from this peculiarity in *Midsummer Night*, in which this identifying feature of "'the most national' of all Norwegian fairy creatures" causes great anguish to a character who learns that the *huldre* he falls in love with has a tail: "'I cannot tell you how I suffered,' he cries. 'Aesthetics and nationalism fought a life and death struggle in my breast.'"

In his collection of Scandinavian folktales, William A. Craigie includes two versions of "The Huldre's Tail." In one, a young man who glimpses the animal feature tactfully acknowledges what he has seen, and although the fairy disappears, the youth is later rewarded with presents and success in business. In the other version, the man sarcastically jokes about the unfortunate appendage: "that's a rare train you have." She becomes angry and he later dies of a fatal illness.

The cow's tail is a tangible image of the *huldre*'s aberrant nature, and in many stories, it falls off as she enters or leaves the church in which she marries a human. Like the mermaid, she wins through marraige to a mortal a soul and the possiblity of eternal salvation. But in addition, the Norwegian tales take their place among a universal group of stories in which a supernatural woman's abnormal physical shape (e.g., the serpent tail of Melusine) speaks of some essential evil that threatens her human husband or from which she pathetically longs to be freed. Sometimes she demands a regular interval during which she must not be seen by her husband, for during this time she assumes her beast form. When he betrays her and learns her secret, she usually leaves him. In Craigie's version of "The Huldre's Husband," the wife inadvertently betrays not her animal form but nonetheless her "nature," again, characteristically repelling the man who had never before glimpsed her true essence. The two had lived very well together and had a child, but suddenly one evening as the child was playing on the hearth, where the woman sat and spun, while the husband was doing something else, something of her wild nature came over her, and she, in a savage mind, said to him that the child would be splendid to spit and roast for supper. The man was scared, and the woman, who noticed that she had made a bad mistake, checked herself and entreated him to forget it; but he didn't. The frightful words were always in his ears; he got by them an ugly glance into his wife's true nature, and the peace of the home was destroyed.

The *huldre*'s tail both symbolizes that which reveals her as a being living only on the fringe of society, as well as that which makes it difficult or impossible for her to adapt to it. Her marginal position also emphasizes the peril of mortal men who encounter her: "mortals and *huldre*-folk may be closely related, but they are essentially different. Every contact with them involves a risk." Conversely, however, the existence of her tail also defines the *huldre*'s vulnerability when she attempts to move securely within human society, for if this tangible proof of her deviant personality is glimpsed, her position is jeopardized and her goals threatened. There is a special joke in the choice of words used by the critic who inadvertently employed an English idiom to speak of Hedda's being "cowed" into submission.

In the context of the *huldre*-tail motif, it is striking to note Hedda's description for Judge Brack of her dreary honeymoon trip and her sense of being trapped in a compartment for two with a companion she already finds unutterably boring:

> *Brack:* Well, then you jump out. And move around
> a little, my lady.
> *Hedda:* I'll never jump out.
> *Brack:* Are you quite sure?
> *Hedda:* Yes. Because there's always someone there who'll . . .
> *Brack* (laughing): . . . who'll look at your legs, you mean?
> *Hedda:* Exactly.

Ibsen could hardly provide Hedda with a cow's tail. But he seems to have come close. The exposure of her legs beneath the long skirt symbolically compromises her desire to live respectably in society as effectively as the disclosure of the *huldre*'s tail compromises hers. It is important to both that they not be fully known.

The Melusine type to which the *huldre* story can be related contains within it a strong antifeminist tradition consistent with the themes of *Hedda Gabler*. The fairy's nature is an exaggerated version of an inherent feminine evil that is at no time so apparent as when a power struggle for dominance ensues. The serpent tail of Melusine has been interpreted by one critic as a phallic image, and her husband's dismay at discovering his wife's secret as an inability to cope with the masculine strength she thus evidences. Interestingly, one of the legends concerning the origin of the *huldre* is that they are descended from Lilith, the first wife of Adam, who departed from Eden because she could not maintain there her equality with her husband. About Hedda, Ibsen specifically says in his notes that she wants to live fully as a man. In the play these masculine tendencies are symbolized by the guns she plays with, offers to Lövborg for his supposedly glorious suicide, and finally turns on herself.

Significantly, guns and other iron objects play an important role in *huldre* narratives. In his early play, *The Grouse in Justedal*, Ibsen evidences familiarity with this theme, and one of his characters, who fears the influence of the fairy folk as he enters their terrain, notes with relief that he is carrying an iron object with him that is his protection (I: 438). Christiansen designates as motif A5a that the human man catches the *huldre* by "throwing iron over her" (*Migratory Legends*). In the variant contained in the collection of legends by Andreas Faye, a collection Ibsen had in his library, a gun replaces the iron object. Craigie uses this version in "The Huldre's Husband": in Nordland the story is told that a "smart fellow got hold of a huldre in the wood" by laying the barrel of his rifle over her. She was baptized, and became his wife. In other stories, men conversely discourage male *huldre* suitors who court their women, or themselves escape from the supernatural folk, by aiming guns directly at them or shooting over the dwellings in which the *huldre*-folk attempt to attach themselves to mortal mates.

Guns and analogous iron objects are thus symbols of male power and dominance. In an early version of *Hedda Gabler*, Judge Brack is as frightened as Tesman of Hedda's use of guns, but in the final version of act 2, he takes out of her hand the pistols which she has been aimlessly shooting. This scene follows the conclusion of act I, when Tesman begs his wife not to touch the lethal weapons, but makes no move to remove them from her possession. Of course, Brack's superior strength of will foreshadows the end of the play, when one of the pistols becomes the means by which he will blackmail Hedda, threatening to expose the knowledge that it was her gun that Lövborg used in the events that led to his death.

It is a mark of Hedda's cowardice that although she possesses guns she does not really use them until her suicide, and even this act has been provoked by the threat of male will. In folklore, the *huldre*'s power to manipulate iron is something she can hide or reveal according to the role she wants to assume in her marriage. Both Craigie and Christiansen tell of the *huldre* who weds a human, is baptized, or loses her cow's tail, and submits to ill-treatment by her husband until she is pushed beyond endurance. "Olav was not nice to his wife. He was quarrelsome and ill-tempered and scolded her from morning till night. She kept quiet and never made a fuss about it." Finally, one day she saw him in a foul mood attempting to fit a horse with a shoe. "Then she took the horseshoe and wadded it up with her bare hands. Then she straightened it out again, fitted it to the hoof, and bent it a little more at the ends." Impressed, or frightened, because it was the forbearance not weakness of his wife that caused her to submit to his misuse of her, Olav reforms and becomes a good husband. In Craigie's version of this story, the wife's power is more straightforwardly expressed:

> So things went on for a time, while the woman suffered and sorrowed. One day she went to the smithy in all friendliness to look at her husband working, but when he began as usual, and they finally came to blows, she, to give him proof of her superiority, caught up an iron rod and twisted it like steel wire round her husband, who had then to give in and promise to keep the peace.

The first reference to guns in *Hedda Gabler* comes at the end of act I when Tesman's wife similarly believes herself to be ill-used. That is, she learns that she will not soon have what she hoped marriage would bring her: the ability to entertain lavishly, a male servant, and a saddle horse. She tells Tesman in what has to be interpreted as a threat that she has "one thing at least that [she] can pass the time with" (7:201). At first he is ecstatic with relief and asks what that might be, to which she answers, "looking at him with concealed contempt," "My pistols" (7: 202). And like the husbands in the huldre stories, he is reduced to abjectness: "No, for the love of God, my darling Hedda . . . don't touch those dangerous contraptions! For my sake, Hedda!"

So long as she had wished to play woman's traditional role, the *huldre* had refrained from demonstrating her potential power to use iron as she could, and the man who captured his fairy bride with his own iron or gun might never have known he might had he not abused his position. Her concealment of strength is a gesture acknowledging her willingness to play her husband's game with his rules. But in *Hedda Gabler*, the heroine's failure to more than toy with her guns indicates not conciliation but cowardice. That she might have used guns to impose her will on the men in her life is revealed in an exchange between Hedda and Lövborg, during which they reminisce about their past and about a relationship that seems never to have advanced beyond teasing provocation:

> *Lövborg:* Oh, why didn't you play it out! Why didn't you shoot me down, as you threatened!
> *Hedda:* I'm too much afraid of a scandal.

The scene is reminiscent of that point in the folktale when the *huldre* wife has succeeded in shoeing the horse by twisting the iron by hand:

> "You're more than a woman, Torgun," said Olav. "As bad as I've been to you more than once, and you haven't hauled off and given me a thrashing! I think that's strange." "I've got better sense," said Torgun.

In both cases the man wonders at the woman's constraint, and in both she responds by indicating a reluctance to abandon her traditional role. This is also true when Hedda later confesses that another, softer emotion had staid her hand. In the end, Ibsen characteristically provides his traditional themes with a twist of their own. Judge Brack "uses" the gun against Hedda as he had earlier taken it away from her, enacting the beginning of the *huldre*-wife tale by in effect capturing his woman with iron or, in this instance, a gun. But instead of using the iron weapon back against the aggressive male, Hedda turns her gun against herself. Yet, symbolically, it is his—Brack's—hands that can be imagined as holding the weapon, and his finger as pulling the trigger. Those who find something heroic about Hedda's final act have not contrasted it with the *huldre*'s demonstration of power, although insofar as gender relationships constantly define the way guns are presented in the play, Ibsen has remained faithful to his folklore.

So long as the *huldre* type was believed (in world folklore) to be a descendant of Lilith or a daughter of Eve, she was also conceived of as part of a malevolent group of female demons who lured men to their doom, kidnapped and destroyed other people's children out of jealousy or spite (Hedda: "Now I'm burning your child, Thea! . . . Your child and Ejlert Lövborg's" [7:250]), and generally posed a threat to a world which found embodied in her all that was evil. But as the centuries passed, two other sets of beliefs arose to color the folklore and affect the literature that grew out of it. The first was that the unfortunate fairy, deprived of God's grace, sought it, and that she longed for salvation. But another view held that rather than being an evil, succubuslike creature without a soul, the fairy was one of the nature spirits that inhabited the visible world, and that like nature itself, she was not malevolent, but benign. Thus her redemption lay not in the church, but in the human mind itself. Moreover, it was she who held out to the mortal world promise of a different kind of salvation, a release from the imprisoning forces of culture. In the nineteenth century, stories such as Andersen's "The Little Mermaid" depicted the otherworldly females as pathetic creatures more often betrayed by men than dangerous to them.

This new view of the supernatural woman arose during the nationalistic resurgence of folklore that was taking place during the nineteenth century. In Norway, too, a "new" *huldre* had made its appearance, and she was, according to Oscar Falnes, formally introduced to the reading public in a review of Landstad's collection of Norwegian ballads. In his study *Norwegian National Romanticism*, Falnes describes a creature who can hardly be recognized as a relative of the dangerous Lilith-like fairy:

> nature's dreamier aspects—the undulating hills of the south and east with their leafy thickets of birch and their shady forests of deep green pine—were symbolized in the wood-nymph, *Huldren*. She was a dainty sprite, refreshing and alluring, delicate and diaphanous, with golden hair set off by eyes of deep blue. . . . Her temperament was melancholy and those who listened to her song and stringed music were moved to sadness and tears. The most striking thing about her (suggesting the gap between Man and nature) . . . was lack of a soul and the circumstances that she had grown a cowtail. The romanticists became thoroughly infatuated with her and she assumed a central place in their nature symbolism. More vividly than any other figure she personified national traits (in nature symbolism there was postulated an intimate relationship between folklore, natural phenomena and national character).

In short, the *huldre* evolved as a national romantic muse, and her soul would have to be won not merely through union with a mortal man but through the *artist*, a theme that would take on explicitness in Ibsen's later plays.

It is possible to see in Ibsen's portrayal of Thea Elvsted an ironically modified version of the new *huldre*:

> Mrs. Elvsted is a slight woman with soft, attractive features. Her eyes are light blue, large, round, and somewhat protruding, with a scared, questioning expression. Her hair is strikingly fair, almost whitish-yellow, and unusually rich and wavy. She is a couple of years younger than Hedda.

As the *huldre* is transformed into the romantic muse so does Thea find her salvation in inspiring the men in her life: as Lövborg tells Hedda after learning that his book was burned, "Thea's soul was in that book."

But the nineteenth-century writer was too sophisticated to reduce to simplistic dimensions the double aspect of the fairy woman, and he usually exploited the ambiguity that surrounded her to express his own relationship to the world of art. In his notes, Ibsen gave Thea, his lady from fairyland, attributes as much at odds with the traditional *huldre* as John Rosmer was with Rosmer Havmand: "Thea Elfsted is the type of conventional sentimental, hysterical petty bourgeoise" (7: 483). He was to alter the spelling of her name, and he may have softened his conception of her. But what nonetheless emerges from *Hedda Gabler* is consistent with other nineteenth-century literature, for to transform the *huldre* into the benign nature spirit is in effect to deprive her of her own symbolism and reduce her to philistine proportions. Heine had so treated the goddess of the Venusberg as a hausfrau in the last part of his "Tannhäuser"; Jean Giradoux had poked fun at a modern world that would pave over a brook to rid itself of mermaids, and his Ondine, forced back to her underseas world, promises her earthly husband to live there as a bourgeoise; and Thomas Mann found in Andersen's Little Mermaid the worst danger the artist could face, pressing art into the service of an everyday world (*Doctor Faustus*).

Ibsen depicts the simultaneous difference and similarity between Hedda and Thea. He wrote in his notes that "Mrs. Elfsted, who forces [Lövborg] into respectability, runs away from her husband. Hedda, who eggs him on beyond the limits, flinches from the thought of scandal" (7: 484). The two women emerge as closely related, if antagonistic classmates, just as the two aspects of the *huldre* had once coexisted:

> *Mrs. Elvsted:* . . . since then . . . we've grown such miles apart. We
> don't meet the same sort of people at all.
> *Hedda:* Well, we must try to bridge the gap again.

Both women prove to be in the end ambiguous characters. Like Hedda, who is both aggressive and cowardly, Thea is also split. She wins where Rebecca West and the Little Mermaid fail and gets her man. But like the seal and swan maidens, she seizes the opportunity to flee both husband and children as soon as the former is absent: "I just packed up a few of my belongings. The essentials. Without letting anyone see. And then I left."

McFarlane points out the "almost indecent haste" with which Thea abandons her family to run after Lövborg. Seeking to realize her "soul" through union with the artist, Thea does seem to display an almost contemptible lack of self. But this view must be posed against the argument that Hedda is an emptied-out version of such Ibsen heroines as Rebecca West and Ellida Wangel. Without Thea's interest in the goals pursued by the men in her life, lacking any other kind of altruism, Hedda is an otherworldly being whose longing for a place in the real world is without the ethical component explicit or implicit in the folklore. Those who defend her on feminist grounds and claim Ibsen as an ally have to ignore Ibsen's own notes, which create a nature-culture conflict along gender lines: "A woman's imagination is not actively and independently creative as is a man's. It needs a little bit of reality to help it along."

The folk traditions on which Ibsen drew have their own discouraging message. The mermaid needs marriage to a man to win a soul; conversely, the woman from the real world, an Agnete, risks her soul when she abandons her own people for the freedom of the otherworld. These stories describe the need for sacrifice, and as Ibsen's next play would make absolutely clear, the sacrifice for art's sake would be exacted from the woman. Perhaps only Kierkegaard paid sufficient attention to the price paid by the merman in the same struggle to unite two disparate modes of existence. But to the extent that it is woman who must choose, to that extent is Hedda Gabler victim, robbed of the sympathetic traits of the new *huldre* and deprived as well of the spiritual quest of the old *hundre*—and thus trapped within a much older tradition of the evil and demonic fairy than the nineteenth century ordinarily remembered.

HAROLD BLOOM

Ibsen: Trolls and Peer Gynt

I found myself recently on the stage of the American Repertory Theatre at Harvard, supposedly discussing Ibsen's *Hedda Gabler*. My fellow performers were an eminent Ibsen scholar (male), an acclaimed Harvard Feminist, and the distinguished and beautiful actress who had just played Hedda. I achieved the success of being hissed by much of the audience when I mildly and amiably observed that Hedda's true precursors were Shakespeare's Iago and Edmund, so that even if the Norwegian society of her day had allowed her to rise to Chief Executive Officer of the firearms industry, Hedda would still have been sadomasochistic, manipulative, murderous, and suicidal, that is to say, her dreadfully fascinating self.

With perhaps some mischief, I added that it made no difference therefore whether Hedda was a woman or a man, and just as actresses have played Hamlet, perhaps some actor would yet play Hedda. The audience was much happier when the scholarly Feminist replied that Hedda was a victim of society and nature, being both unhappily married and unwillingly pregnant. "She is trapped in a woman's body" became a refrain, as did the notion that society victimized Hedda by giving her nothing to do.

My Feminist opponent was not particularly original; nor was I. Brigid Brophy had anticipated us both back in 1970 by saying that Hedda's tragedy could have been avoided had she "become commander-in-chief of the

Norwegian armed forces," but I think the formidable author of *Black Ship to Hell* (one of my favorite books) was mistaken. Whether commanding an army or arms factory, Hedda would have acted like her forerunners Iago and Edmund. Her genius, like theirs, is for negation and destruction. Again like them, she is a playwright who writes with the lives of others. Her intelligence is malign, not because of social circumstances but for her pleasure, for the exercise of her will. If she resembled anyone that Ibsen had ever known, it was Ibsen himself, as he was aware.

It is no accident that *Hedda Gabler*, written in Munich in 1890, is the masterpiece of the Aesthetic Age, that perilous transition between the Democratic and Chaotic. Iago, pridefully savoring his debasement of Othello, and Edmund, detachedly contemplating the gullibility of his father Gloucester and his brother Edgar, are in league with Hedda hoping ardently that Løvberg has shot himself, at her urging and with her pistol, in proper style. Elevating Iago to Othello's second in command and Edmund to Gloucester's heir would only have delayed the tragedies they animate; other starting points would have been generated. Hedda as armaments minister or as field marshal would still have found another impetus for destroying Løvberg and herself.

All this is intended as a prelude to the most crucial element in Ibsen's canonicity: his social colorings are only a mask for his conversion of Shakespearean tragedy and Goethean fantasy into a new kind of Northern tragicomedy, a dramatic poem overtly High Romantic in *Brand* and *Peer Gynt*, yet subtly just as High Romantic in *Hedda Gabler* and *The Master Builder*. The shadows of *Hamlet* and of *Faust* fall upon all of Ibsen throughout the half-century of his career as dramatist. His canonicity, as well as his playwright's stance, have everything to do with his struggle to individuate his own poetic will and almost nothing to do with the social energies of his age. Irritable and cranky, ruthless in devotion to his gift, the not very charismatic Ibsen resembles Goethe only to the degree that both renounced some of their most vital impulses in order to practice their art without impediment. Ibsen charmed almost no one; Goethe charmed everyone, himself included. Like Shakespeare, Ibsen had the mysterious endowment of the true dramatist, which is to be able to lavish more life on a character than one possesses oneself. Goethe's only persuasive dramatic creation is his own personality, or Mephistopheles insofar as he is Goethe. There is no one in Goethe's plays or dramatic poems like Brand, Peer Gynt, Emperor Julian, Hedda Gabler, Solness. Demoniac or trollish beings, they are intensely rammed with life, a Shakespearean panoply of roles without rival in modern literature. But they carry an un-Shakespearean burden, which is the playwright's disapproval. Eric Bentley, nearly half a century ago, isolated this central peculiarity in

Ibsen: "he wrote works which were more and more subjective and difficult and which bore within them a concealed condemnation of modern man, including the poet himself."

This condemnation is directed even more, as Bentley implied, at the public, who suffer through their stage surrogates precisely what Ibsen wishes them to suffer. Kierkegaard, who had a strong if oblique effect on Ibsen, distinguished between two despairs: that of having failed to become oneself, and the greater one, of having indeed become oneself. Ibsen's protagonists quite definitely have become themselves. Except for Peer Gynt, they end in despair. Ibsen labored mightily to make Peer Gynt despair, but this is the one character who got completely away from him and entered the literary space inhabited by Hamlet, Falstaff, Lear's Fool, Bernadine (of *Measure for Measure*), Don Quixote and Sancho Panza, and only a few others.

Part of the odd comedy of *Peer Gynt* as dramatic poem ensues from watching Ibsen working hard but vainly to make himself, and us, disapprove of or dislike Peer. Falstaff's wit justifies his every fault, mitigates his life, until we reflect upon it; and who has time for such reflection while Falstaff is on stage? Peer's endless energy and insouciance keep him going against adversaries as preternaturally formidable as the troll king, the Great Boyg, the Button-Molder, and the Strange Passenger, as well as against all merely human opponents. Whether in the theater or in the study, we side with Peer, indeed are absorbed into the great Gyntian self.

Ibsen is the exemplary dramatist of the Aesthetic period because, far more subtly even than Chekhov, let alone Strindberg, Wilde, and Shaw, he intuited how to perspectivise his characters through aspects of our perceptions and sensations. He is the democratic heir of the aristocratic Goethe, and though he could not equal *Faust, Part Two* as a dramatic poem, he possessed the secret that Goethe never learned, how to revive poetic drama in the post-Enlightenment. The mythologies of *Faust, Part Two* were too remote for dramatic immediacy; Ibsen relied instead upon an occult Norwegian folk mythology that functioned for him the way the Freudian mythology works for many of the writers of our Chaotic Age.

Ibsen's dramatic psychology centers upon the figure of the troll, suddenly popular again in children's dolls. The wild-haired little imps that I pass in the storefronts have, however, a rather more benign aura than Ibsen's trolls, who are authentic demons. In an early essay on folk ballads (1857), Ibsen noted that popular writing in his nation had favored "fantastic travels to the home of the trolls . . . war with trolls," which puts us into the world of *Peer Gynt*. Reading Ibsen and watching him performed, I am overwhelmed by the impression that Ibsen's trolls are not, to him, ancient fantasies or modern metaphors. Like Goethe, Ibsen believes in his *daimones*, in the preternatural sources of his own genius. Trolls are not, as some critics have suggested, Ibsen's equivalent of the Freudian unconscious. They are closer to the later Freudian mythology of the drives, Eros and Thanatos, and since *we* possess the drives, we are partly trollish in our nature. But Ibsen is a monist where Freud tries to be a dualist; our alternating desires for life and death, in Ibsen's view, are not the human element in us. Since the drives are nevertheless universal (or at least a universal mythology), trolls cannot be simply ogres, as, say, the mountain trolls are in *Peer Gynt*. Peer himself is a borderline troll, and Hedda Gabler and Solness, as we will see, are trolls except for their merely societal timidities. In *Brand*, the girl Gerd is someone we both admire and abhor, because the human in her, all that is not troll, is an authentic spiritual prophetess. Something fundamental in Ibsen, a sly uncanniness uneasily allied to his creativity, is pure troll.

I do not think Ibsen would have agreed with some of his modern scholars in their definitions of trolls. Muriel Bradbrook called the troll "the animal version of man," but the healthy animal in the endlessly active Peer Gynt rejects the trolls. Rolf Fjelde, whose version of *Peer Gynt* is the one I will use, goes beyond Bradbrook by saying of the troll, "in recent history he ran the death camps." Ibsen's trolls are personally very nasty indeed, particularly in *Peer Gynt*, but they are closer to sadistic, disturbed children than to systematic technocrats of genocide. Most simply, trolls are *before* good and evil, rather than beyond it.

The most formidable humanized troll in Ibsen is Hedda Gabler, and Hedda cannot be called evil. That would be as uninteresting as saying that her precursors Iago and Edmund are wicked fellows. Doubtless Ibsen thought of Shakespeare's hero-villains, Macbeth included, as being trolls; but that is not a very Shakespearean myth. In Iago and Edmund, as in Hedda, there is a playfulness gone rancid, and insofar as the sublime Falstaff yields to a certain rancidity, a trollishness appears in him also. The opposite of trollishness is wit and the high spirits that sheer wit can engender. Sir John, witty to the end, never transmutes into a troll, whereas the sadistic clown of *As You Like It*, Touchstone, is little better than one.

Trollishness, whether in Ibsen or, as he partly teaches us to find it, in Shakespeare, is a dialectical matter. Like the Goethean daemonic, it is destructive of most human values, yet it seems the inevitable shadow side of energies and talents that exceed the human measure. Hedda Gabler, whose ambiguous sexuality includes sadistic desires for Thea Elfstead, ultimately descends from Lilith, Adam's first wife according to Jewish esoteric tradition. In one account, Lilith abandoned Adam in Eden because she declined further sexual intercourse in the missionary posture, as we have come to call it. When Ibsen noted that Hedda desired to live altogether as a man, he implied that his tragic protagonist was in Lilith's line, since Norwegian folk-lore traced hidden female trolls (huldres) as the daughters of Adam's first wife. Again the point is not Hedda's supposed evil nature, but her preternatural allure. Properly directed and acted, Hedda should be as coldly fascinating and nihilistically seductive as Edmund, and should have the power of turning something in each of us into a Goneril or a Regan. Her trollishness is her glory, however sinister.

Criticism or performance that converts Ibsen into a social reformer or moralist is destructive of his aesthetic achievement and threatens his authentic place in the Western dramatic canon, one second only to Shakespeare and perhaps Molière. More even than the later Shakespeare, Ibsen is an occult or visionary playwright. From start to finish he writes romance, even if the flamboyance of *Brand*, *Peer Gynt*, and *Emperor and Galilean* seems to vanish in the bourgeois, democratic tragedies that became Ibsen's characteristic work. In abandoning poetry for prose, Ibsen says he was yielding to modernity; but nothing in his nature was at all yielding. George Bernard Shaw deceived himself and others in proclaiming a social Ibsen; I cannot think of any other Western dramatist of true magnitude who is as consistently weird as Ibsen. A strangeness that refuses domestication, an eccentric vision, really a baroque art—Ibsen manifests these qualities as does every other titan of the Western Canon. As with Milton or Dante or Dickinson or Tolstoy, so it is with Ibsen: we have lost sight of his originality because we are contained by that individuality; we have been partly formed by Ibsen. Shakespeare is necessarily the largest instance of this phenomenon. But Ibsen, early and late, remained more Shakespearean than he cared to recognize.

Critics generally agree that Ibsen's first canonical play is the ferocious *Brand*, composed in Italy in 1865, when the dramatist was thirty-seven. More even than *Peer Gynt*, which followed it, *Brand* seems a play for the theater of the mind and not for any actual stage. It now has a peculiar glory in English, because the version by the poet Geoffrey Hill (1978) is much the finest Ibsen available to us as poetry. Hill, a master of savage eloquence, is a martyrologist, and his temperament, as manifested in his own poems, is peculiarly Brandian. He declines to call his *Brand* a translation, but it surpasses any purported translation we have.

What Hill demonstrates sublimely is that Brand is sublimely unbearable; when he dies at the end, in an avalanche, the audience or readers can only be relieved that the doom-eager priest will not be able, following the highest of principles, to destroy anyone else. On this central issue of his tragedy, Ibsen is hidden or equivocal: is Brand's God only a magnified Brand?

If one believes (as I do) that every god, Yahweh included, was once a man (the central insight of Joseph Smith, the Mormon prophet), one reflects on the truth of the mad girl Gerd's final conviction that Jesus never died but instead became Brand. Brand is the Norwegian or Viking Jesus, even as American religionists worship no Jesus of Nazareth, but the American Jesus. W. H. Auden, striving for an eminent Christian orthodoxy, condemned Brand as an idolater, hardly an Ibsenite judgment:

> . . . our final impression of Brand is of an idolator who worships
> not God, but *his* God. It makes no difference if the God he calls
> his happens to be the true God; so long as he thinks of him as his,
> he is as much an idolater as the savage who bows down to a fetish.

Gerd's reading of Brand is not Ibsen's and yet remains more relevant to the play than Auden's interpretation does. Brand's God is his only to the extent that any prophet's or mystic's God is his own. Whatever Brand's relation to his God, it isn't the relation that renders him unbearable. His human relations, starting with his mother, are hopeless, including his marriage, since Agnes is shown as falling in love not with the man but with the hero of faith.

However Norwegian Brand is or was, his religion seems very American and post-Christian to me. We learn little about Brand's God, but there is just enough to show us that Brand and God exist together in a mutual solitude, whether of one self or of two. Auden sees in Brand the not wholly successful representation of an apostle, but Ibsen's Brand is no apostle of anyone. Like Ibsen himself, like Peer Gynt, Brand is a trollish self. Ibsen is a dramatic genius, and Brand a very persuasive representation of that fearful phenomenon, a religious genius. Peer Gynt, like Don Quixote and Sir John Falstaff, is something else, a genius of play, what Huizinga called *homo ludens*. Brand's nearest parallel is Julian the Apostate, another fascinating but ultimately unloving and unbearable genius of the spirit.

In both figures, as in nearly all of Ibsen's major protagonists, there are qualities that remind us of oddities in Ibsen's own trollish nature. I have a good many friends who are authentic poets, novelists, and playwrights, and many possess a considerable number of eccentricities; but none of them keeps a poisonous scorpion under glass upon his or her writing desk, plying it with fruit. Ibsen was neither Brand nor Emperor Julian, but he was a master builder knowingly in league with trolls. And while he evidently intended Peer Gynt to be only a self-parody at best, the universalism of Peer is very nearly a full brother to Hamlet, Falstaff, Don Quixote, Sancho Panza.

Far more than Goethe's Faust (whom Ibsen greatly admired), Peer is the one nineteenth-century literary character who has the largeness of the grandest characters of Renaissance imaginings. Dickens, Tolstoy, Stendhal, Hugo, even Balzac have no single figure quite so exuberant, outrageous, vitalistic as Peer Gynt. He merely *seems* initially to be an unlikely candidate for such eminence: what is he, we say, except a kind of Norwegian roaring boy, marvelously attractive to women (in his youth), a kind of bogus poet, a narcissist, absurd self-idolator, a liar, seducer, bombastic self-deceiver? But this is paltry moralizing, all too much like the scholarly chorus that rants against Falstaff. True, Peer, unlike Falstaff, is not a great wit (though Peer can be very funny). But in the Yahwistic Biblical sense, Peer the scamp bears the Blessing: more life. Brand is doom-eager, a Viking death-ship in himself. Peer is a warmth bringer, though not exactly a light bearer. Ibsen makes this palpable in the wonderful pathos of the death scene of Peer's fierce and loving mother, who is comforted by Peer's playful tenderness as she expires, a scene that overtly contrasts with Brand's obnoxious and principled refusal to ease the dying of his own miserly and miserable mother.

Much of the critical reaction to *Peer Gynt* consists simply of seeing Peer as Brand turned upside down. Since Brand's essence is "No compromise!" the Gyntian self is identified with trimming, in a weak interpretation of the Great Boyg's injunction: "Go round about." Peer is a multiplicity of self-indulgences, but hardly a compromiser as such. As befits the Democratic Age, Peer is the natural man—all too natural. He is also, like Brand and Julian the Apostate, the preternatural man, driven by trollishness and by the need of transcending trollishness. We don't much like Peer toward the end on shipboard, being wolfish about the crew; or the shipwrecked Peer, drowning the cook with a touch of gusto. But for the most part Peer provokes our affection. His violent side reflects not only his trollishness, but his mythological origin and status as troll killer.

Ibsen professedly derived his Peer Gynt from a quasi-historical hunter, Per Gynt, who is the hero of a Norwegian folktale. The hunter encounters the Great Boyg, a mysterious and invisible troll who is a bent, snakelike presence; but unlike Ibsen's Gynt, who has to follow the Boyg's injunction to go around it, the folktale hero slays the Boyg. Subsequently, this ferocious hunter slaughters the trolls who make love to the herd girls, the same passionate women who entice Ibsen's Peer Gynt. The playwright softens the violence of the original Per, while retaining the hero's reputation as yarn-spinner and storyteller. Ibsen's Peer is a nineteenth-century Norwegian peasant, child of a declining family, not an uncanny hunter, except in his fantastifications. These yearnings are hardly to be taken as an indication that Peer is what W. H. Auden interpreted him as being, the artist-genius as a new kind of dramatic hero. Ibsen's Peer is neither artist nor genius, and Auden brilliantly insisted on getting this wrong:

the Peer we see on stage has no appetites or desires in the ordinary sense; he plays at having them. Ibsen solves the problem of
presenting a poet dramatically by showing us a man who treats
nearly everything he does as a role, whether it be dealing in slaves
or idols or being an Eastern Prophet. A poet in real life would
have written a drama about slave trading, then another drama
about a prophet but, on the stage, play acting stands for making.

The Peer we encounter in Ibsen's pages is consumed by wonderfully
ordinary appetites and desires and is certainly much more a natural man than
a poet. Yet Auden's insight remains; Solness in *The Master Builder* is an architect, while Rubek in *When We Dead Awaken* is a sculptor. As for Løvberg's
burnt-up manuscript in *Hedda Gabler*, neither we nor Ibsen estimate the
cultural loss to be very great. Auden looks for the nonexistent poet in *Peer
Gynt*, because Ibsen seems to have an intimate relation to this protagonist,
more than to Brand or to Emperor Julian. Part of the mystery of human
aesthetic Ibsen is that among all his characters he seems most heavily
invested in Peer Gynt and Hedda Gabler. He is Hedda, as Flaubert is Emma
Bovary. The relation to Peer Gynt is very different and abides in the slash
mark between identity/nonidentity. If one winds around again to Shaw's
association of Peer Gynt with Don Quixote and Hamlet, the phenomenon is
aesthetic universalism, transcending national canons. Hamlet is probably not
a representation of Shakespeare's own imagination; Macbeth is closer to that
prophetic intensity. The Don and Cervantes no one need speculate upon, for
Cervantes memorably ends his epic romance with an overt declaration: "For
me alone Don Quixote was born, and I for him. He knew how to act, and I
knew how to write. We two alone are as one."

It would startle us to substitute "Peer Gynt" for "Don Quixote," and
Ibsen would never have done so. Yet truly for Ibsen alone was Peer Gynt
born, and Ibsen for him, even though neither perhaps (in Cervantes' sense)
knew how to act. Other plays by Ibsen achieve tragic eminence, but nothing
else is so fecund. Eric Bentley, nearly half a century ago, accurately termed
Peer Gynt "a masterpiece and a delight" and encouraged us to interpret this
grand dramatic poem with a little sympathy. I like best Bentley's word
"delight."

Ibsen's contemporaries did not appreciate acts 4 and 5, which are the
glory of the work, never surpassed by Ibsen as invention, the essence of
poetry. The last two acts together are considerably longer than the first three
together and transcend the saga of the young Peer. Acts 1 through 3 show us
Peer at twenty, vitalistic and unstoppable, contending with neighbors and
with trolls. Judging himself unworthy of Solveig because of his trollish

amours, and isolated by the death of his mother, Peer goes into exile, and the play becomes surrealistic, perhaps irrealistic, closer to Beckett than to Strindberg. The gorgeous and hilarious act 4 opens on the coast of Morocco, proceeds into the Sahara Desert, and ends in a Cairo madhouse. Peer is now a splendidly corrupt middle-aged Americanized slave trader, hosting an outdoor dinner for equally corrupt cronies—British, French, Prussian, and Swedish—to whom he expounds the Gyntian moral philosophy:

> *The Gyntian self—it's an army corps*
> *Of wishes, appetites, desires,*
> *The Gyntian self is a mighty sea*
> *Of whim, demand, proclivity—*
> *In short, whatever moves my soul*
> *And makes me live to my own will,*
> *But just as our Lord had need of clay*
> *To be creator of the universe,*
> *So I need gold if I'm to play*
> *The emperor's part with any force.*

The troll in Peer has triumphed, since pragmatically he has followed the Troll King's injunction: "Troll, to yourself be—enough!" rather than the human motto: "Man, to yourself be true!" In trollish consistency, the Greek revolt against the Turks being under way, Per reverses Byronic heroism and proposes financing the Turks. When his associates flee with his gold-laden yacht and then explode with it, he praises God, while lamenting that the Deity is scarcely economical.

The hero of the first three acts is now more clearly a hero-villain, but he is also consistently funnier and even more likable, because his rueful misadventures touch so tellingly on a universal strain in human fantasies. Knowing still that he somehow remains elect, the scamp Peer clambers up a tree, where we see him fighting off monkeys as if they were so many trolls. With his customary insouciance he next wanders through the desert and meditates on improving it. Peer, we suddenly see, is the link between Goethe's Faust and Joyce's Poldy Bloom. Each dreams of a new domain, reclaimed from ruined nature; and Faust's seaside kingdom, Gyntiana, and Poldy's New Bloomusalem in the Nova Hibernia of the future are all best summed up by Peer:

> *In the midst of my sea, on a rich oasis,*
> *I'll reproduce the Nordic races.*
> *The dalesman's blood is royal almost;*

Arabian crossings will do the rest.
Within a cove, on a shelving strand,
I'll found Peeropolis, my capital.
The world's obsolete! Now the ages call.
For Gyntiana, my Virgin land!

Ibsen mingles farce, fantasy, and a yearning pathos when Peer goes on to cry out for a crusade against Death, a presage of the marvelous quest of act 5. Fate (and Ibsen) bring Peer the stolen horse and robes of the emperor of Morocco. Sublimely mounted and attired, he goes off to become a prophet, surrounded by dancing girls led by Anitra, a particularly attractive celebrator of the Gyntian self. As prophet, Peer is very nearly fulfilled but falls into the quotidian when he attempts a more secular satisfaction with the wily Anitra, who runs off with the horse and the prophet's wealth, while gratifying poor Peer not at all. We like Peer all the better for his quick bounce back from his latest erotic humiliation:

To try to stop time by skipping and dancing;
To fight the current by preening and mincing!
To strum the lute, take love for a fact,
Then end like a hen—by getting plucked.
That's conduct to call prophetic frenzy—
Plucked! Oh Lord, I've been plucked all right!

His prophetic career over, Peer sets himself to be an old historicist, a skimmer-off of history's cream. As a new Vico, he seeks "the sum of the past" and goes to Egypt to hear the Statue of Memnon welcome sunrise. Peer's impulse is a parody of Faust's in *Part Two* of Goethe's poem, which haunts Ibsen's acts 4 and 5. Instead of Goethe's extraordinary revivification of the classic, with Faust as the lover of Helen, we get Peer as Norwegian tourist, who writes in his notebook,

The statue sang. Heard definite tones,
But can't figure what it all means.
A hallucination, obviously.
Nothing else worthy of note today.

Instead of carrying Peer into the dark backward abyss of classical history, Memnon reminds him only of the Troll King. What ought to be an even more imposing confrontation with the Great Sphinx at Giza again fails as world history and seems to Peer only another encounter with the Great

Boyg. The Oedipal answer to the riddle "What is Man?" is given not by Peer but by Begriffinfeldt, head of the Cairo madhouse, who is also visiting the Sphinx in search of understanding (as Begriffinfeldt's name literally means). The search is over when Begriffinfeldt proclaims Peer the Emperor of Interpreters, who has solved the riddle of life by saying of the trollish Sphinx, "He's *himself*." Baffled but forever willing, Peer finds himself in the Scholar's Club or madhouse where Begriffinfeldt locks the keepers in a cage and releases the inmates, making a grand anti-Hegelian pronouncement: "Absolute Reason / Died last night at eleven o'clock."

Reason is dead, and the shocked Peer reigns in its place and receives the demented homage of Huhu, a language reformer; of a fellah, who carries the mummy of King Apis on his back; and best of all, of Hussein, a cabinet minister who lives in the illusion that he is a pen. For Ibsen, these were brutal contemporary political satires, but they live now in their own inspired lunacy. Peer sends Huhu off to interpret the Moroccan apes with whom he had struggled earlier, and instructs the fellah to hang himself in order to become like King Apis. Amiably as the Huhu matter turns out, the actual suicide of the fellah horrifies Peer, and a second suicide, by the penman Hussein, is too much altogether and causes Peer to pass out. In a sublimely sordid apotheosis, Begriffinfeldt crowns the unconscious Peer with a wreath of straw, and all hail the Emperor of Self as act 4 ends.

I cannot think of a twentieth-century play that equals *Peer Gynt* act 4 as a revival of the tradition of Aristophanes and of *Faust, Part Two*. Ibsen's verve is unfailing as he surges from one outrageous invention to another. Whatever it is that Peer represents, we do him wrong to invoke Augustinian moralizings, as some of the best Ibsen critics have done. Ibsen is more a scorpion than a moralist and, in this play, more of a Dionysiac than we have understood. Eric Bentley is perhaps a touch too harsh on Peer, harsher than Ibsen was:

> *Peer Gynt* is a counter-Faust. It shows the other side of Faustian striving, the striving of modern careerism with all its vast implications. In his gay unscrupulousness, his adventurous egoism, and his amiable immorality, Peer Gynt is the Don Quixote of free enterprise and should be the patron saint of the National Association of Manufacturers.

Peer, in one phase, was indeed a great robber baron, but ultimately he is too vitalistic and metamorphic to abide in any role, and his self-absorption produces a pragmatic disinterestedness. Peer is a genius of play, trollish and manic play. Ibsen, like Cervantes and Shakespeare, is not interested in the

Fall of Man. Trollishness is not a rebellion against God, even when it manifests itself in men rather than in trolls. Act 4 of *Peer Gynt* is as anti-Christian
as it is anti-Hegelian; absolute reason and absolute spirituality die together
at midnight, while the battered Peer lives on.

Whatever his critics think, Ibsen does not regard Peer as a failure or a
hollow man. *Faust, Part Two* is an even greater dramatic poem than *Peer
Gynt*, but unlike Faust, Peer is the triumphant representation of a personality. What Ibsen values in Peer is what we should value: the idiosyncractic
that refuses to be melted down into the reductive or the commonplace,
which is the agon of act 5 of the play. I dissent strongly from a view now held
by many, expressed most forcefully by Michael Meyer in his *Ibsen on File*
(1985):

> Whether one regards Peer as having died in the madhouse or in
> the shipwreck, Act V surely represents either the unreeling of his
> past life in his mind at the moment of death or (which is perhaps
> the same thing) the wandering of his soul in purgatory.

Ibsen's Peer Gynt does not die, either in the madhouse or in the shipwreck; he is still very much alive when the final curtain falls. Peer, like
Odysseus and Sancho Panza and unlike Don Quixote and Falstaff and Faust,
is a survivor, as befits the precursor of Leopold Bloom. Ibsen cheerfully
buries Brand under an avalanche, but he cannot bear to kill Peer Gynt. The
great trolls, Hedda Gabler and Solness and Rubek, must all die; trollish Peer,
who is Ibsen's sense of life, must live. All of act 5 is a refusal of death by water,
of meltdown, of purgatorial suffering. Not for Peer Gynt the Faustian apotheosis into an angelic and womanly sphere; instead Ibsen provides a return to
the woman who becomes at once mother and much belated bride.

Critics and directors need not fear that this is melodramatic and
sentimental; it is rather Ibsen's final outrage in an endlessly outrageous
drama. The trolls could not destroy Peer because he had women backing
him, and the Strange Passenger and the Button-Molder are thwarted by
the same Byronic and Goethean enigma. Peer's relation to Aase, his
mother, and the saintly Solveig is knowingly obscured by Ibsen, since we
are far likelier to remember the protagonist's erotic adventures, human and
trollish. The connecting element is gusto, for which Ibsen forgives Peer
almost everything.

Act 5 darkens Peer, giving him his first ugly moments in the play. Part
of the lasting strangeness of *Peer Gynt* is that it is more a trilogy of dramas
than a single work. The twenty-year-old Peer of the first three acts is a heroic
vitalist, uncanny enough to be part troll in his energies and desires. Act 4's

middle-aged Peer is both a matured humorist and a scoundrelly scamp, and his fantastic adventures just barely stay within natural bounds. The supernatural pervades the final act, in which the aged Peer, at some cost to his humor, is at once more rancid and more poignant than ever before. Although *Peer Gynt* is Ibsen's most original and least Shakespearean play, this double development in Peer parallels Falstaff's fortunes as the second part of *Henry IV* ebbs to its conclusion.

The return to the sea and to the mountain valleys of Norway has much, but not all, to do with the changed atmosphere of the final act. Old age—Peer's and, by a prolepsis, Ibsen's—sets the bleakness of a cosmos where death is a constant intimation. Like Goethe in *Faust, Part Two* (to whom is he again indebted), Ibsen has a frankly elitist vision of immortality. The great mass of souls are melted down into a common fund, from which fresh life can receive its spirit; but the great, creative souls retain their individuality after death. This concept goes back to Petrarch, but Goethe and Ibsen enliven it with a desperate twist into literalism. The question then becomes: What is the greatness of Peer Gynt, now at his most savagely trollish, that justifies his holding off the Strange Passenger and the Button-Molder? It is one thing for Gretchen (and Goethe) to save Faust, but why is it even more persuasive that Solveig (and Ibsen) save Peer Gynt?

Ibsen, to his dramatic credit, does not make this problem easy for us. Peer for the first time is unpleasant to confront, unless one happens to be the rather grisly Strange Passenger, who requests the gift of Peer's corpse for the purposes of unsavory research, and who utters the memorable comfort to the hero: "No one dies halfway through the last act." But two-thirds of the way through the last act Peer meets the Button-Molder, who shapes the rest of the play. Ibsen's debt to Goethe here was shrewdly worked out in 1942 by A. E. Zucker, who rightly compared the Button-Molder's tone to that of Mephistopheles. Ibsen's inventiveness matches Goethe's in sardonic and macabre humor and has the added force of a lifelong obsession going back to Ibsen's own childhood. As a boy, Ibsen had used a casting ladle in a game of button molding, just as Aase, early in the play, says that the childish Peer had done the same. When the Button-Molder tells Peer, "You know the craft," he touches a source where early fascination mingles with terror. The metaphor involved is Biblical and prophetic, implying purification more than punishment, though this "purification" ironically consists in the loss of self-identity, a particular horror for Peer (and for Ibsen).

"Friend, it's melting time" is the Button-Molder's wry remark to Peer, and part of the Button-Molder's curious charm is his patience, his willingness to be postponed until the next crossroads. He knows that Peer will encounter the haggard and deposed Troll King before that rendezvous and will again hear the trollish word: *enough*. "Troll, to yourself be enough" pragmatically ensues in "Friend, it's melting time." At their second meeting, the dialogue between Peer and the Button-Molder takes a turn that Ibsen's critics sometimes tend to Christianize. Peer, in honest confusion, asks what is it "to be yourself," and the Button-Molder replies with too easy a paradox: "To be yourself is to slay yourself."

But why should we think that the Button-Molder speaks for Ibsen, or rather for the play? There is no protagonist anywhere in Ibsen who achieves selfhood by suicide, including Rubek at the end of *When We Dead Awaken* and Hedda Gabler. No literary artist was less interested in slaying his own self than Ibsen, and I take it that the true point of the Button-Molder is that he is wise enough to accept perpetual deferment. For how can you melt Peer Gynt down into the communal? So much does Peer fear so unlikely an end that he offers himself up to a curious character called the Lean One, Ibsen's version of Mephistopheles; but the Lean One thinks that Peer is not worth damnation, at least incognito. The famed Peer Gynt, Quixotic emperor of himself, is another matter, and the Lean One goes off southward in search, misdirected by the unrevealed Peer.

The increasing separation between the actual and the legendary Peer begins to seem the play's final center. For a third time the Button-Molder yields, and the advent of Solveig, at once Gretchen and Beatrice, transforms the situation. Still, the drama ends in an antiphony of voices, Solveig's and the Button-Molder's, moving to cancel each other out. The Button-Molder promises a meeting at the final crossroads, while Solveig embraces Peer, promising an endless regressiveness. There is little reason to associate Ibsen with the endorsement of either promise. For him, and for us, the play concludes in irony, that is to say, meaninglessness. Peer is neither saved nor doomed to a final meltdown. Instead, he is to sleep and dream. Certainly, he will not be enough to and in himself, and he will have been purged; but will he be himself when asleep in Solveig's lap?

Peer Gynt is about five hundred lines longer than the uncut Hamlet, though compared to *Faust* it is a brief work. Clearly, *Peer Gynt* is Ibsen's *Hamlet* and his *Faust*, the play or dramatic poem in which the full range of an imagination is exposed. With *Brand* as its prelude and *Emperor and Galilean* as its huge epilogue, *Peer Gynt* is the center of Ibsen, containing everything he had, everything he quarried for the prose plays of his supposedly major phase. The canonicity of *Peer Gynt* is to me one with its trollishness, even as the best of the prose plays are the most trollish, *Hedda Gabler* in particular.

To return to Ibsen's trollishness is to return to Ibsen the dramatist, for the true quintessence of Ibsenism is the troll. Whatever it meant in Norse folklore, the troll in Ibsen is the figure for his own originality, the signature of his spirit. Trolls mattered most to Ibsen because it can be so difficult to tell them from people, a difficulty augmented in Ibsen's later plays. The difficulty, at least for Ibsen, was neither a moral nor a religious matter. Is Brand a troll? The question is irksome but hardly meaningless, and it ceases to be irksome when we ask it concerning Hilde Wangel, Rebecca West, Hedda Gabler, Solness the Builder, and Rubek, among others.

Trollishness, for and in Ibsen, is a question of psychic cartography. The daemonic is its own category in Goethe, but it does not pervade everything. With Ibsen there are no boundaries, and we do not know who is altogether human and who is contaminated by the Northern demons. We tend, however, to be most interested when the characters are trollish, and the formula in Ibsen therefore becomes something close to the hidden principle that the dramatic is another name for the preternatural. That is very unlike what Ibsen is supposed to be; but the actual Ibsen, as a playwright, resembles his own serpentine troll, the Great Boyg. That should teach us, at the least, to stop terming Peer Gynt a moral weakling, an evasive compromiser, an unrealized self. He is a borderline troll, fascinating and vitalizing, and so is Ibsen. Eric Bentley long ago emphasized that the later Ibsen was a realist outside, a vast phantasmagoria within. Bentley, of course, was right: in *Brand* and *Peer Gynt* and *Hedda Gabler* the inside and the outside cannot be distinguished, and we are given ghostlier demarcations, keener sounds, than in any dramas since.

MICHAEL GOLDMAN

Eyolf's Eyes: Ibsen and the Cultural Meanings of Child Abuse

What are we to make of the current celebrity of child abuse? It is disconcerting to realise that child abuse provides the model topic for TV's confessional shows; it is intimate, embarrassing, disturbing, as shamefully riveting as television itself. The subject may seem in danger of a kind of trivialization—as if its seriousness were tainted by its daily role in the theater of tears presided over by the Geraldos and Oprahs. But this kind of theater, no less than that of the Elizabethans and the Greeks, reflects a cultural urgency. And child abuse seems to make a special connection to that urgency.

I think the surging interest in child abuse is not an accident or a fad, but a sign of its central role in the problematic of our culture. By "our culture" I mean, not simply TV or the nineties, but a familiar atmosphere of rather long historical duration, that dominant tissue of interests and concerns which emerges with the French Revolution and continues today. Broadly conceived, it is that sense of the human situation which makes Buchner and Ibsen and Dostoevsky and Freud and Beckett and Picasso immediate to us—and to each other—in ways that Voltaire and Bach and perhaps even Shakespeare are not. They are immediate because they breathe an atmosphere of difficulty we recognize as our own. Child abuse intersects many strands of that difficulty—social, psychological, philosophical, political—in surprising and important ways.

From "Eyolf's Eyes: Ibsen and the Cultural Meanings of Child Abuse" by Michael Goldman from *American Imago* 51:3 (Fall 1994): 279–306. Copyright © 1994 Johns Hopkins University Press.

There is, for example, the suggestive link between child abuse and poststructuralism. It's been noticed that the issue of child abuse regularly raises the question—did it really happen? This is often thought of as an instance of the general problem of philosophical undecidability, of the gap between truth and representation. But I want to suggest that the question of child abuse—the very possibility of child abuse—inherently carries with it an element of undecidability. Not because of the nature of reality, but because of the specific reality of abuse. Not, as it were, the general puzzle, did the tree fall in the forest? but that child abuse specifically interferes with knowing if trees fall. Child abuse is an assault on reality itself. Victims of child abuse typically lose their ability to distinguish between memory and fantasy. The result is a deep impairment of the sense of identity, a loss of the capacity to construct a self or to determine what is real.

This mixture of doubt, rage, and imprisonment in fantasy, and the experience of this as a permanent condition—all characteristics of the mentality of the abused child—has in our day best been encapsulated in the "always already" of Derrida. This phrase, perhaps the most famous in the lexicon of deconstruction, implies an inevitable belatedness affecting all experience, a forced reliance on someone else's prior representation for all our information about reality. Shengold calls his book on child abuse, *Soul Murder*, and traces the origins of that phrase to a nineteenth century study of Kaspar Hauser, the famous "wild child" from Nuremberg. "Always already" reminds me of Kaspar Hauser's phrase for his jailor and tormentor, "The man who was always there." Hauser was imprisoned, as it were, by belatedness itself.

The person who feels utterly cut off from reality (and thus for whom the question, "Did it really happen?," can never be decided) is in the position of this notoriously abused child. It is probably no accident that Hauser captured the European imagination at the dawn of the modern period—and that it was to describe him that "soul murder," a term now so common in the literature of child abuse, was coined.

Through these connections, both child abuse and deconstruction take their place in an easily neglected historical perspective—as parts of a long-developing anxiety that seems to increase as our century draws to its close. From Marx to Freud to Foucault, from the fantasies of schizophrenics to our familiar worries about the influence of advertising, a certain kind of apprehension keeps recurring. This is a feeling of belatedness, of being controlled from outside—a feeling that instead of thinking one is being thought, that there is no substantial reality to hold on to, either externally or internally—that we live not in a world of stones and trees and living air, but in a prisonhouse of words, other people's words.

Such anxiety and belatedness enjoy a curious status in academic culture today. Associated with lively and original methods of analysis, with new ways of producing new books and teaching old materials, they take on the very privilege which, by definition, they seek to undermine. They treat the impossibility of clarity and meaning as if it were clarity and meaning itself. For literary studies in particular, arriving by way of writers like Derrida, Foucault, and Lacan, they carry the weight of disciplines imagined (especially by students of literature) to be weightier, more primary, even as they dissolve to paralyzing inadequacy the very notions of intellectual substance and primacy themselves. So what is in fact a mastering and destabilizing unease, an historically accelerating loss of confidence or savor, an oscillation of rage, indifference and despair, becomes confused with a philosophical advantage, a place from which to lever the unfortunately vanishing world.

As such, the analogy with symptoms of child abuse does much more than simply illuminate the uses and pitfalls of poststructuralism. It helps us, in fact, to understand why we're so interested in child abuse. For no matter how important the facts of abuse are, to say nothing of the problems of its victims, we need also to understand our attraction to the subject—why we are interested in it now, what other cultural problems it focusses and symbolizes.

Modern History and the Vulnerable Child

The wounded child peers at us through all the luxuriant growth of nineteenth century literature, from Blake to Dosteovsky, from Dickens to Rimbaud. And the wound is a mark of power and horror, a ministry of fear felt as transformingly in Freud as in Wordsworth. Ibsen is especially important here, for he grasps the centrality of the subject as well as anyone in the century, and we will see that his treatment of it is perhaps the most comprehensive of all. But first it is important to locate the theme historically.

Did Europe in the nineteenth century begin to abuse its children as never before, or did it rather begin to acknowledge how widespread that abuse was, indeed that its culture might be founded on child abuse? The question is of course unanswerable, but unanswerable in a way that goes to the heart of child abuse, because it reproduces the cruel undecidability inherent in the crime. The history of child abuse can never be written, because the abuse itself is inscribed in fantasy, in the intertwined fantasies of victim, abuser, and observer—because the reader of any such history is trapped inside the fantasy in which the abuse has its defining life.

This is not to deny the physical reality of assaults on children—but the physical reality of abuse is rarely the point. As a physical reality abuse is simply that, assault. The radical damage of child molestation goes far beyond the physical damage, which may indeed be nonexistent. It takes place in the determining mental life of the child, in the imagination, or rather at the base of the imagination—and it is on such foundational traumas to the imagination that the mental life of the adult is built. This is as true of the less specifically sexual examples of child abuse—child labor, the deprivations and oppressions of family life—as it is of molestation itself.

It is of all these abuses that the nineteenth century seems to become aware—either to see it everywhere as a social problem, a new evil born of industrialism, or perhaps simply to discover it in its heart. The question is unanswerable—did Halvard Solness, Ibsen's Master Builder, pause on his upwardly mobile track to commercial success to crush an impressionable thirteen-year-old girl to his body and kiss her on her lips, or was there simply a moment when, simultaneously, she imagined it and he desired it? We never know, we can never know, but it destroys them both.

Here it is useful to recall another damaged child, whose appearance in a long-unpublished play by a precocious German medical student uncannily anticipates not only Ibsen but the whole course of modern drama. Near the end of Buchner's *Wozzeck*, Wozzeck desperately promises his bastard son a toy horse. The boy pulls away and Wozzeck asks the Idiot who is tending him to buy him a "horsey." The child doesn't yet know or perhaps doesn't understand that his father—tormented, exploited, cruelly experimented upon by his superiors—has murdered his mother. IDIOT. [shouting joyously] Hop! Hop! Hip-hop, horsey! He runs off with the child. His mother is dead, his father sure to be executed. Whatever future we can contemplate at this moment hangs on this child. Do we feel hopeful, sympathetic, repelled, crushed, numb? Where is the story going, where does it leave us?

The child offers an undefended surface to an obscure and threatening process which seems recognizably modern. His figure, at risk, innocent, but almost sinister within its innocence, seems so easily to absorb the entire chronicle of complex abuse which Buchner has made out of the story. It juxtaposes the child with all the social and psychological forces that have pushed Wozzeck toward his crime, and with the unspecified consequences of the crime still to come. One modern name for the process that the child confronts is history.

Buchner's first play, *Danton's Death*, written a year earlier when he was twenty-one, was about the French Revolution. *Wozzeck* is set a generation later, in the Germany of Buchner's own day, and the child seems easily a figure for history's victim. But he seems also a bad seed from which history may explode. The implied sense of history here is new. For it is not a sense of history as fate, or as conflict, or even as a chain of events which is evoked by this child—but rather of history as a certain kind of scientific construct. What lies behind it is the distinctly modern sense of history as a complex causal process—a working out of forces whose secular explanation it is the burden of modern consciousness to undertake. This notion of history seems to emerge in Western thought as a response to the French Revolution.

The French Revolution offered a new model for anxious political reflection—of an inexplicable cataclysm of which we were all descendants. More precisely, it was the model of an unexplained catastrophe which should be explicable. It was a secular event and evidently the result of a play of forces of exactly the type that enlightened secular thought considered susceptible of analysis.

For Marx, the French Revolution was the event which made necessary the life project of historical explanation. No previous moment in history had created the same burden of difficulty, and it is no surprise that vast systems, like Hegel's, of making sense of events as parts of an historical process, emerge so soon after the Revolution and are so full of the shock waves it unleashed.

A distinctive feature of the Revolution was that the event seemed to move as if to an agenda of its own. Not God's agenda; by then there could be no patience with such an explanation. Yet it did not seem governed by man's agenda either, though clearly a horde of intentions had flooded into it. Nevertheless, it was not just a disturbance, a stone thrown into the pool of time. Rather, it possessed momentum, direction, logic, as if propelled by something embedded in the very process of its unfolding, a life of its own— a life to be attributed to history itself, to be explained by a science of what shaped history.

Let us think again of Wozzeck's bastard child riding/being carried off on his imaginary horse, fading away, a final silhouette of the drama. Is he the product, the pathos, or the source of the process we have been witnessing? How can we tell the dancer from the dance? At this moment we may remember that the Yeats poem, "Among School Children," from which this famous evocation of undecidability is taken, is also about children and what happens to them in the adult world:

> *O chestnut tree, great rooted blossomer,*
> *Are you the leaf, the blossom, or the bole?*
> *O body swayed to music, o brightening glance,*

How can we know the dancer from the dance? Yeats's question and his poem refer, of course, to history and society and the unappeasable restlessness of human desire, but they are also the end of a sequence of "questionings" in which figures of adult power and sexual intensity have hovered over children, concerned to draw meaning, energy, and radical satisfaction from them.

In Yeats as in Buchner, troubled by the image of a vulnerable child, we find ourselves confronting history. We could take a similar path through Wordsworth's long autobiographical poem, "The Prelude," where the young man, shocked by the cruelties of the Revolution, overstimulated by the experience of urban crowds, reconstitutes himself as a poet by remembering moments of overwhelming childhood stimulation by "nature"—a nature figured as threatening, beautiful, parental, as ravished and ravishing, sometimes menacingly external, sometimes thrillingly internal to the poet/child. Or we could connect Dostoevski's memory/fantasy of the raped child in the bathhouse to his tormented relation with Western "Enlightenment." The point is that, regularly, wound round the figure of the wounded child we find an anxiety about history, society, and the self which rises from the traumas of the French Revolution and anticipates some of the central questions of modern culture. The child functions as a center of fantasy in which we are all implicated, all betrayed.

We can, then, usefully distinguish two things that are being explored in this essay. First, the figure of the wounded child as the intersection of many strands of social thought. Second, this child as a peculiarly empowering figure, whose wound speaks for us and to us not simply of guilt and/or desire, but of a power to engage, even to change the secret life of our times. I have so far tried to suggest briefly some of the ways in which the points are true. Now I want to focus extensively on one example, that of Ibsen, not so much to arrive at a critical understanding of the playwright as to explore the specific power he derives from imagining the wounded child.

Ibsen's Abused Children

Child abuse is an almost obsessive theme in Ibsen, and I want to approach its resonance in his drama by concentrating on a curious and, I think, revealing feature of the way he represents it. I am referring to the fact that in the two plays in which Ibsen extensively presents the sufferings of a damaged child, he links the subject to an equally extensive imagery of sight and seeing.

To be a poet is to see, said Ibsen, famously. It is a claim that has powerful relevance for his theatrical art. The world his "realistic" plays show us is insisted upon in massive, seamless visual detail. We are made responsible for seeing every square inch of the stage. Instead of paying attention to a few selected props (a crown, a skull) as we are on Shakespeare's stage, we must be aware of every object in continuous relation to every other object. The latest books are on the round table in the center of a parlor that looks out into another room, full of plants, beyond which we see a fjord.

At the same time, seeing, for Ibsen, implies a powerful ethical force, as even the preceding account of visual realism suggests. Ibsen's other famous epigram about poetry is [angstrom] dikte, det er [angstrom] holde dommedag over seg selv. To write poetry—or plays—is to hold a doomsday judgment on oneself. If to be a poet is to see, then for Ibsen it is a kind of seeing that implies a pitiless intensity of self-examination.

But one can go much further than this, and approach Ibsen by trying, quite specifically and concretely, to understand the dramatic power of his pitiless gaze, what it means as a material aspect of his technique. And here is where we will be most helped by looking at the interplay in his work between the motifs of seeing and of childhood suffering. For much of the harsh power of Ibsen flows from a complex sense of seeing attached to the figure of the wounded child. In his plays it is as if we saw and were seen with a vision that draws its energy from the wounds themselves—we stare, we are stared at, we see with the victim's eyes, we see the abuse, we see ourselves as abusers, we see our abusers—all with a vengeful, liberating, unblinking ruthlessness.

The Wild Duck: Portrait of a Retouched Daughter

Produced in 1884, five years after *A Doll's House* had catapulted Ibsen into European recognition, *The Wild Duck* left many in its audience confused. Perhaps no play in the past two centuries had so disconcertingly mixed comedy with painful emotional content. Equally disconcerting was the way it directed much of its mockery at a figure who seemed to embody Ibsen's own presumed zeal for social reform. Gregers Werle, the rebellious son of a rich businessman, attaches himself to the family of his old friend, Hjalmar Ekdal, urging them to follow a program of honesty and truth in all things, especially their own relationships. Gregers' bungling efforts to persuade the vain and self-dramatizing Hjalmar to follow his "summons to the ideal" would seem comical except that they lead to the suicide of Hjalmar's beloved, if carelessly exploited daughter, Hedvig. Bewildered by Gregers' insistence that she sacrifice her pet wild duck to prove her love for her father, the fourteen-year-old turns the pistol on herself.

The Wild Duck abounds with references to sight and seeing. We are frequently reminded that the living room of the Ekdal family, where most of the action takes place, doubles as a photographic studio. The reference to photography has seemed to many to suggest the superior accuracy of realism, and Ibsen did at one point refer to himself as a photographer, but the emphasis is much less on the reality of what is seen than on distortions of the visual process. Hedvig Ekdal may have inherited her weak eyes from Gregers' father, for old Werle was her mother's lover, but it is Hjalmar who endangers her sight by allowing her to take over his work retouching photographs.

Hjalmar's occupation as a retoucher clearly extends to all the narratives by which he constructs and justifies his life. His daughter and wife cooperate in this; indeed they work always to soothe him, to make him look good—to allow him a vision of himself as breadwinner, scientific genius, self-sacrificing father. Both Hjalmar and his father are given to grandiloquent, literary phrases that lend their lives an aura of romance and heroism. Gregers accuses his father of trying to compose a false picture ("Tableau of father with son") but is equally guilty of distortion in his portrait of Hjalmar as a man of unusual moral qualities. The sardonic Dr. Relling, with his theory of the "life-lie," claims to see a similar process of self-delusion at work universally—but even this theory allows Relling to retouch some unflattering features of his own existence.

In *The Wild Duck*, seeing is not so much a question of what, objectively, is to be seen, but of what is behind the eyes, of whose eyes one sees with:

> *You've seen me with your mother's eyes. . . .But you*
> *should remember that those eyes were—clouded at*
> *times.*

As this speech of old Werle's suggests, retouching is not simply a matter of hypocrisy or convenient self-deception. It rises from the cloudiest springs of human disposition, from our most crippling needs and passions. Just as the play, for all its humor, is not simply comic, so the drive to retouch is located by Ibsen not simply in the human comedy of saving appearances but in deep and deeply deformed sources of imagination and desire. A child is at the center of *The Wild Duck* because the adult efforts at retouching that shape its action are all linked to the volatile and distorted psychic life we bring with us from childhood.

We come to understand this in part through the childhood histories of certain characters—Hedvig, Gregers, Hjalmar—and we feel it through the powerful subtextual currents Ibsen requires of his actors, but we also experience it in our own visual efforts with the stage picture—notably with its most spectacular feature. For there is a major element in the stage set that is constantly changing its appearance, constantly distracting and teasing us with altering contours and valences. Huge, complex, partially obscured, located at the back of the stage where it can't help being noticed but can't fully be observed, the garret where the duck is housed in an artificial forest literally upstages the photographer's studio. It is at once ludicrous and romantically evocative.

What is usually forgotten in discussions of the stage set in *The Wild Duck* is the way it engages the audience. We don't simply respond to the loft room, we try to look at it. There are things there we can't quite see but wish to see, even when we're supposed to be looking somewhere else. It is the most complex and subtle stage set ever devised, certainly without parallel in theatrical history at the moment Ibsen created it. He suggests its complexity—its dynamic engagement with the audience—in the stage directions:

> *The doorway opens on an extensive irregular loft room*
> *with many nooks and corners . . . Clear moonlight streams*
> *through skylights into certain parts of the large room; others lie*
> *in deep shadow.*

> *Morning sunlight shines through the skylights. A few*
> *doves fly back and forth; others perch, cooing, on the rafters.*
> *Chickens cackle now and then from back in the loft.*

Not only does the loft look different at different times of day, but it keeps us looking and noticing. We see it in at least four different lights. It invites curiosity, theatrical wonder, mixed feelings. The irregularity, the nooks and corners, the moonlight and shadow evoke romantic associations, but also an effort to peer into what is not clearly seen—in part because it is not clearly lit, in part because it is at the back, beyond our clearest view, in part because of the way the characters describe it. The birds and animals moving around in it are an attraction and a distraction. We will look for them, strain to see them, glance away to follow their flight or movement, even when there is something going on in the foreground we should be focussing on. It is a process something like thinking over one's personal history or trying to remember a dream—the uncertain, groping attempt to separate fantasy from memory.

The play of light and dark and of animal life off in the background, as we strain to see it, makes it mysterious, fascinating, "a world of its own" as

Hedvig calls it. Yet at the same time the loft is associated with a sense of delusion, self-deception, failure, pathetic limitation. We are watching, not bears in a forest, but rabbits in an urban attic, a piece of ingenious yet amateur carpentry, filled with the cackling of chickens as well as the cooing of doves, a source of embarrassment as well as interest for Hjalmar and Gregers, something which like all "live" animals in the theater, both heightens and threatens the illusion, an effect which reminds us simultaneously of theater as magic and theater as contraption.

Hedvig finds it a mysterious and wonderful world, and so it's associated with the rich, volatile imagination of a sensitive adolescent on the threshold of sexual maturity. But it's also something that her father has made, and though, as such, it's an escape from his responsibilities (we see him tinkering with it when he should be retouching photographs), at the same time it shows Hjalmar at his best, the little boy who loves constructing toy-like mechanisms. And our involuntary engagement as spectators in this huge contraption implicates us in his escapism. Indeed, why should we call it involuntary, since we have come to the theater, the place of such "realism" and ingenuity, of our own free will?

The attic, then, combines the shabbiness and deceit of theater with its transfiguring power. It operates as a kind of reminder of the mental life we bring with us from childhood—the imaginative background which, poisoned and enfeebled as it may be, continues to affect us through our adult life. One process that seems everywhere figured in *The Wild Duck*, that seems central to Ibsen's view of life and which perhaps becomes clear to him for the first time as he writes this play, is that of people coming up injured from the depths of childhood.

The chief examples of this process are, of course, Hedvig, Gregers and Hjalmar, and part of the play's originality lies in the way it shows the two adults drawing on their own childhood injuries to fatally damage the child. In particular, the scenes between Gregers and Hedvig are crucial. Hedvig's journey to suicide has to be convincing, and it depends on Gregers' being able to reach her at her most private depth of fantasy. Gregers can do this because he instinctively shares her fantasy world, because he literally talks her language.

Gregers understands how Hedvig's mind works because, like his half-sister, he has passed a lonely childhood, brooding on fantasies. Like her, his grasp of reality is not firm, and so they become partners in a fatal *folie à deux*, the first of several examples in Ibsen. The encounter is fueled by histories and feelings from which Gregers is alienated, including whatever vengeance he may be seeking on his father's bastard daughter and perhaps even on his envied childhood hero, Hjalmar, who has become his father's protegé.

We mustn't forget that, like Hedvig, Gregers is also an abused child. As Ibsen says in his worknotes for the play, Gregers "experiences the child's first and deepest sorrows—sorrows of family—everyday anguish of family life." Hedvig was the name of Ibsen's sister, the one member of his family to whom he felt close. And he has given to Hedvig many details from his own childhood experience, especially of the fantasy world into which he withdrew. In *The Wild Duck* she pores over the very books that fascinated Ibsen as a child. But in the play Ibsen has made her brother—made himself, that is—into a stepbrother, a twisted and vengeful character, responsible for a suicide which, like little Eyolf's a decade later, punishes a self-absorbed, sensual parent.

But there is also a social dimension to Hedvig's victimization. Exploited like many child laborers, she endangers her eyes (and thus becomes more isolated) so that Hjalmar may live in relative leisure. His sudden anger at her is heightened by his suspicion that he in turn has been exploited by the wealthy Werle. Indeed, the fantasy world of the garret is a compensation for the Ekdals' descent in class, which has closed the forests to them and locked them in a shabby urban life. Gregers, moreover, sees himself as a social reformer (he began his career distributing pamphlets to his father's employees), but his projects become increasingly identified with the bitterness he has carried with him since childhood and with his fatal, unseeing assault on Hedvig's imagination.

With Gregers as with all the characters, one gets the sense of two juxtaposed modes of action: the relatively conscious effort to retouch the picture—to reform, meddle, tidy up, arrange and interpret life; and a more unconscious stumbling or groping in the depths. There is a strong premonitory image of this early in the play, at the end of Act One:

> GREGERS.   Look, your gentlemen friends are playing
> blindman's bluff with Mrs. Sorby. . . .
> (Laughter and joking from the company
> which moves into view in the inner room)

This is the same stage space that will become the garret room in the succeeding acts. It has remained brightly lit and largely unoccupied for most of Act One, which now closes on the arresting picture of a dozen well-dressed, well-fed adults groping about blindly in a children's game in this large light-filled area. The audience, at this point, may tentatively assign the image a rather superficial satirical, socially "progressive" meaning, easy mockery of the local plutocrats. This might well be the way Gregers would see it, and we tend to see things with his eyes at this moment in the play. But the image carries more power than that. The light-filled room projects a suggestion which will be heightened by both the duck and the garret and by what we come to share of the characters' lives. For if we all come up injured from the depths of youth, we retain something of those depths—something of their wildness, expansiveness, mystery, authenticity, though in a wounded or tainted form. Life for all of us is a blindman's bluff, a child's game now played by grown-ups whose groping mocks and mimes the lonely bewilderments of childhood. And that is both the comedy and the pity of it.

Eyolf's Eyes

"To be a poet is above all to see." But what, in this world of blindman's bluff, does it mean, to see? What kind of seeing is possible? What is to be seen? And if every adult is a wounded or tainted child, who tends to see things with the wounded and tainted eyes of those who initially abused him—then who in the end is doing the seeing that constitutes the play? More particularly, in the theater, who are we when we see, who sees for us, as us? In the last two acts of *Little Eyolf* (1894), Alfred and Rita Allmers are tormented by an image of their dead son, the crippled Eyolf, who has wandered away from them and drowned while they were absorbed in their own problems. The event is all the more painful because it echoes an earlier moment of neglect. Ten years earlier, Alfred and Rita, absorbed in love-making, had left the infant Eyolf alone, sleeping on a table, from which he fell and crippled himself. It is the mark of this wound, the boy's crutch, that floats to the surface of the fjord at the end of Act One, to signal Eyolf's drowning, accompanied by the grotesque shout of "Krykken flydder" (the crutch is floating) from the ragged children on the shore. What haunts both parents, however, what they cannot help seeing, is a vision of Eyolf's eyes. "The eyes, the eyes," cries Allmers, and it is this fierce impression of Eyolf's accusatory gaze that breaks him, as it breaks his wife.

It is not hard to read *Little Eyolf* as a child's fantasy of vengeance on his parents through suicide, a notion that becomes irresistible if we know something of Ibsen's life and other work. Feeling neglected, shut out from the parental circuit of love, the child imagines, "how they would suffer if I died; then they would regret how they have treated me, then I would be even with them for what they have done."

Fuelled by *Little Eyolf*, we may think of Ibsen's theater as the seeing place for the child's vengeance, where the force of the action is a kind of seeing vengeance on the adult world, on us and through us. We see with the eyes of the child, and at the same time we feel the child's gaze directed on us.

This doubled intensity is an important part of Ibsen's power. The unblinking focus of the claim against us is reinforced by the sweeping assault on the elders and masters by whom we are limited and denied.

But the picture of childhood damage in *Little Eyolf* is a complex one. There is not one Eyolf in the play, but two. As a child, Allmers' sister, Asta, was called Eyolf—in what itself may have been another scenario of abuse involving Allmers. Here, however, it becomes important not simply to summarize the story, but to catch the expository rhythm by which we become aware of the peculiar sexual history of Allmers and his sister. For this is a revelation that masks as an evasion.

The day after Eyolf's death, Asta and Allmers fall into a kind of reverie as she sews a mourning band on his arm.

ASTA.	Now the left arm.
ALLMERS.	Thank you.
ASTA.	Yes, it's customary.
ALLMERS.	Well—then go ahead.

(She moves closer and begins to sew.)

ASTA.	Hold your arm still. I don't want to prick you.
ALLMERS.	(half smiling). It's like old times.

Why does Ibsen—always very sparing, very pointed in his gestural notations—introduce this piece of business? The answer is that it allows a reenactment, a kind of regression to the intimate scenes of their life together. Suddenly we are watching a pair of isolated, devoted children, prematurely freed from parental supervision. Their story unfolds for us, with a physical accompaniment that brings the old emotions to life, "distracting" Allmers from his sorrow.

Poor, orphaned early, Alfred Allmers had to care for his little sister while he was still a student. She in turn, though eleven or twelve years his junior, looked after him, mended his clothes, shared his struggles and ambitions, was his constant companion. To share his life even further, she chose— or was persuaded—to take part in a curious masquerade:

ASTA.	But then when you went to college—(Smiles involuntarily.) Imagine, that you could be so childish.
ALLMERS.	You think I was childish!

ASTA.	Yes, it seems so to me, really, looking back on it. You were embarrassed you didn't have a brother. Only a sister.
ALLMERS.	No, it was you. You were embarrassed.
ASTA.	Oh yes, I was, a little maybe. And I guess I felt sorry for you—
ALLMERS.	Yes, you must have. So you hunted up those old clothes I had as a boy—
ASTA.	Those nice Sunday clothes, yes. You remember the blue blouse and the knee pants.
ALLMERS.	(his eyes lingering on her) I remember so well the way you dressed up and walked around in them.
ASTA.	That was only when we were at home alone.

This piece of cross-dressing gained her the male name she would have possessed if she had been born a boy—Eyolf.

And so, half-way through the play we learn suddenly, almost casually, the real significance of its title. At this point we may begin to wonder just which damaged child stands at the center of the drama.

The dialogue just quoted itself masquerades as a comforting reminiscence, but it is subtextually charged. This is clearly felt when Allmers and his sister come to the question of the reasons for Asta's transvestite disguise. Allmers, the long-blocked author of an unwritten treatise on Human Responsibility, is eager to disclaim responsibility here. Both are embarrassed.

In a moment of passionate lovemaking with Rita, perhaps the only such moment in his life, Alfred has betrayed the secret behind the name Eyolf—and now he confesses this to Asta, who is shocked. So powerful is this moment for them both, that in order to avoid it Allmers must change the subject back to the child's death:

ASTA.	Alfred, you've never told any of this to Rita, have you?
ALLMERS.	Oh, I think I did tell her once.
ASTA.	No, Alfred, how could you!
ALLMERS.	Well, you know—a man tells his wife everything—nearly.
ASTA.	Yes, I suppose so.
ALLMERS.	(as if waking with a start strikes his forehead

and jumps up). Oh! that I can sit here and
[forget Eyolf's death]—

It is a moment of authenticity, but also a flight from embarrassing truth.
What began as an apparent evasion now must be evaded in turn.

At this point we may already guess something that will only be
confirmed later in the act—that the moment when the secret of Asta's trans-
vestism was revealed was the very moment when little Eyolf was crippled.
Alfred surrendered the information to Rita as a kind of tribute in the after-
glow of orgasm. But even in this dialogue between brother and sister there
can be no doubt of its oblique sexual intensity.

Eyolf's accident, which has initially been associated with sexual guilt,
a retribution for Allmers' surrender to Rita, now seems to punish an even
more deeply concealed guilt over his relation with Asta. And the sexual
implications of both revelations are complex. Asta's male disguise seems at
once an avoidance and a release of sexual desire. In the usual Ibsen configuration of two women—one passionate, the other sexually cool—Asta seems
at first to play the latter role, especially by contrast with Rita, and her boyish
disguise seems to further cover her sexuality. But of course it is also a sexual
release, a game by means of which Alfred and his sister could both disguise
and indulge their attachment.

ALLMERS.	I had no passionate feelings for you at the start.
RITA.	What did you feel for me then?
ALLMERS.	Terror [Schreck].

And at his single moment of unencumbered sexual response to Rita, Allmers
has felt compelled—or enabled—to yield up the secret of his relation with
Asta.

Toward its end, the play behaves as if its deepest secret were a
simpler one: that Asta and Allmers were soulmates, but because they thought
they were brother and sister they never told their love and—tragically—
Alfred married Rita, in part to provide for Asta. But as so often in Ibsen this
is really a piece of sentimental dramaturgy promoted not by the author, but
by the characters concerned. It constitutes a touching interpretation of their
relationship, but what we actually see of their behavior reveals two sexually
dysfunctional and potentially destructive people—sister now moving like
brother into marriage with a partner whose passion she cannot return.

It is hard not to blame Alfred for his sister's fixation at an early stage
of sexual development and to find something chilling in his passing her

private name on to his child—and the secret of the name to his wife. For it is in the originally secret relation of the two Eyolfs that Rita's resentment of her son seems to have begun, and in this light Alfred's confession to Rita may represent less a token of love than a revenge on her sexual power. It certainly cripples Eyolf in more ways than one.

Ibsen sketches Eyolf's neglect with his usual unsparing eye and lets us see how each of many separate blows takes its toll. Eyolf is and always has been a pawn in a slippery sexual game played by the three adults responsible for his upbringing.

We may also see an intensifying counterpoint in the story of Asta and Allmers if we consider the play as expressing the fantasy of the child or, even more powerfully, of the author who can fantasize simultaneously as both father and child. Here, in the condensed and overdetermined imagery of a dream, one can see the dynamics of a terrible battle between the two generations. Sexually threatened by the power of the mother's sexuality, the father displaces his feared castration onto the child. The child in turn fantasizes himself as his father's true love-object, a forbidden "sister," who bears the child's own name and dresses in male clothing. Thus he makes his father desire him rather than his mother, and then punishes him by rejecting his overtures.

Once again it is useful to return to a vivid moment and explore how it projects a performance life. I have in mind a passage late in the play, which involves a difficult subtextual challenge for the main actor:

> RITA.   Didn't you use to call her Eyolf? It seems to
>   me you confessed that once—in a private
>   moment. (coming closer.) Do you remember
>   it, Alfred—that wildly beautiful hour?
> ALLMERS.   (recoiling, as if in dread) I remember noth-
>   ing! I won't remember!

Allmers here seems haunted, not as Ibsen's fearfully crouching characters usually are, by emptiness, but by a fullness he seeks to deny. And for the actor here, the key question is what he seeks to empty out: what is it that Allmers refuses to remember?

To begin with, he is recoiling from the memory of the intensity of the sexual event, from the sensations of "that wildly beautiful hour." But he is also trying not to remember his betrayal of Asta, along with the suppressed sexual content of that relation. Of course he recoils, too, from the memory of Eyolf's accident, another betrayal. And the memory of his pleasure must be intensely distasteful because he now finds her unattractive.

So that tremendous moment, which gnaws at him and governs his response, even as he seeks to deny it, becomes a paradigm of the kind of alienated memory that Ibsen made the cornerstone of modern acting. It is the point in his past toward which run all the motifs of evasion in Allmers' life, the desires and deceptions he has kept from himself. It is the navel of his dream.

Has Allmers sexually maimed his sister and then memorialized that abuse in his child? And abused himself and his wife as well, for it is no accident that the disfigured boy becomes the final block to sexual fulfillment for Allmers and gives him a weapon to punish Rita for her sexual energy, indeed for the wealth he has received from her.

It is this wealth which gives the play its social dimension. Rita's fortune has enabled Eyolf to lord it high above the other children in the play, who are damaged by poverty and beaten by their parents. Indeed, the cries which accompany the news of Eyolf's suicide are their cries, initially mistaken for the noisy quarrels with which they reproduce their fathers' violence towards them. Dramatically, this makes for an extraordinary effect. For it is as if the sexual tension of the wealthy parents passes into a quarrel which becomes, first, the wild cry of the oppressed children and then the voice of Eyolf's death.

The scene is worth examining in detail. A terrible argument between Allmers and Rita has been interrupted as Asta and her devoted suitor, the uncomplicated road builder Borghejm, come in from the garden. But the awful half-articulated threats that Allmers' sexual coldness has drawn from his wife ("I'm almost tempted to wish . . . " "Rita! I beg you, don't be tempted into anything evil.") hang in the air as they enter:

RITA.	I'll bet it's the evil eye that's played tricks on you here. . . .
BORGHEJM.	You believe in the evil eye, Mrs. Allmers?
RITA.	(huskily). If I'm vile and evil, Alfred, it's your doing. (Confused shouts and cries are heard from far off down by the water.)
BORGHEJM.	(going to the doorway). What's the excitement—?
RITA.	Look, all those people running out on the pier.
ALLMERS.	What is this?

Propelled by the misery of her marriage with Allmers, Rita's hatred of Eyolf seems to break the confines of realism and explode outward in the cries from below that announce the death of her son. We have, then, a scenic orchestration that fuses intense impressions of inner and outer violence, of individual psychology and social condition.

Drawing on the accumulated impact of such associations, the final pages of *Little Eyolf* articulate a connection between child abuse, sexuality, and history that is central to Ibsen's vision. Like many of his plays, *Little Eyolf* includes a kind of fantasy version of the modern social project, in this case the children's home Alfred and Rita vow to create in memory of their dead son. The class warfare that, at least in their minds, is another possible cause of Eyolf's death (the poor children refused to save him because they hated him) will be assuaged by a program of education, love and generous subvention. But Ibsen has forced us to see an ironic underside to this project, to question both its motives and chances for success—just as he does with Lovborg's history of the future or Borkman's ode to capitalist expansion or Solness' homes for human beings, or indeed that early bitter parody of social betterment, the Captain Alving whorehouse/home for sailors.

Each of these optimistic enterprises is inextricably bound up with the tainted and ambiguous individual desires that have helped generate it. We feel them as products of evasion and self-delusion, as well as of oblique and thwarted sexual impulses. The liberal movement toward liberty and enlightenment is glimpsed as the enactment of a corrupt and damaging fantasy.

Like the Alving orphanage, or the pedant Tesman's attempt to recreate Lovborg's scientific vision of the future, the children's home Allmers and Rita promise to create has a dubious likelihood of success, since the talents and desires of its founders are so removed from what they intend. Allmers and Rita hope to dedicate themselves to social compassion. But their desire is clearly a product of their guilt and rage, a response to abuse both suffered and inflicted.

The children's home that they contemplate takes its place as the last in a series of disturbing substitutions. The children are substituted for little Eyolf, who was substituted for Asta, who substituted for a boy and was fathered by the man who replaced Allmers' father in his mother's bed. And there are similar substitutions in Allmers' intellectual life—philosophy, the mountains, the "infinite"—all choices that help him keep what "gnaws" at him at a distance. The most powerful figure for the threat Allmers seems to spend his life evading is the Rat-Wife, "the old woman with a dog in the bag" who visits the house in Act One and so fascinates and repels the crippled child. She offers to get rid of "anything here that nibbles and gnaws"; Eyolf follows her out of the house and to his death. Clearly the threat takes various forms in the play, and their overlapping suggests they are related: the sexual threat embodied in Rita, death, guilt, money, class hatred. Against all of them, Allmers marshals an ineffectual rhetoric of denial and transcendence—the law of change, the stillness of the mountains, the life work on "responsibility," social amelioration.

This interplay of threat and evasion reflects a complex vision, but its unitary force is perhaps best appreciated if we think of it quite literally as a vision, an intensity of seeing in the theater, for which Eyolf's staring eyes offer a partial but powerful emblem. Indeed, the final instants of the play present a crucial problem which can only be solved by grasping the peculiar texture of the moment—a texture that can be best expressed in terms of the pressure of seeing exacted by the scene.

In a sense, all final moments in drama invite us to take a long last look. Even a quick blackout only sharpens the afterimage. The end of a play inevitably reminds us of the special status of the theater as a theatron or seeing-place; we feel the peculiar attentiveness of our own gaze with unusual sharpness as we are about to break it off. Some plays, however, seem to heighten the intensity of our stare, to make us dwell on what we are seeing. The stop-action finales of Beckett and Chekhov underline a frozen image. Shakespearean tragedy draws our attention to what we see at the end— Hamlet borne off by four captains, the heavy loading of Desdemona's bed. Shakespearean comedy, on the other hand, places more emphasis on ongoing process, the celebration to come, the general happy exit. Ibsen is unusual in the extent to which he not only invites a long look as the final curtain approaches, but makes us aware that we are looking and of the shifts and edges that enter into our perception as we watch.

How is the final moment of *Little Eyolf* to be staged? Rita reaches out her hand to her husband, and says, "Thanks." The flag has been raised, they speak of raising their eyes "upwards," but their gaze remains level. They have agreed to take on the task of caring for the poor, abused children on the beach, but in a context that makes clear that this is a desperate move to fill the emptiness in their lives.

The emptiness in this final scene rises, of course, from the terrible experience of loss Allmers and Rita have undergone, but it also seems to flow from Allmers' experience in the mountains, which he describes early in the first act and now returns to at the end. Structurally, this motif seems to operate like a secret in a well-made play; it emerges in pieces, contested, guessed at, and worried over by the central characters—but unlike the well-made device, the ultimate "meaning" of Allmers' journey—if it has one—is never clearly revealed. But the imagery of that journey is powerfully present in the closing moments of the play.

Throughout Ibsen's career, the high waste lands of Norway

provided him with a complex symbol, varying somewhat in meaning over the years, but almost always carrying a core of anguish about the potentials of human aspiration and artistic achievement. The vidde is a place where the artist can stand alone, looking down with a detached aestheticism on the ordinary scene of human desire and suffering. In Ibsen's long poem, "On the Vidde," the artist on the heights watches his mother's house burn down, concerned only with how the scene might be framed and rendered.

The vidde is a place of emptiness and isolation; it is also a place of stillness/silence. And both terms, "tomt" and "stillhet"—each crucial in Ibsen's lexicon—echo through *Little Eyolf*'s final scene. "Tomt" is Ibsen's most frequent marker of existential fear and isolation. "Stillhed" carries an ambiguous though equally anxious charge. It can describe the peace, the freedom from sexual agitation that Rebekka West attributes to the effect on her of the spirit of Rosmersholm; but for her it is also a source of radical sexual inhibition. Immediately after describing the stillness she has found at Rosmersholm, she concludes that the Rosmer way of life "kills happiness."

So just as the remoteness of the mountains can imply a callousness or suppression of affect that the idea of artistic detachment fails to disguise, so their stillness can also imply human inadequacy. Is the stillness Rebekka finds at Rosmersholm a good thing? It seems a surrender to Rosmer's own suspect desexualization. And the stillness of the vidde certainly fits in all too neatly with Allmers' eagerness to stake out a rationale for escaping the sexual demands of his passionate wife. Allmers has claimed to find some transcendent value in the "stillhed" of the mountains in which he got lost, though Rita has wondered if he wasn't simply scared by his experience. In the last act, though, with Allmers having acknowledged his bitterness and sense of inadequacy, one feels in his concluding evocation of the traditional counters of transcendence a clear sense of their emptiness, their unresponsiveness:

RITA.   Where should we look, Alfred?
ALLMERS.   Upward—toward the mountain peaks.
                         Toward the stars. And toward that great
                         silence.
RITA.   (extending her hand to his). Thank you!

Of course they do not look upward. They stare, as Eyolf stares, as we in the audience stare, straight ahead.

I am talking about the scene as something to be seen. And certainly all the features of the stage picture are important. But the intensity of the image here depends less on the specific visual configuration than on the intensity of the acting. There is a need for absolute honesty in performance, which is the vehicle by which the pressure of Eyolf's eyes can be felt by us as we watch the scene.

What do we see? Ourselves, powerfully, vengefully revealed. We watch the tragic triviality of two normally selfish, greedy, weak, abnormally insistent human beings caught in a moment of more consciousness than they can stand. ("I can't bear it" is another key phrase in Ibsen.) Their tenderest, most socially positive affirmations are tainted, their lives are built on a foundation of abuse. Alfred may be telling the truth, may at least be trying to tell the truth, but he can only use his old language of lies. Somewhere, far to the North, the confident young engineer, Borghejm, will be blasting roads through the stillness of the mountains, but at his side will be the pretty, recessive wife who does not love him, permanently scarred by her older brother's sexual games and her own complicity in them. Here, night is falling though the flag flies high. Rita and Alfred's hands may at any moment touch, but the voices of possible meaning, of possible hope, are silent.

The Modern Family at Twilight, or What Alice Knew

Little Eyolf ends in twilight, an atmosphere especially appropriate to the kind of melancholy with which Europe was coming to invest the career of post-enlightenment civilization. From Wagner to Spengler to *The Waste Land*, twilight became a recognized symbol for the decline of modern culture. One may also think of the prologue to *Alice in Wonderland*, another sunset-drenched scene of belatedness in which stands the figure of a pre-pubescent, sexually invested nineteenth century child, the center of a fantasy that the modern world has found as commanding as it is evasive.

Was the caress of Charles Dodgson's eyes, of his camera, of his narrative, a form of child abuse? Once more, what seems most striking about this well-known example is its deep undecidability. Nor does it seem accidental that the problem of Dodgson's relation with Alice Liddell and her little friends is so strongly connected to the emergent science of photography. Dodgson's great portrait of Alice as a beggar girl is an unexpectedly powerful icon of its epoch, teasingly weighty in its subject's unreadable not-quite-passivity, which at once resists and invites our scrutiny. The eyes flick "knowingly" toward us. Can we preserve her innocence by saying she has been posed? Is her look simply a mechanical gesture, produced by the same respectable adult hand that has bared her shoulder and arched her tummy and spread her knees? What knowledge did she put on with Dodgson's power? We are pulled in many directions here, by the archaizing costume and the new technology, the sensuality and the propriety, the Oxford mathematician and the little girl, the absent recorder and his sexualizing eye, the absent little girl and hers. There is a dizzying mixture of advance and regression, which is echoed in the many transformations of the two Alice narratives.

Dodgson, the classic Victorian curate, would invite his little girls for tea and then take pictures of them in various stages of undress. The Victorian setting would seem once more to be part of a pair of opposites—until one realizes that the tension, the doubleness I have been describing is itself at the heart of the Victorian moment. What is more a combination of advance and regression than the world of a Trollope novel? All its ostensibly backward-looking manners and mores, its fox hunts, its code-driven ladies and gentlemen, its inarticulate romances and parliamentary debates, ride the bucking rhythms of unfathomable change—the rhythm of the railroads, the Reform Bill, and female restlessness.

For us, though, the point is that what we call Victorianism is but a special instance of Western bourgeois life. The tension that invests the body of Alice Liddell is the same we find in Little Eyolf or Hedvig Ekdal. The bourgeois family was and remains an advanced social formation. Like capitalism, though it constantly demands modification, it has not been improved upon. And yet it is terrifyingly regressive, a cave in which parents and children can hide, except from each other, a rabbit hold from which it is hard to escape. The old bachelor's hand squeezes the bulb, and with the flash we find ourselves, children of the French Revolution and the modern family, staring at our own image—vulnerable, arrogant, half naked, new, reflecting an unfathomable knowledge—our secret self in the image of a beautiful child, always already abused.

THOMAS F. VAN LAAN

Ibsen and Shakespeare

In April 1852, six months after Ole Bull hired Ibsen to work for the Norwegian Theater in Bergen as a "dramatisk Forfatter" [dramatic author], the theater sent him, in company with two of its actors, on an extended study tour to Denmark and Germany so that he could become familiar with advanced theater practices. From Copenhagen he reported, in a letter of 16 May to the theater's management, "Med Hensyn til Repertoiret have vi været meget heldige. Vi have saaledes seet Hamlet, samt flere af Shakspeares Stykker, ligeledes af Holbergs,—samt "Naar Damer føre Krig, En Søndag paa Amager, Slægtningerne, o. fl." [With regard to the repertory, we have been very fortunate. We have seen *Hamlet* as well as other plays by Shakespeare, likewise some by Holberg—as well as *Bataille de dames* [by Scribe], *A Sunday at Amager, The Relatives*, and others.] The other plays by Shakespeare performed at Copenhagen's Royal Theater while Ibsen was in town, all of which he apparently saw, were *King Lear, Romeo and Juliet*, and *As You Like It*, the last no doubt in the form of *Livet i Skogen* [Life in the Forest], an extensive reworking of Shakespeare's play into conventional formulas by the Danish theater-hack, Sille Beyer. In Dresden, he could have seen *Hamlet* again, the Tieck-Mendelssohn production of *A Midsummer Night's Dream*, and *Richard III*, but there he was short of money and had to pay to attend the theater, so we do not know whether he actually saw any of these productions.

From "Ibsen and Shakespeare" by Thomas F. Van Laan from *Scandinavian Studies* 67:3 (Summer 1995): 287–305. Copyright © 1995 Society for the Advancement of Scandinavian Study.

His letter from Copenhagen clearly indicates that he knew about Shakespeare, the prominence of *Hamlet* among his plays, and his importance to the realm of drama, but as far as can be determined, this trip may well have given him his first real acquaintance with Shakespeare's work. For there is no conclusive evidence that prior to 1852, before which he had written his first two plays, *Catilina [Catiline]* and *Kjæmpehøien [The Burial Mound]*, he had ever seen or read any Shakespeare, and indeed what evidence there is suggests that he probably had not.

Before his trip abroad, Ibsen's first real opportunity to attend the theater came during his stay in Christiania from April 1850 to October 1851. During this period, he could have seen approximately seventy plays at the Christiania Theater, but, amazingly, not one of them was by Shakespeare. Nor were any plays by Shakespeare performed by the Norwegian Theater in Bergen during his first six months in residence. As a matter of fact, during his entire stay in Bergen from 1851 to 1857, the Norwegian Theater put on only one "Shakespearean" play, Sille Beyer's *Livet i Skogen* (in September 1855). As a whole, this record of what was performed in Norway's two leading theaters between 1850 and 1857 also suggests the unlikelihood of Shakespeare's having been staged by a traveling company in Skien or Grimstad.

Ibsen could, of course, have read Shakespeare, and there is reason to suppose that he was prompted to do so shortly after his arrival in Christiania. The first review of *Catilina*—written during 1849 but published in 1850—stated that its author "synes at vilde bebude en vis shakespearisk Kraft og Alvor" [seems to wish to proclaim a certain Shakespearean power and seriousness] and makes other references to Shakespeare, most importantly when claiming that *Catilina* is the equal of *Coriolanus* in capturing a particular feature of Rome: "hiin Gjæring, hiin Bølgebrydning mellem de modsatte Partier, hiin gjensidige Higen efter Magt og Rettigheder, der baade var den romerske Storheds Amme og Giftblanderske [that tumult, that clashing of the waves between the opposed factions, that mutual craving for power and privilege that was both the wet nurse and the poisoner of the Roman grandeur]. The author of the review, Paul Botten-Hansen, then only twenty-five years old and already one of Norway's most widely read and well informed students of literature, befriended Ibsen shortly after his arrival in Christiania. Given Botten-Hansen's interest in and knowledge of Shakespeare, it is reasonable to suppose that he urged the promising dramatist to develop his gift by reading Shakespeare's plays.

However, if such urging occurred, no evidence suggests that Ibsen followed through. Certain facts, moreover, seem to indicate that he did not. Books were hard to come by for an extremely poor student living in

Christiania at that time. The best source was the university library, which owned copies of Shakespeare in at least English (which Ibsen could not read), German, and Danish. According to library registers, several of these volumes were checked out to various patrons during 1850 and 1851 but not to Ibsen. In fact, his name does not occur anywhere in the registers for these years. I suspect that since he had not passed all the parts of the entrance examination necessary to become a fully matriculated student, he was not allowed to borrow books from this library. Having passed part of the exam, he was entitled to become a nominal student and a member of the student society, which maintained a small library of its own. But his was a sorry fate if he had to rely entirely on this institution as his half-satiric, half-lamenting article about it in the society's own newspaper in April 1851 makes painfully clear. Another indication that he was not reading Shakespeare at this point in his career is the lack of any mention of his name in his various prose writings from the period, even in the theoretical pieces in which it would have been highly appropriate. Nor is there any allusion to or echo of Shakespeare in any of the poems written prior to 1851, a fact made particularly notable because of the frequent reminiscences of other writers—Oehlenschläger, Wergeland, Welhaven, and others—which tend to serve as a detailed record of his reading.

Many have claimed that *Catilina* reveals prominent traces of *Julius Caesar* and that Ibsen, therefore, must have been familiar with Shakespeare's work by 1849 while he was living in Grimstad and at work on *Catilina*. This is, however, a highly dubious claim. Books, especially translations of foreign works, were in very short supply. Later Grimstad had a small circulating library but apparently not during Ibsen's sojourn there. Many of the wealthy homes probably had private collections of books, but Ibsen was not welcome in most of these homes. Those who think he read Shakespeare in Grimstad suppose that he had access to the texts through Georgiana Crawfurd, "an old Scottish lady," who lived in Grimstad and let Ibsen borrow books from her personal library. Since she could read Shakespeare in English, however, it seems unlikely that she would own translations of his plays in the languages that Ibsen understood. In any event, the many supposed parallels cited as proof of Ibsen's use of *Julius Caesar* in writing *Catilina* have a much more plausible explanation: Shakespeare and Ibsen drew on the same general area of Roman history, and the parallels already existed in their material or are otherwise accounted for by it. To write *Catilina*, Ibsen could have learned everything he needed to know from Schiller's *Die Räuber* and the plays of Oehlenschläger. If Ibsen had been influenced by *Julius Caesar*, *Catilina* would have been, in my opinion, a much better play than it is.

It should also be mentioned that Ibsen's second play, *Kjæmpehøien*, which he began before he left Grimstad for Christiania, resembles *The Tempest* in its portrayal of a father and daughter living alone in a remote location being visited by a group that includes a young man with whom the daughter ultimately becomes romantically involved. Few, if any, however, have cited *Kjæmpehøien* as evidence of Ibsen's knowledge of Shakespeare, and I do not find in this play any conclusive traces of *The Tempest*. The resemblance is most likely the result of coincidence.

Ibsen told Henrik Jæger, when the latter was interviewing him for his 1888 biography, that the only dramatists he could remember reading before he wrote *Catilina* were Holberg and Oehlenschläger. He may also have told him that he had definitely read no Shakespeare, but this is not entirely clear from what Jæger writes on the matter: "Der er ting i 'Catilina' som kunde lede tanken hen paa Shakespeares romerske tragedier; specielt kunde man i sidste akt fristes til at tænke paa sidste akt af 'Julius Caesar'; men Ibsen kjendte dengang kun Shakespeare af navn; nogen inflydelse fra den kant kan der altsaa slet ikke være tale om" [There are things in *Catiline* that could bring to mind Shakespeare's Roman tragedies; in particular, one could in the final act be tempted to think of the final act of *Julius Caesar*; but at that time Ibsen knew Shakespeare only by name; there can thus be no talk whatever of any influence from that quarter]. We are accustomed to discount Ibsen's claims about his reading, especially when they conflict with our theories, but perhaps we would do better to take him at his word.

Just as the 1852 study tour brought Ibsen his first real exposure to Shakespeare, it also occasioned a discovery that proved very important for Ibsen's growing knowledge of Shakespeare: Hermann Hettner's volume entitled *Das moderne Drama*. This book surveys the various types of tragedy, domestic drama, and comedy. It was written in order to teach the would-be dramatist—as well as mediocre dramatists already plying their trade—the laws of dramatic art, and it is loaded with sound practical advice, especially about what not to do. According to Jæger, Ibsen found it "meget interessant og vækkende" [very interesting and inspiring]. A particularly important feature is Hettner's frequent reference to models of what he considered good artistic practice. He draws on several dramatists including Sophocles (*Oedipus Tyrannus* and, since Hettner was heavily influenced by Hegel, *Antigone*), Goethe (*Faust* and *Torquato Tasso*), Schiller (*Wallenstein*), and Hebbel (*Maria Magdalena*), but most of his models are plays by Shakespeare. As examples of the psychological character tragedy, he discusses *Julius Caesar, Antony and Cleopatra*, and especially singles out *Coriolanus* as an unrivaled model of the type; his extensive analysis of this play is extremely laudatory going so far as to state that its third act is "vielleicht das Grøßte, das Shakespeare gedichtet hat" [perhaps the greatest that Shakespeare has written]. His models for the tragedy of passion are *Hamlet, Macbeth*, and *Othello*. For domestic tragedy, he offers as ideal examples *Romeo and Juliet, Othello*, and—despite the rank of the protagonist—*King Lear*. And for the *Märchenlustspiel (eventyrkomedie)*, his ideal models are *The Winter's Tale, The Tempest*, and especially *A Midsummer Night's Dream*, which he felt was in most respects "wohl die zarteste Dichtung, die jemals die Phantasie eines Menschen ersonnen hat" [no doubt the most delicate poem that the human imagination has ever conceived].

It seems highly probable that Ibsen, who so desperately wanted to write good drama, would have been inspired by these models to develop his familiarity with Shakespeare through reading either the Tieck-Schlegel German translation or the Danish translation—though at the time still incomplete—by Foersom, Wulff, and others. In any event, the first three of the six plays that Ibsen wrote for the Bergen theater suggest that he was indeed becoming familiar with Shakespeare.

1. *Sancthansaften (St. John's Night)*, which he was writing during his study trip in 1852, is an *eventyrkomedie*; most of it is entirely accounted for by Danish examples of this type with which Ibsen was familiar, but those who have found it to be influenced by *A Midsummer Night's Dream*, which Ibsen could have seen in Dresden, seem justified by at least one detail of the play: the magical juice that the Nisse uses to alter the vision of the mortals.

2. The revised version of *Kjæmpehøien*, written in 1853, moves the action from the coast of Normandy to an island in the Mediterranean, thereby making the basic situation even more like that of *The Tempest*, and a few of its minor touches suggest that Ibsen may well have read Shakespeare's play before undertaking his revision. What most indicates the possible influence of Shakespeare on this revision, however, is its great superiority to the original version in characterization, the nuanced modulation of the dramatic action, and the unprecedented (for Ibsen) creation of verse that is expressive of the speaker and of what is happening to the speaker as he or she speaks. Even so, in its revision, *Kjæmpehøien* continues to be far more a homage to Oehlenschläger than to Shakespeare.

3. The most obvious influence on *Fru Inger (Lady Inger)*, written in 1854, is Scribe, but this play also has definite Shakespearean traces. The often expressed claim that its protagonist is a Hamlet figure involves only vague parallels, but Shakespeare seems clearly present in this play in probable echoes of *Macbeth* (especially Lady Inger's fifth-act display of

madness, which is highly reminiscent of Lady Macbeth's sleepwalking scene), the density of the historical texture, and an occasional tendency to employ image clustering and other verbal devices characteristic of Shakespeare, especially the punning linking of "Kongemoder" and "Kongemorder" [king's mother and king's murderer].

Ibsen's years in Bergen also saw two other extremely important indications of his increasing familiarity with Shakespeare. In 1855, the year after he wrote *Fru Inger*, Ibsen became a member of an exclusive literary and social club, the 22 December Society. Its records note that on November 27, he "holdt Foredrag over W. Shackspear og hans Indflydelse paa den nordiske Kunst" [gave a lecture on W. Shakespeare and his influence on Scandinavian art]. Unfortunately no copy of this lecture or account of its contents survives. The second manifestation of the ever larger role Shakespeare was gradually assuming is the briefer of his two poems entitled "Kong Haakons Gildehal" ("King Haakon's Guildhall"), which was published in 1858 after Ibsen had returned to Christiania but which Seip believes was written in Bergen in 1856.

Du gamle Hal med de Mure graa,
Hvor Uglen bygger sin Rede;
Saa tidt jeg dig seer, maa jeg tænke paa
Kong Lear paa den vilde Hede!

Han gav sin Døtre Kronens Skat,
Han gav dem sit dyreste Eie,—
De jaged' ham ud i den sorte Nat
At færdes paa vildsomme Veie.

Du Hal, som tynges of Tidens Vægt,
Du maatte det Samme friste,—
Du gav en utaksom Efterslægt
Den dyreste Skat du vidste.

Du gav os Erindringens gyldne Høst,
En Saga med Billeder rige,—
Men spored' du vel i noget Bryst
En taksom Tanke at stige?

Der Maatte du stande, som Albions drot,
Til leeg for de kaade Vinde;

I Sekler peb Stormen med Haan og Spot,
Omkring din graanende Tinde.

Nu snakkes jo lydt om at Folket er "vakt";
Det prøver vel Feilen at vette;
Saa flikkes med Pjalter din Kongedragt,—
Du har alt en Narre Hætte!

Og derfor, du Hal med de Murc graa,
Hvor Uglen bygger sin Rede,—
Saa tidt jeg dig seer, maa jeg tænke paa
Kong Lear paa den vilde Hede.

(You ancient hall with your walls of gray,
Where the owl builds its nest;
Whenever I see you, I must think about
King Lear on the wild heath!

He gave his daughters the precious crown,
He gave them his dearest possession—
They drove him out into the black night
To wander the desolate ways.

You hall weighed down by the weight of time,
You had to endure the same—
You gave an ungrateful posterity
The dearest treasure you knew.

You gave us memory's golden harvest,
A saga with images rich—
But did you detect in any breast
A grateful thought to arise?

You had to stand there, like Albion's king,
At the mercy of wanton winds;
For ages the storm whistled with scorn and derision,
Around your graying pinnacle.

Now there's loud talk that the people are "awakened";
They'll try no doubt to correct the fault;
So with rags will be patched your kingly garb—

You already have a fool's cap.

And therefore you hall with your walls of gray,
Where the owl builds its nest;
Whenever I see you, I must think about
King Lear on the wild heath.)

The poem reflects a profound experience of King Lear, especially in its exploitation of Shakespeare's linking of Lear with his fool. If Ibsen had not read the play since seeing it in 1852, the performance certainly made a great impression on him, and he had done much thinking about it. What makes the poem important is the momentous leap it represents in his development as a poet. Here for the first time in his poetry, he reaches beyond the materials of his poetric roots—the themes, diction and images of Wergeland, Welhaven, and Oehlenschläger, of the revolutionary fervor of 1848, and of Norwegian national romanticism—to something from another culture to serve as a means of illuminating and understanding native traditions. For the first time in his poetry, instead of recycling the inherited comparisons of his literary forbearers, he creates a highly original metaphor for what he wants to represent. And for the first time since committing himself to national romanticism, instead of praising his people for carrying within them the spirit of their heroic past, he criticizes them for their failure to live up to it.

A final indication from the Bergen years of the increasing importance of Shakespeare to Ibsen, but of considerably less significance, is the faint echo of *Hamlet* in "Om Kjæmpevisen og dens Betydning for Kunstpoesien" [On the Heroic Ballad and Its Significance for Poetry], a lecture given at the 22 December Society in February 1857 and published in May of that year. The echo is heard in Ibsen's contrast of the romantic or Christian view of life with that of the sagas: "Den romantiske Livsanskuelse derimod gaar en anden Vei, den hylder Shakspeares Sætning: 'at der findes Mere mellem Himmel og Jord, end Philosopherne veed af at sige'" [The romantic view of life, on the other hand, goes a different way, it upholds Shakespeare's maxim: "That there is more between heaven and earth than the philosophers are able to speak of"]. Shakespeare actually wrote, "There are more things in heaven and earth, Horatio/Than are dreamt of in your philosophy" or in the Danish translation available at the time, "Der er' fleer' Ting i Himlen og paa Jorden,/ min venn, end Jeres Philosopher drømme." Ibsen's version may be the result of imperfect memory or the affected indifference to exact quotation that certain writers cultivate, but it is more likely the result of second-hand acquaintance with "Shakspeares Sætning."

The three final Bergen plays—*Gilden på Solhaug* (1855) [*The Feast at*

Solhaug], *Olaf Liljekrans* (1856), and *Hærmændene på Helgeland* (1857) [*The Vikings at Helgeland*]—suggest that this first unequivocal impact of Shakespeare on Ibsen did not penetrate very deeply insofar as his dramatic work is concerned, for only the last of them, begun in Bergen but finished in Christiania, manifests any discernible trace of Shakespeare: Ørnulf's directions to his son Thorolf about how to behave at the feast in Hjørdis's hall:

> *te dig høvisk i gildehuset, så jeg har hæder af dig. Unødig tale skal du ikke fore; men det du mæler, skal være hvast som en sværdsæg. Vær vennesæl sålænge godt vises dig; men ægges du, da skal du ikke tie dertil. Drik ikke mere end du kan bære; men vis heller ikke hornet fra dig, når det bydes med måde, på det at du ikke skal holdes for en kvindekarl.*

(bear yourself in courtly wise in the feast-house, that I may have honor by you. Needless talk you shall not utter; but what you do speak shall be keen as a sword's edge. Be friendly as long as good is shown you; but if you are goaded you shall not keep still about it. Drink no more than you can bear; but do not put the horn by either when it is offered in measure—so that you shall not be held for a womanish man).

There is also little trace of Shakespeare in his next play, *Kjærlighedens Komedie* [*Love's Comedy*], which he did not write until 1862, five years after his return to Christiania. Falk's retort to Lind, "Du ogsaa, Brutus?" when he too succumbs to the community's conventional ideas about marriage, is, in all probability a reflection of popular parlance rather than a conscious allusion to "Et tu, Brute?" in *Julius Caesar*. On the other hand, the miscellaneous prose Ibsen wrote in Christiania during 1857–63, which mentions Shakespeare frequently and usually significantly, clearly reveals that his knowledge of and preoccupation with Shakespeare were continuing to develop.

His review of Andreas Munch's *Lord William Russell* (December 1857) begins by arguing that "af den sande historiske Tragedie have vi ingen egentlig Ret til at kræve Historiens Fakta, men vel dens Muligheder, ikke Historiens beviselige Personer og Charakterer, men Tidsalderens Aand og Tænkesæt" [of the true historical tragedy we have no proper right to demand the facts of history, but indeed its possibilities, not history's demonstrable personages and characters, but the era's spirit and way of thinking]. And to support this claim he points out that "Schillers 'Wilhelm Tell', 'Wallenstein', 'Maria Stuart' o.s.v.ere uhistoriske, ligesaavel som Shakspeares 'Macbeth' o. Fl.; thi omendkjønt disse Værker fremstille historiske

Kjendsgjerninger, saa hviler dog Fremstillingen paa en fuldstændig
Ophævelse af baade den skildrede og enhver anden Tidsalders og Tidsaands
Eiendommeligheder" [Schiller's *Wilhelm Tell, Wallenstein, Maria Stuart* and
so forth are unhistorical, as are likewise Shakespeare's *Macbeth* and others; for
although these works represent historical facts, the depiction nevertheless
rests on a complete cancellation of both the portrayed and the characteristics
of every other era and spirit of the time]. Later in the review, he mentions a
critic writing in *Christianiaposten* who argued for "et Korstog mod de
Beyerske Bearbeidelser [av Shakespeare], som forlængst have vundet Borg-
erret paa Kjøbenhavns Scene, og derfra naturligviis fundet Veien til os" [a
crusade against the Beyeresque adaptations {of Shakespeare} that have long
since won the rights of citizenship on Copenhagen's stage and therefore, of
course, found their way to us]. And later still, while considering whether "en
Person kan virke dramatisk ved at være Gjenstand for Handling ligesaavel
som ved at være den Handlende" [a character can seem dramatic by being
the object of action just as well as by being the one who acts], Ibsen writes,
"i Hamlet er det netop Hovedfigurens Mangel paa Handledygtighed, som
betinger det Heles dramatiske Virkning" [in Hamlet it is precisely the
protagonist's lack of capacity for action that determines the whole dramatic
effect].

        While discussing the Christiania Theater's repertory in "De to Theatre
i Christiania" (March 1861), he laments that "Med den ægte Shakspeare gav
man sig ikke ifærd, her hjalp man sig med de Sille-Beyerske Tidsmæs-
sigheder" [one had nothing to do with genuine Shakespeare, here one made
do with the Sille-Beyeresque modernizations]. He also laments the tendency
of the Christiania audience to respond with enthusiasm to what it neither
likes nor understands out of fear of seeming to lack good taste—as, for
example, in

> *Jubelen og Beundringen over en mangelfuld Udførelse af et saakaldt
> shakespearsk Skuespil, som man alligevel kun delvis forstaar. Man
> har jo baade læst og hørt at Shakespeare skal være en stor Forfatter;
> den gode Tone byder altsaa at finde Smag i ham; at det er en forloren
> Shakespeare, der bydes, gjør Intet til Sagen, da man ikke kjender den
> ægte, og at man ikke ret kan faa Tag i de mange Skjønheder, han jo
> skal indeholde, undskylder man for sig selv derved, at disse samme
> Skjønheder ligger meget høit. Ligeoverfor Ens Sidemænd paa
> Tilskuerbænken skjules deslige Selvbekjendelser lettest under et
> febrilsk Bifald.*

[the jubilation and admiration in response to a highly deficient

performance of a so-called Shakespearean play, which, nevertheless, one only partly understands. One has, after all, both read
and heard that Shakespeare is a great author; good form thus
decrees finding him to one's taste; that it is a sham Shakespeare
that is offered does not make any difference since one does not
know the genuine, and that one cannot rightly make out the
many beauties he is supposed to contain one justifies to oneself
on the basis that these beauties are very lofty. Face to face with
one's fellow spectators, self-confessions of this sort are most
easily concealed by fervent applause].

His attempt to fathom the frame of mind of the theater public in his
review of Augier's *Diana* (November 1862) occasions the observation that
"Anderledes, end bagefter opfundne, er nok forøvrigt aldrig den selvbevidste
ledende Tanke tilstede i Massens Stemninger; den er tilstede paa samme
maade, som vor Tids tydske Dybsindigheder over Shakespeare var tilstede
for hans egen Selvbevidsthed" [To be sure, the self-conscious ruling thought
is never present in the moods of the masses otherwise than as something
formulated after the fact; it is present in the same manner that the German
profundities of our day concerning Shakespeare were present for his own
self-consciousness]. And his delight in the excellence of Christian Jørgensen's
performance of Richelieu and of the ensemble playing between him and the
actress who played Diana prompts him to ask, "Hvorfor lader man ikke
Macbeth komme til Opførelse? Saaledes indrettet og forkortet, som
Dramaturgerne nutildags er enige om at give Stykket, vil det med
Anstændighed kunne besættes, men det er naturligvis en Selvfølge at man
maatte benytte Lembches Oversættelse, og ikke Foersums" [Why don't they
let *Macbeth* be performed? Arranged and abridged as the dramaturgs are in
agreement about giving the play nowadays, it can be respectably mounted,
but it of course goes without saying that one must use Lembche's translation
and not Foersom's].

Note must also be taken of Ibsen's explanation to Peter Hansen in an
important letter from October 1870 that his life in Rome—during his first
stay there between 1864 and 1868—was one "som ikke kan sammenlignes
med noget andet end stemningen fra Shakespeares 'As You Like It'" [that
cannot be compared with anything other than the mood of Shakespeare's *As
You Like it*]. The important point is that he actually writes "As You Like It"
and not "Livet i Skogen."

Taken together, the references I have cited demonstrate a deepening
knowledge and experience of Shakespeare and his works, some of which is
surely accounted for by the implications of the assertion: "men det er

naturligvis en Selvfølge at man maatte benytte Lembches Oversættelse, og ikke Foersums." Edvard Lembche's complete translation of Shakespeare was based in part on the existing translations by Foersom and others and soon became the standard nineteenth-century Danish translation. It began to come out in 1861, and Ibsen appears to have been reading it as it came out. The most important result of his deepening experience with Shakespeare during these years is the play he wrote in 1863, *Kongs-emnerne* [*The Pretenders*], which is by far his most overtly Shakespearean play. I find almost certain echoes in *Kongs-emnerne* of *3 Henry VI, Richard III, 1 Henry IV, Henry V, Hamlet, King Lear*, and *Macbeth*. Shakespeare's history plays in general are echoed by the concern in *Kongs-emnerne* with the nature of kingship and the qualifications required by the role. And *Richard II*, with its focus on the transition from the Middle Ages to the modern era, its simultaneous tracing of the contrasting careers of Richard and Bolingbroke, and its ultimate development as the tragedy of Richard, seems clearly to have served Ibsen as a direct model for *Kongs-emnerne*.

But perhaps the most striking evidence for Ibsen's having come fully under the influence of Shakespeare in writing *Kongs-emnerne* is its form. In his preceding tragedy, *Hærmændene på Helgeland*, from 1857, he had finally perfected the dramatic structure he had been working toward in *Catilina* and *Fru Inger*, the structure that we know so well from his last twelve plays, the great dramas of contemporary life. This structure features his famous retrospective method in which crucial aspects of the past are gradually revealed until late in the play the protagonist, responding to these revelations, enters into a course of action designed to reclaim the past by transforming the situation it has shaped. Ibsen abandoned this structure not only for *Kongs-emnerne* but also for the three succeeding plays of what Meyer calls "the great epic quartet": *Brand, Peer Gynt*—which also deliberately misquotes *Richard III* with "Mit Rige,—mid halve Rige for en Hest!" [My kingdom—half my kingdom for a horse!] and recalls the mood and movement of Shakespeare's late romances—and *Kejser og Galilæer* [*Emperor and Galilean*], which recalls *Macbeth*, especially in Emperor Julian's being assured of his invulnerability by an equivocal prophecy. All four plays are expansive, dense works that unfold gradually in a manner characteristically Shakespearean, and all four veer toward the extended monologue as the primary unit of dramatic expression. They also tend to begin, not in the midst of things, as with *Hærmændene*, but with the event or events that form the point of departure for the action. The past continues to exercise some influence in them, but it has a much smaller role than in *Fru Inger, Hærmændene*, or the dramas of contemporary life, and, as in Shakespeare, it is usually represented as part of the stayed action. *De unges Forbund* [*The League of Youth*], which Ibsen wrote between *Peer Gynt* and *Kejser og Galilæer*, is not of the same magnitude as the plays of the epic quartet, but in other respects, it too is an example of Shakespearean form.

Ibsen used Shakespearean form for over ten years and then abandoned it as abruptly as he had taken it up. *In Samfundets støtter* [*Pillars of Society*], his next play after *Kejser og Galilæer*, he returned to the dramatic structure he had perfected in *Hærmændene* and, with the possible exception of *En folkefiende* [*An Enemy of the People*], continued to use it for the rest of his career. The dramas of contemporary life also lack conspicuous echoes and traces of Shakespeare, but in my view did not disappear with these plays, as has been maintained, but like Ibsen's earlier romanticism and his poetry went underground. Various Ibsen critics, such as Brian Johnston and Errol Durbach, have found traces of Shakespeare in one or another of these plays, but I have something much more extensive in mind. I see many of the dramas of contemporary life contributing to the creation of a new, modern version of tragedy. One of the most interesting features of them in this respect is that in play after play, Ibsen shapes his contemporary middle-class action in such a way that sometimes particular details, sometimes the action as a whole echo elements of a familiar major tragedy of the past. The result is a non-explicit, deep-structural allusion suggesting that the contemporary middle-class action is as legitimate for tragedy as the more heroic action of the famous tragic drama it implicitly echoes. Appropriately enough, given the influence of Hegel and Hettner, *Et dukkehjem* [*A Doll House*] and *Gengangere* [*Ghosts*] allude to dramas by Sophocles—respectively *Antigone* and *Oedipus Tyrannus*—while *Bygmester Solness* [*The Master Builder*] alludes not to a specific work but rather to the type of traditional tragedy exemplified by the Faust plays, *Macbeth*, and Aeschylus's *Prometheus Bound* to which Ibsen's play seems explicitly to allude in a speech by Solness. But most of the tragedies from the past that Ibsen alludes to are by Shakespeare: *Coriolanus* in *En folkefiende*, *Othello* in *Vildanden*, *Macbeth* in *Rosmersholm*, *Antony and Cleopatra* in *Hedda Gabler*, and *King Lear* in *John Gabriel Borkman*. The play alluded to by *Når vi døde vågner* [*When We Dead Awaken*] is also by Shakespeare, although it is not a tragedy but one of his romances: *The Tempest*. The subtlety of this kind of use of his Shakespearean materials indicates to me that this is the period in which Ibsen most has them at his command.

In order to clarify what I mean by these deep-structural allusions, I will briefly describe three of them. *En folkefiende* almost certainly gets its title from *Coriolanus*. Shakespeare's protagonist is called "chief enemy to the people," "enemy to the people and his country," and "The People's enemy," the last of which comes out "Folkets Fiende" in Wulff's translation (though not in Lembche's, which uses "Avindsmand"). More important, *En folkefiende* also calls to mind much of the content of Shakespeare's play. Dr. Stockmann's confrontation with his community in Act Four might well have been modeled upon the scenes from the third act of *Coriolanus*, the act that Hettner so admired, in which its protagonist must face the people and their tribunes in the market place in order to be elected consul. Stockmann's virtual exclusion from the life of the community and his vague talk of emigrating to America form an appropriate parallel for the ultimate outcome of Coriolanus's confrontations, his being literally banished but verbally redefining this banishment by choosing to seek "a world elsewhere." Stockman's talk of how his opponents ought to be destroyed and their community leveled, is within the particular circumstances of Ibsen's play, a remarkably close echo of Coriolanus's eventual preparation to lead a force against Rome with the intention of accomplishing what Stockmann only talks about. And the visits to Stockmann in the final act by a series of self-interested tempters who want him to change his mind about the baths recalls the series of emissaries from Rome who call upon Coriolanus in the final act to get him to change his plan so that they will be spared.

The allusion to *Othello* in *Vildanden* is a function of action, structure, and genre. In both, the primary action concerns a central character who convinces another that his wife has been unfaithful; the second, acting from a sense of outrage and feeling fully justified, causes the death of an innocent female whom he continues to love but also considers villainous. Both plays begin with the first of these central characters seeming to be the protagonist, but in both attention gradually shifts to the second central character: from Iago to Othello and from Gregers to Hjalmar. Although *Othello* is a tragedy, it has many of the characteristics of the kind of traditional comedy of intrigue in which an old husband with a young wife is outwitted—Machiavelli's *La Mandragola* is a prime example. Generically then, both *Othello* and *Vildanden* generically unite comedy and tragedy, in effect deriving tragedy from a base of comedy.

The extended allusion to *Antony and Cleopatra* in *Hedda Gabler* involves theme, situational and character parallels, and the linear structure of the action. Central to Shakespeare's tragedy is the antithesis between Rome and Egypt, which ultimately is a conflict between two separate worlds: the first preoccupied with establishing and maintaining order, acting in terms of regimen and duty, and amassing possessions and power; the second with the free and spontaneous search for pleasure and the cultivation of personal honor based on heroic action. This conflict is echoed, on a smaller scale, in *Hedda Gabler* in the two opposing worlds of, on the one hand, the Tesmans, Thea Elvsted, and Brack and, on the other, Hedda and Løvborg. In the area of character parallels, Brack, constantly manipulating others to gain power over his world and all its inhabitants, behaves much like Octavius Caesar, while Thea, who reclaims Løvborg for the social order but cannot hold him, recalls Octavius's sister Octavia in her brief marriage to Antony. The resemblance of Løvborg to Antony and Hedda to Cleopatra results not only from their seeking pleasures frowned on by the controlling social order, but also, and more emphatically, from the way in which the action of Ibsen's play matches that of Shakespeare's. Løvborg, like Antony, is called upon to affirm his world's values through suicide but, also like Antony, botches the job leaving Hedda, like Cleopatra, alone. Each of the heroines is, thus, left during the final act at the mercy of the Caesar-figure with responsibility of affirming her world's values by herself, if they are to be affirmed at all. Hedda's response, like Cleopatra's, is an elaborately staged suicide.

Ibsen does not, however, merely echo his Shakespearean materials. He typically gives them a twist that puts his own individual stamp on them. Stockmann does not ultimately seek his "world elsewhere" but instead decides to remain where he is in order to do battle with his community from within. Ibsen's Iago—Gregers Werle—creates mischief not from deliberate malevolence but from a desire to do good. His Othello— Hjalmar Ekdal—aspires to high language of a sort that Shakespeare's hero speaks naturally, but with Hjalmar the effect is at best sentimental and at worst farcical. Ibsen also gives the shift in protagonists in *Othello* a further dimension by ultimately shifting to a third protagonist when, at the end, he replaces Hjalmar with Hedvig. And in *Vildanden*, unlike *Othello*, the element of comedy threatens, though without wholly succeeding, to over-whelm the tragedy. In *Hedda Gabler*, the characteristic Ibsen twist is most evident in the antithesis between the two worlds, for his parallel to Rome, most emphatically embodied in Tesman and his aunt, is a world that has long since lost sight of the kind of aspirations that Shakespeare's Octavius Caesar still comprehends, even though he finds them inconvenient to adhere to himself. There is definitely not, I believe, any twist in Ibsen's setting Hedda parallel to Cleopatra but rather a straightforward drawing on Cleopatra's triumph as a means of sanctioning Hedda's final act. Ibsen's tendency to give the Shakespearean materials a stamp of his own is apparent at least as early as *Kongs-emnerne*. Here Skule, in yearning for a son so that he can solidify his stolen kingship, echoes Macbeth's lamenting his not having a son to inherit the crown he has seized. Ibsen's twist, so typical of him, is to provide Skule with a son and to make the acquisition of this son the chief cause of disaster.

Ibsen's twists are but one manifestation of a central and very impor-tant fact of his use of Shakespeare. The plays in which Shakespeare's pres-ence can be detected—even *Kongs-emnerne*, where his presence is most evident—are still very much Ibsen's own. At the same time, the presence of Shakespeare makes these plays much richer than they would be without it. Shakespeare's presence was a profound and long-lasting aspect of Ibsen's work, and while Ibsen had a thing about ghosts, in this case the ghosts were friendly spirits, even tutelary ones.

Chronology

1828	Born in Skien, Norway on March 20, to Marichen and Knud Ibsen, a merchant
1834–35	Father's business fails and the family moves to Venstoep, a town a few miles outside of Skien.
1844	Becomes assistant to an apothecary in the seaport town of Grimstad.
1846	Illegitimate son born to Else Sofie Jensdatter.
1849	Writes first play, *Catiline*.
1850	Enters the university in Christiana, now the city of Oslo, and writes second play, *The Warrior's Barrow*.
1851	Joins newly formed National Theatre in Bergen, where he will stay for the next six years.
1852	Writes *St. John's Eve*, a romantic comedy.
1853	*St. John's Eve* is performed in Bergen but fails.
1854	Writes *Lady Inger of Oestraat*, a historical tragedy.
1855	*Lady Inger of Oestraat* is performed at Bergen and also fails. Writes the romantic comedy *The Feast at Solhaug*.
1856	*The Feast at Solhaug* is performed at Bergen, which garners a small measure of success. Writes *Olaf Liljekrans*.

1857	*Olaf Liljekrans* is performed at Bergen. It is not a success. Writes *The Vikings at Helgeland*.
1858	Marries Suzannah Thoreson. *The Vikings at Helgeland* is staged and is a small success.
1859	A son, Sigurd, is born.
1860–61	Suffers poverty and despair and is unable to write.
1862	Writes *Love's Comedy*. The National Theatre in Bergen goes bankrupt. Awarded university grant to gather Norwegian folk songs and tales.
1863	Takes part-time job as literary advisor to the Danish-controlled Christiania Theatre. Writes *The Pretenders*, and is granted a government stipend.
1864	*The Pretenders* is staged at the Christiania Theatre and is a success. Moves to Rome, and remains abroad for the next twenty-seven years.
1865	Writes *Brand*.
1866	*Brand* published to critical acclaim, bringing Ibsen fame throughout Scandinavia.
1867	Writes *Peer Gynt*. Its publication garners even greater praise than *Brand*, and increases Ibsen's recognition as a playwright.
1868	Moves to Dresden.
1869	Completes *The League of Youth*.
1871	Publishes a volume of poetry, *Poems*.
1873	Completes *Emperor and Galilean*, begun nine years prior.
1874	Moves to Munich.
1877	Completes *The Pillars of Society*, which is widely acted in Germany.
1878	Returns to Italy for a year.
1879	Writes *A Doll's House*. Returns to Munich for a year.
1880	Moves to Italy.
1881	Writes *Ghosts*. The play is rejected by theaters and publishers in response to public outrage against its exploration of free love and venereal disease.

1882	Writes *An Enemy of the People*. *Ghosts* is performed in the United States.
1884	Writes *The Wild Duck*.
1885	Returns to Munich, and visits Norway for the first time since 1874.
1886	Writes *Rosmersholm*.
1888	Writes *The Lady from the Sea*.
1890	Writes *Hedda Gabler*.
1891	Resettles permanently in Norway.
1892	Writes *The Master Builder*. His son marries Bergliot Björnson.
1894	Writes *Little Eyolf*.
1896	Writes *John Gabriel Borkman*.
1898	First volumes of collected works published in Copenhagen.
1899	Writes *When We Dead Awaken*.
1901	Suffers a stroke and is partially paralyzed.
1903	Second stroke leaves him helpless and dependent.
1906	Dies in Christiania, Norway, on May 23, at the age of seventy-eight.

Contributors

HAROLD BLOOM is Sterling Professor of Humanities at Yale University and Professor of English at New York University. His works include *Shelley's Mythmaking* (1959), *The Visionary Company* (1961), *The Anxiety of Influence* (1973), *Agon: Towards a Theory of Revisionism* (1982), *The Book of J* (1990), *The American Religion* (1992), and *The Western Canon* (1994). His forthcoming books are a study of Shakespeare and Freud, *Transference and Authority*, which considers all of Freud's major writings. A MacArthur Prize Fellow, Professor Bloom is the editor of more than thirty anthologies and general editor of five series of literary criticism published by Chelsea House.

E. M. FORSTER (1879–1970) is author of the novels *A Passage to India* (1924), *Howard's End* (1910), and *A Room With a View* (1911). His critical works are published in two collections of essays, *Abinger Harvest* (1936) and *Two Cheers for Democracy* (1951).

FRANCIS FERGUSSON has collaborated on translations of the plays of Sophocles and is the author of many works of drama criticism, including *Literary Landmarks* (1975), *Shakespeare: The Pattern in His Carpet* (1970), *Dante* (1966), *The Human Image in Dramatic Literature* (1957), and *The Idea of Theater* (1949).

ERIC BENTLEY is emeritus Brander Matthews Professor of Dramatic Literature at Columbia University. His critical works include *The Brecht*

Commentaries (1987), *The Playwright as Thinker* (1946, 1987), *In Search of Theater* (1953), and *The Life of the Drama* (1964, 1991).

UNA ELLIS-FERMOR was Professor of English at Bedford College, University of London, until her death in 1958. Her translations include *The Master Builder*, *Rosmerhold*, *Little Eyolf*, and *John Gabriel Borkman*.

MICHAEL MEYER is a leading contemporary Ibsen scholar. His works include a three-volume biography of Ibsen (1967–71) and translations of his plays.

JOHN NORTHAM has published numerous articles on Ibsen's plays.

RICHARD GILMAN has been Professor of Drama at Yale, and received the George Jean Nathan Award in 1972. He is author of *Common and Uncommon Masks* (1971) and *The Confusion of Realms* (1969). His articles and essays on the theater have appeared in *The New Republic*, *Commonweal*, *Newsweek*, *American Review*, and *Performance*.

SVERRE ARESTAD is emeritus professor of Scandinavian languages, and former chair of the Department of Scandinavian Language and Literature at the University of Washington. He has been editor of *Scandinavian Studies* and published widely on Danish, Swedish, and Norwegian drama and novels.

ROBERT BRUSTEIN is Professor of English and Harvard University and drama critic for the New Republic. He has been artistic director of the American Repertory Theatre and director of the Loeb Drama Center at Harvard, and former dean of the Yale Drama School and founder of the Yale Repertory Theatre. He has received the George Jean Nathan Award in drama criticism and the George Polk Award in journalism.

INGA-STINA EWBANK is translator into English of *Three Chamber Plays* by August Strindberg (1997), and is author of *Shakespeare's Liars* (1984), *Shakespeare, Ibsen and the Unspeakable* (1976), and *Their Proper Sphere: A Study of the Bronte Sisters as Early-Victorian Female Novelists* (1966).

BARBARA FASS LEAVY is Professor of English at the City University of New York, Queens College. She has recently published *La Belle Dame sans Merci and the Aesthetics of Romanticism*, a study of mermaid and fairy mistress themes in Romantic literature.

MICHAEL GOLDMAN is the author of *Acting and Action in Shakespeare's Tragedies* (1985), *The Actor's Freedom: Toward a Theory of Drama* (1975), and *At the Edge; Poems* (1969).

THOMAS F. VAN LAAN is the author of *Role-Playing in Shakespeare* (1978) and *The Idiom of Drama* (1970).

Bibliography

Anderson, Andrew R. "Ibsen and the Classic World," *Classic Journal* XL:4 (January 1916): 216–225.

Anderssen, Odd-Stein. "Before the Centenary of *Peer Gynt*," *World Theater* XII:4 (1963-64): 281–300.

Arestad, Sverre. "Ibsen and Shakespeare: A Study in Influence," *Scandinavian Studies* (August 1946).

——— . "Ibsen's Concept of Tragedy," *PMLA* (June 1959).

——— . "*Peer Gynt* and the Idea of Self," *Modern Drama* (September 1960).

——— . "Ibsen's Portrayal of the Artist," *Edda* (June 1963).

——— . "Ibsen, Strindberg and Naturalistic Tragedy," *The Theatre Annual* (1968).

Arup, Jens. "On *Hedda Gabler*," *Orbis Litterarum* XII:1 (1957): 4–37.

Bentley, Eric. "Henrik Ibsen: A Personal Statement," *Columbia University Forum* I (Winter 1957): 11–14.

Brustein, Robert. "Henrik Ibsen," *The Theatre of Revolt*. Boston: Little, Brown and Company, 1964.

Bull, Francis. "The Influence of Shakespeare on Wergeland, Ibsen, and Bjornson," *The Norseman* 15 (1957): 88–95.

Davis, Rick. "Ibsen in a Box," *American Theatre* 11 (May–June 1994): 62–65.

Deer, Irving. "Ibsen's Brand: Paradox and the Symbolic Hero," *The Lock Haven Bulletin Series* I:3 (1961): 7–18.

Downs, Brian W. *A Study of Six Plays by Ibsen*. 1950. New York: Octagon, 1972.

——— . *Ibsen: The Intellectual Background*. New York: Macmillan, 1947.

Dukore, Bernard F. *Money and Politics in Ibsen, Shaw, and Brecht*. Columbia: University of Missouri Press, 1980.

Durbach, Errol. "Nora as Antigone: The Feminist Tragedienne and Social Legality," *Scandinavian-Canadian Studies / Etudes scandinaves au Canada* 5 (1992): 29–41.

———— , ed. *Ibsen and the Theatre*. London, 1980.

———— . *A Doll's House: Ibsen's Myth of Transformation*. Boston: Twayne, 1991. 40–55.

Englestad, C.F. "Henrik Ibsen and the Modern Theater," *World Theater* VI:1 (1957): 5–26.

Gerland, Oliver. "Psychological Models for Drama: Ibsen's *Peer Gynt* and the Relational Self," *Mosaic* 29 (June 1996): 53–73.

Hurrell, John D. "*Rosmersholm*, The Existentialist Drama and the Dilemma of Modern Tragedy," *Educational Theater Journal* XV:2 (May 1963): 118–124.

James, Henry. "Hedda Gabler," "The Master Builder," "Little Eyolf," "John Gabriel Borkman," *The Scenic Art*. Ed., Allan Wade. New York: Hill and Wang, 1957.

Johnston, Brian. "Three Stages of *A Doll House*," *Comparative Drama* 25 (1991): 311–328.

Joyce, James. "Ibsen's New Drama" *[When We Dead Awaken]*, *The Critical Writings of James Joyce*. Ed., Ellsworth Mason and Richard Ellman. New York: Viking Press, 1959.

Kaufmann, F.W. "Ibsen's Conception of Truth," *Germanic Review* XXXII (April 1957): 83–92.

Koht, Halvdan. "Shakespeare and Ibsen," *Journal of English and Germanic Philology* XLIV:1 (January 1945): 79–86.

———— . *Life of Ibsen*. Translated by Einar Haugen. New York: Benjamin Blom, 1971.

Lowenthal, Leo. "Henrik Ibsen," *Literature and the Image of Man*. Boston: Beracon Press, 1957.

MacFarlane, James Walter. "Henrik Ibsen," *Ibsen and the Temper of Norwegian Literature*. London: Oxford University Press, 1960.

Mayerson, Caroline W. "Thematic Symbols in *Hedda Gabler*," *Scandinavian Studies* 22:4 (November 1950): 151–160.

Quigley, Austin E. "*A Doll's House* Revisited," *Modern Drama* 27 (1984): 584–603.

Raphael, Robert. "Illusion and the Self in *The Wild Duck*, *Rosmersholm*, and *The Lady from the Sea*," *Scandinavian Studies* 35:1 (February 1963): 37–50.

Reinert, Otto. "Sight Imagery in *The Wild Duck*," *Journal of English and Germanic Philology* LV:3 (July 1956): 457–462.

Schechner, Richard. "The Unexpected Visitor in Ibsen's Late Plays," *Educational Theater Journal* XIV:2 (May 1962): 120–127.

Svendsen, Paulus. "Emperor and Galilean," Trans. Allen Simpson. *Edda* LVI (Hefte 4, 1956): 336–350.

Tennant, P.F.D. "Ibsen as a Stage Craftsman," *Modern Language Review* XXXIV:4 (October 1939): 557–568.

Thompson, Alan Reynolds. "Ibsen as Psychoanatomist," *Educational Theater Journal* III:1 (March 1951): 34–39.

Valency, Maurice. *The Flower and the Castle: An Introduction to the Modern Drama: Ibsen and Strindberg*. New York: Macmillan, 1963.

Whicher, Stephen. "The World of Ibsen," *The Commonweal* LXIV:17 (July 27, 1956): 417–419.

Acknowledgments

"The Task of the Poet" by Henrik Ibsen from "Speech to the Norwegian Students, September 10, 1874," from *Masterpieces of the Modern Scandinavian Theatre*, ed. Robert W. Corrigan, trans. Evert M. Sprinchorn. Copyright © 1967 by Evert M. Sprinchorn.

"Ibsen the Romantic" from *Abinger Harvest*, © 1936 and renewed 1964 by Edward M. Forster, reprinted by permission of Harcourt Brace & Company.

"*Ghosts*: The Tragic Rhythm in a Small Figure" by Francis Fergusson from *The Idea of a Theater* by Francis Fergusson. Reprinted in *Ibsen: A Collection of Critical Essays*, ed. Rolf Fjelde. Copyright © 1965 by Prentice-Hall, Inc.

"Ibsen: Pro and Con" by Eric Bentley from *Theatre Arts* XXXIV:7 (July 1950): 39–43. Copyright © 1950 by John D. MacArthur.

"Introduction to *Hedda Gabler* and Other Plays" by Una Ellis-Fermor from *Henrik Ibsen: Hedda Gabler and Other Plays*, trans. Una Ellis-Fermor. Copyright © 1950 by the Estate of Una Ellis-Fermor.

"Introduction to *The Pillars of Society*" by Michael Meyer from *Henrik Ibsen: The Pillars of Society*, translated from the Norwegian by Michael Meyer. Copyright © 1963 by Rupert Hart-Davis.

"The Wild Duck" by John Northam from *Ibsen: A Critical Study* by John Northam. Copyright © 1973 by Cambridge University Press.

"Ibsen and the Making of Modern Drama" by Richard Gilman from *The Making of Modern Drama: A Study of Buchner, Ibsen, Strindberg, Chekov, Pirandello, Brecht, Beckett, Handke* by Richard Gilman. Copyright © 1974 by Richard Gilman.

"The Fate of Ibsenism" by Robert Brustein from *Critical Moments: Reflections on Theatre and Society 1973–1979* by Robert Brustein. Copyright © 1978 by Robert Brustein.

"The Ibsen Hero" by Sverre Arestad from *The Hero in Scandinavian Literature from Peer Gynt to the Present*, eds. John M. Weinstock and Robert T. Rovinsky. Copyright © 1975 by the University of Texas Press.

"*Brand*: The Play and the Translation" by Inga-Stina Ewbank from *Ibsen: Brand: A Version for the Stage* by Geoffrey Hill. Copyright © 1981 by the University of Minnesota Press.

"Hedda Gabler and the *Huldre*" by Barbara Fass Leavy from *Ibsen's Forsaken Merman: Folklore in the Late Plays* by Per Schelde Jacobsen and Barbara Fass Leavy. Copyright © 1988 by New York University Press.

"Ibsen: Trolls and *Peer Gynt*" by Harold Bloom from *The Western Canon: The Books and School of the Ages*. Copyright © 1994 by Harold Bloom.

"Eyolf's Eyes: Ibsen and the Cultural Meanings of Child Abuse" by Michael Goldman from *American Imago* 15:3 (Fall 1994): 279–306. Copyright © 1994 Johns Hopkins University Press.

"Ibsen and Shakespeare" by Thomas F. Van Laan from *Scandinavian Studies* 67:3 (Summer 1995): 287–305. Copyright © 1995 Society for the Advancement of Scandinavian Study.

Index